HANNAH MORE

By the same author

THE CHARITY SCHOOL MOVEMENT
A Study of Eighteenth-Century Puritanism in action

HANNAH MORE IN 1787

From the portrait by Opie. "Opie made cruel havoc of female beauty, he could not catch a trait of feminine grace or delicacy. He hit [Hannah More's] likeness, but had lost all the fine expression of her countenance."—RICHARD POLEWHELE, *Traditions and Recollections* (1826) p. 77.

HANNAH MORE

BY

M. G. JONES
LITT.D
Fellow of Girton College

CAMBRIDGE
AT THE UNIVERSITY PRESS
1952

CAMBRIDGE UNIVERSITY PRESS
Cambridge, New York, Melbourne, Madrid, Cape Town,
Singapore, São Paulo, Delhi, Mexico City

Cambridge University Press
The Edinburgh Building, Cambridge CB2 8RU, UK

Published in the United States of America by Cambridge University Press, New York

www.cambridge.org
Information on this title: www.cambridge.org/9781107622043

First published 1952
First paperback edition 2013

A catalogue record for this publication is available from the British Library

ISBN 978-1-107-62204-3 Paperback

CONTENTS

LIST OF ILLUSTRATIONS

Plates

Map

PREFACE

THE main sources for the life of Hannah More are the four volumes of the *Memoirs of the Life and Correspondence of Mrs Hannah More*, including some pages of her Diary, edited by William Roberts, Esq., and published in 1834, and Miss More's own works published between 1773 and 1825. Roberts's *Memoirs* were subjected, during and after his lifetime, to severe and not unmerited criticism. Few persons could have been less well equipped to write Miss More's memoirs or to edit her letters. He possessed neither literary grace nor constructive gifts. He was not always informed, and as comparison of some of the published letters with their originals shows, he corrected Miss More's letters and diary when in his judgement they required emendation. Far more questionable was his unfortunate omission of that part of her letter to the Bishop of Bath and Wells, during the Blagdon Controversy, in which she admitted her participation in Holy Communion at the Presbyterian Meeting House in Bath—an omission presumably intended by Roberts to safeguard her reputation, but which, instead, impugned Hannah More's most striking characteristic, her honesty.

Contemporary letters make clear that some at least of Miss More's contemporaries regarded Roberts as an unsuitable choice as her biographer and were unwilling to lend him letters of Miss More in their possession. 'Hannah More', said Miss Marianne Thornton in her *Recollections*, with characteristic vigour,

calls Sir Thomas Acland in one of her notes 'the recreant Knight of Devonshire', which Roberts, thinking uncivil, I suppose, altered to 'the excellent and estimable Sir Thomas Acland', two words which that playful woman never used in her life. Somewhere she began a letter to me, 'When I think of you I am gladerer and gladerer', which he, thinking it bad English, has done into 'I am very glad'. Now if such an oaf as that will write a book at least he should be honest.

'Had it been possible for any literator, with Mrs More's correspondences at his command, to produce an uninteresting book', wrote the *Quarterly* in a trenchant review of the *Memoirs* in November 1834,

we are obliged to confess our belief that the task must have been accomplished by Mr Roberts. . . He writes with the confusion and verbosity of one whose brain has been less exercised than his hand. He sees and therefore describes few things clearly, nor has he any notion what the things are concerning the history, manner and deportment of such a person as Hannah More that her biographer ought to have made it his business to describe. . .

Apart from, and in addition to, Roberts's technical deficiencies, his strong Evangelical sympathies distorted his interpretation of Miss More. Everything that is not in keeping with his conception of an Evangelical saint is suspect. Hannah More leaves his hands as the austere, sanctimonious precisian which the nineteenth century was excused for disliking. His extravagant and undiscriminating enthusiasm for her did nothing to rehabilitate her in the eyes of posterity.

Other contemporary biographies of Hannah More merit attention. The *Life of Hannah More* by Henry Thompson, Curate of Wrington, Somerset, which appeared in 1838, is a carefully annotated work. He knew Miss More only in the last years of her life, but Wrington parish, in which her home at Barley Wood was situated, supplied him with new and interesting details. As an orthodox Churchman, antipathetic to Evangelical 'enthusiasm', his study of her life is a useful corrective to that of Roberts.

The *Life of Hannah More* by the Reverend William Shaw, Rector of Chelvey, Somerset, published in 1802, is of interest mainly as an illustration of the scurrilous practice, discernible throughout the later eighteenth and early nineteenth century, of destroying reputations by calumny and vituperation. Hannah More's success in galvanizing some of the 'lazy clergy' of the Mendips to support her schools aroused vehement opposition among those who disapproved of the schools and their founder. His *Life* sets out to disparage her. Much, but not all, of it is easy to refute. It portrays the mind of its author rather than that of his subject.

Preface

Of the several nineteenth- and twentieth-century biographies of Hannah More, that of Charlotte Yonge in 1888 is still the best. It is written with Miss Yonge's distinctive charm, and is of peculiar interest as a High Churchwoman's view of an Evangelical, but it adds little to the history of Hannah More's life as related by Roberts and Thompson. A recent life of Miss More by Miss M. A. Hopkins of Connecticut, U.S.A. (1947) has made use of some hitherto unknown letters of Hannah More found in libraries and museums and in private hands in England and America.

Each of these biographies has its particular value, but a study of Hannah More's correspondence reveals a woman of far richer personality and of greater significance in the history of her time than has been commonly acknowledged. Her correspondence was carried on with a remarkable galaxy of men and women, who, between them, represented the different interests of the age and who sought her friendship and valued her opinion. Her letters to them emerge triumphantly from the biographies. Clear, vivid, informative, free from pose and affectation, they have a refreshing spontaneity, some wit and shrewd judgement of men and affairs. Those printed by Roberts are but a fragment of those written by her, as the appearance of her letters in memoirs of the last hundred years and the discovery of MS. letters hidden away in private collections bear witness. As recently as May 1951, three hundred MS. letters written by Miss More to Richard Hart-Davis, M.P. for Bristol, 1812-31, were sold by auction. Like all good letter-writers, she adapted her matter and her style to meet the tastes of her correspondents, and in so doing revealed herself. 'I have a particular notion about correspondence,' she wrote. 'I would not give much for what is called a fine letter even from those who are most gifted in writing. What I want in a letter is a picture of my friend's mind and the common sense of his life . . . I have the same feeling in writing to him.' No one who has read the great letter-writers of the eighteenth century would deny her letters high praise. They have been curiously neglected by historians of the eighteenth century. Hannah More's *Works*, the second main contemporary source

ix

for her life, were published in collected editions in 1801 and again in 1819, 1830, 1853, and 1864. Their literary value, in contrast to that of her letters, is negligible, but as 'documentaries', stretching over half a century of national life, they invest the revolutionary changes in religion and manners with which she was primarily concerned with a rare dynamic quality.

Finally, there are the innumerable references to Miss More in the letters and memoirs, published and unpublished, of her contemporaries. Collected together they present formidable proof of the extraordinary importance which the men and women of her time attached to this pious and public-spirited woman and her opinions. To students of eighteenth-century history her long life, stretching from 1745 to 1833, her innumerable public activities, and her relations with all sorts and conditions of persons supply a valuable cross-section of English social and religious history in the years under review.

M. G. J.

CAMBRIDGE
August 1952

ACKNOWLEDGEMENTS

I am much indebted to the late Sir Edward Anson, Bart., to the late Brigadier-General H. Biddulph, to Mr E. M. Forster, Mr C. Becher Pigot, Lord Templewood and Mrs Ivo Hood, Dr J. A. Venn and Mr C. E. Wrangham for permission to use manuscript materials in their possession: to Miss Rhoda Power and Miss Anderson-Scott for their generous help, and to others of my friends in England and the United States of America, who have given me information.

M. G. J.

PART I

BRISTOL

'Boast we not a More?'
Legend at the Theatre Royal, Bristol

CHAPTER I

THE SCHOOL IN PARK STREET

'What, five women live happily together! I will come and see you.'
Dr Johnson to Sally More (1776)

(i)

THE five More sisters, Mary, Elizabeth, Sarah, Hannah, and Martha, were pious, intelligent, and highly competent young women.[1] Educated by their parents, they were sent out into the world unusually well prepared to earn their living. Little is known of their parents.[2] Mary Grace, their mother, daughter of 'a creditable farmer' at Stoke, near Stapleton, Bristol, was a woman of vigorous character. Jacob More, her husband, a man of gentle birth, was born at Thorpe Hall, a 'substantial family mansion' at Harleston, near Bungay, Norfolk, in 1700, and, becoming a good classical scholar at Norwich Grammar School, then under Samuel Parr's brother, intended to take Holy Orders. Differences of opinion in religion and politics, for Jacob More was a Tory and High Churchman, in the eighteenth-century meaning of the term, while his mother was a zealous Nonconformist, and the unfortunate issue of a lawsuit which 'blasted his hopes' of succeeding to a family estate at Wenhaston, Suffolk, sent him from the East to the West of England to seek a livelihood. There, through the patronage of Norborne Berkeley, Esq., later Baron Bottetourt, the local magnate at Stoke Park, he became master of a poorly endowed charity school at Stapleton,[3] three miles outside Bristol, married Mary Grace, taught his schoolboys and his five daughters, and invited relays of unfortunate prisoners, whom the persistent French Wars deposited in the neighbourhood, to polish his children's knowledge of the French language. His daughters, well equipped, established

3

one of the best-known schools for girls in the eighteenth century, and retired from their labours in 1790 with a comfortable competence.

Sally's gay recital of the conversation she and Hannah enjoyed with Dr Samuel Johnson in 1776 provides the best contemporary account of their adventure:

After much critical discourse, he turns round to me, and with one of his most amiable looks, which must be seen to form the least idea of it, he says 'I have heard that you are engaged in the useful and honourable employment of teaching young ladies.' Upon which with all the same ease, familiarity and confidence we should have done, had only our own dear Dr Stonhouse been present we entered upon the history of our birth, parentage and education, shewing how we were born with more desires than guineas, and how, as years increased our appetites, the cupboard at home began to grow too small to gratify them: and how, with a bottle of water, a bed and a blanket, we set out to seek our fortunes: and how we found a great house with nothing in it, and how it was like to remain so till, looking into our knowledge-boxes, we happened to find a little *larning*, a good thing when land is gone, or rather none: and so, at last, by giving a little of this little *larning* to those who had less, we got a good store of gold in return but how, alas, we wanted the wit to keep it. 'I love you both,' cried the inamorato, 'I love you all five. I never was at Bristol. I will come on purpose to see you. What, five women live happily together! I will come and see you. I have spent a happy evening. I am glad I came. God for ever bless you: you live lives to shame duchesses.'[4]

And, though Boswell does not mention it, Dr Johnson, attended by Boswell, paid his promised visit to the sisters in April 1776.[5]

The school was opened at No. 6 Trinity Street, one of the best quarters of the old city, in 1757. The parents, who had followed their children to Bristol, set up a private school for boys on Stony Hill,[6] an arrangement which assured to their daughters parental guidance combined with independence. Mary More, aged nineteen, a grave and mature young woman, was the governess of the establishment. Betty, a shadowy figure, as housekeepers are apt to be, cared for the domestic side of the school. The three younger sisters, Sally, Hannah, and Patty, when they had ceased to be the pupils of their elders and had reached years of discretion, were the under-governesses. With the help of visiting masters for French,

4

Italian, dancing, and music and with the hindrance of a succession of ignorant and incompetent assistant mistresses, they formed the teaching staff. 'I thought', wrote Hannah from London in 1783 to Mary More, 'that Mrs Garrick would drop with laughing when I read in Sally's letter that you spent all your leisure in teaching the *governesses* to read and write. It struck her fancy mightily.'[7]

The sisters were fortunate in the time and place of their venture. The second half of the eighteenth century witnessed a remarkable degree of interest in the education of boys and girls, on what may be termed, to distinguish it from the instruction in the petty schools and the endowed and subscription English charity schools, a secondary level of education. Primarily, this interest may be ascribed to the steady rise in wealth, numbers, and influence of men engaged in trade and commerce on an ever-growing scale. The expansion of commerce and banking, the development of a colonial empire, and, above all, the rapid growth of industrialism, were creating a new social order. Not sufficiently coherent in the 'fifties and 'sixties to form a class, in the modern sense of the term, the most prosperous members of the middling classes were, in mid-century England, beginning to rival the landed aristocracy and the 'estated gentlemen' in wealth, while the remainder enjoyed a considerable means of well-being. To education they made a characteristic contribution in the support they gave to the private venture school or academy, whose education differed from the almost exclusively classical education of the old endowed grammar school. Instruction in mathematics, commercial arithmetic, history, geography, and modern languages, with or without the classic tongues, was the response of the schoolmaster to parents who demanded an education which would fit their sons directly for the counting-house, the factory, and, with the rapid growth of retail trade, the counter. As early as 1760, Joseph Priestley, himself a representative of the new interests, held that 'the severe and proper discipline of the grammar school had become a topic of ridicule. Few young gentlemen, except those who were destined for some of the learned professions, were made to go through the rigours of it.'[8] The remarkable work of the private venture schools for boys, some of which were socially select and of high intellectual standards, others of which were conducted by men who, often without character or qualifications, undertook to give instruction in any subject to any pupil able to pay the fees, has not yet been adequately studied or appreciated. Good and bad, they succeeded so well in meeting the requirements of the age that the decline of the endowed grammar school, restricted by law and by the Church from adapting its curriculum to modern demands, may in great part be attributed to them.

The growing interest in the education of girls in the eighteenth century received support of a like nature from the same source. It was this support which explains the remarkable popularity of the private venture schools for girls. Schools, some of them offering a high standard of education for girls, may be found here and there in the seventeenth and early eighteenth century, but in general the education of girls was then, except in the charity schools, lamentably neglected. Some gentlemen's daughters received instruction at home from their parents or from their brothers' tutors, some, when so rare a bird could be found, from an educated family governess. Some few attended the more select of the schools in existence, but the majority had no education at all and, according to Richard Steele, were not ashamed of their illiteracy.[9] Dean Swift, expressing in 1723 his usual contempt for the 'generality of women', alleged that 'not one gentleman's daughter in a thousand could read or understand her own natural tongue.' Nor could they converse. 'When both sexes meet; if the men are discoursing upon any general subject, the ladies never think it their business to partake in what passeth';[10] and it might be asserted without fear of contradiction that the daughters of the comfortable middling classes, precluded by law or custom from attending the grammar schools, and by fear of loss of caste from attending the endowed or subscription charity schools for the poor, were in no better case. Yet, half a century later, Dr Johnson could assert, 'All our ladies read now.'[11] So marked a change in the intellectual position of gentlemen's daughters may be

6

ascribed in part, as Lady Mary Wortley Montagu ascribed it, to 'the frequency of the mixed Assemblies', which her granddaughters enjoyed in the 'enlightened' 'sixties. They provided 'a kind of Public Education, which I have always considered', added this good feminist, 'as necessary for girls as for boys.'[12]

But 'the enlarged way of thinking', which, she held, the mixed assemblies fostered, benefited only the select few who attended them. More potent as an influence in breaking down female illiteracy was the 'superfetation' of literature[13]—a spate of new books, novels in chief—which offered to women a delight so new and desirable that the labour of learning to read was forgotten in the pleasures it assured. The novel had created a new reading public. Moreover, since it was, in general, descriptive of fashionable life, it introduced to families rising in the world standards of feminine accomplishments—reading, writing, deportment, dancing, music, drawing, needlework, and the elements of foreign languages—to which they paid the sincerest form of flattery. Private venture schools for girls, usually boarding-schools for all or part of the pupils, met the growing demand for feminine education of this kind. They appeared rapidly in the second half of the eighteenth century. Differing from one another in the social standing of their pupils, and in the fees charged, they one and all provided an almost identical curriculum in accomplishments. 'The plan is the same,' lamented a correspondent of the *Sentimental Magazine* in 1773, 'the daughter of one of the lowest shopkeepers at one of these schools, is as much miss and young lady as the daughter of the first Viscount at the other.'[14] Little schools with an inscription on the door 'Young ladies Boarded and Educated' were so numerous and had become so common that they created throughout England a quasi-system of education for girls, which remained until late in the nineteenth century their chief means of instruction. Women of all sorts and conditions, with or without character or intellectual qualifications, found in the private venture school a not too ill-paid means of livelihood. Among them the More sisters, who set up their school on the crest of the wave, held an honourable place.

The School in Park Street

Equally fortunate were the sisters in the neighbourhood of their enterprise. 'Boeotian Bristol' was, throughout the greater part of the eighteenth century, a favourite subject of opprobrium to the *intelligentsia* who visited it or lived within its walls. Its dirt, wealth, ostentation, and absorption in money-making, so that the 'very parsons learned to turn the penny',[15] its indifference to the sciences and the arts won it unrelieved reproach. But in the 'sixties and 'seventies Bristol was beginning to bestir itself and prepare for its Augustan Age in the 'nineties.[16] In the 'seventies a group of leading citizens formed the Bristol Library Society, one of the first in the kingdom, for the diffusion of literature; men distinguished for their eminence in literature and science were invited to visit the city and address its citizens. Nor could a city, however indifferent to the arts, ignore the interest aroused by the alleged discovery of the Rowley papers, when all England was divided upon their authorship, for was not Chatterton a Bristol boy? Even more remarkable as a sign of awakening interest was the opening of the famous Theatre Royal in King Street, financed by fifty public-spirited Bristol gentlemen. The elegant and beautifully proportioned little theatre was proclaimed by Garrick to be the 'most complete of its dimension in Europe'. From its opening to the close of the century it was one of the most prosperous in the provinces. Every leading actor of the later eighteenth century, it is said, with the exception of Garrick, played upon its boards, and many of them were trained by William Powell, the actor-manager, and his successors.[17]

The More sisters were active participants in the city's new interests. The school, unlike most schools, was a centre of intellectual life. The sisters, educated and intelligent, read widely; they attended the public lectures with enthusiasm and did their part in entertaining the distinguished visitors to the city. Charitable and generous, they befriended the unhappy Chatterton's mother and sister after his death,[18] and, regarding the stage, as their mentor Addison had done, as an agent of the good life, they frequented the Theatre Royal and, on occasion when *King Lear* or other plays suitable for young ladies were performed, marched the whole school to the theatre.

The School in Park Street

The response of the prosperous citizens of Bristol to the sisters' venture was immediate and continuous. The school was in striking contrast to those depicted by Southey in his *Reminiscences* as characteristic of girls' schools in the West of England. Five well-educated schoolmistresses of piety and high character put it in a class by itself. Bristol citizens sent their daughters, and even their sons in their tender years. The highly respected Mrs Edward Lovell Gwatkin, wealthy and well connected, sent her daughter; Old Cottle, the bookseller, his two girls; the cousins of William Turner, squire of Belmont, Wraxall, were among the boarders; the 'lovely and unfortunate Perdita',[19] daughter of John Darby, a prominent West India merchant; the daughter of William Powell; and later, Selina Mills, daughter of Thomas Mills, the bookseller, and mother of Lord Macaulay, were among the pupils. From the 'seventies Hannah More's social and literary successes in London extended the clientèle of the school. It began to draw its pupils not only from the families of Bristol merchants and tradesmen but from the gentry and professional classes, 'from Land's End to John o' Groats'. 'Several ladies of fortune and discernment', wrote the editor of *Public Characters*, 'gave their support to the sisters, sending their daughters and advertising the school to their friends, so that many families of rank received their education in it.'[20] In 1767 the sisters moved out of Trinity Street and built for themselves a commodious school-house in the fashionable and newly developed district of Park Street, where they remained until they retired in 1790.[21] Mrs Elizabeth Montagu, who visited the Mores at Bristol in 1781, paid her tribute to the sisters and the school:

I passed a most agreeable day with Miss Hannah More and her three sisters. They are all women of admirable sense, and unaffected behaviour, and I should prefer their school to any I have ever seen for girls, whether very young or misses in their teens.[22]

It was left to Dr George Horne, at the time Dean of Canterbury and later Bishop of Norwich, whose daughter, little Sally Horne, was a boarder at the school, to put on record the acknowledgements of the parents for an education firm in principle and polished in accomplishments 'after the similitude of a palace'.[23]

9

The School in Park Street

An adventure such as this of five penniless and inexperienced young women required for its success not only intelligence and character, with which the More sisters were amply endowed, but patronage, and it is a testimony to the high reputation of Jacob More and his daughters that at no time in their scholastic career did they lack this essential of eighteenth-century success. It is clear, in the light of later events, that the ducal family of the Beauforts was interested in Jacob More and his daughters. Norborne Berkeley, later Baron Bottetourt, uncle of the fifth duke, was patron of the Stapleton endowed charity school and had appointed Jacob More to the mastership. The wife of the fifth duke gave her patronage to Hannah More when she called upon her in her modest lodging in Henrietta Street, Covent Garden, and thereby established her in London society.[24] One of the most influential men in the Bristol of his age, Josiah Tucker, Rector of St Stephen's and Dean of Gloucester, was a warm friend of the sisters. Bishop Warburton's epigram that trade was Tucker's religion is remembered when Bishop Newton's commendation of him as the pattern parish priest is forgotten. To crowded congregations of his wealthy parishoners at St Stephen's he propounded economic and political doctrines which made him, before the appearance of the *Wealth of Nations*, the most discussed political economist of his day.[25] His interest conferred no small benefit upon the school. For Hannah he had unbounded admiration. He acknowledged her masculine quality of common sense by talking to her as an equal on private and public affairs.

'Our dear Dr Stonhouse', the sisters' next-door neighbour in Park Street, constituted himself their guide, philosopher, and friend early in the history of the school.[26] Wealthy, well connected, 'with elegant manners' and a reputation as one of the most eloquent preachers in the Kingdom, the rector of Great and Little Cheverell, Wilts, held a lectureship at All Saints Church, Clifton, and was a conspicuous figure in Bristol society. He was a patron of incalculable value to the sisters in their adventure. They, for their part, were of one mind in their love and admiration for him as friend and priest. The portrait of the good clergyman in *The Shepherd of Salisbury Plain*, one of the happiest of Hannah's tracts, may be regarded as the composite picture of their next-door neighbour. It was he, said Hannah, in later years who 'first awakened me to some sense of serious things'. He guided her reading in the works of Christian evidence and Christian devotion, introducing her to Anglican and Nonconformist classics, the 'judicious Hooker', Jeremy Taylor, Thomas Wilson, Richard Baxter, and Philip Doddridge; yet it was he who, admiring her 'dramatic genius', prevailed on his old friend, David Garrick, to consider her plays for the London stage, an action curiously out of keeping with his Evangelical leanings.

The names of four of the five members of the 'Bright Sisterhood', as Lord Macaulay dubbed the sisters, appear but seldom in the *Memoirs of the Life and Correspondence*. Many of Hannah's letters to them were carefully filed by Patty; theirs to her, it must be presumed, were not preserved. The forceful, uncompromising, ardent character of Hannah's most dearly loved sister, Patty, her untiring zeal and dry humour live in her notable *Mendip Journal*, and there were not lacking men and women whose considered opinion it was that she was the 'spiritual genius' of the family.[27] The elder sisters depend on occasional contemporary references for their portraits. Mary More, who carried on her shoulders the heavy responsibility of the school and the care of her young sisters, was a woman of sober dignity and trenchant speech. To her careful religious training Hannah owed much.[28] Betty, except when hospitality was concerned, does not emerge from the family background. Of 'a reserved disposition', she was the complement to Sally More, 'a sprightly gay-tempered creature whose vivacity age could not tame'. 'The wild and unrestrained wit' of this rather noisy young woman not seldom alarmed her sisters' sense of propriety. David Garrick, her 'dear, dear friend', considered her sense of humour greater than that of any woman he knew. It was rumoured that in her youth she had written two novels, and that in her old age she was a 'furious politician'.[29] The sisters appear consistently as kindly, cheerful women of excellent good sense.[30] They looked well after their pupils while the school was in being, and in later years identified themselves with Hannah's religious and philanthropic interests. Their strong individuality did not prevent them from living together for sixty years in 'uninterrupted harmony'.[31]

The fourth daughter, Hannah, born in 1745, was from childhood regarded by her parents, sisters, and friends as the genius of the family. Delicate though she was as a child and throughout her long life, her remarkable vitality did much to compensate for a lack of physique. Her letters disclose a vivacious and impulsive young woman, overflowing with affection and generosity. Parents and sisters were devoted to her, admired her, and coddled her with, at times, suffocating care. It is not given to every woman to be a hero to her sisters. This singular achievement Hannah accomplished without apparent effort. She, on her part, paid graceful deference to her parents and elder sisters, she was the life-long confidante of Patty, and the delighted admirer of Sally's humour. Her pleasing appearance[32] was matched by a quick wit, a catholic taste for 'sensible nonsense', a charm of manner and an immense capacity for hero-worship which enabled her to make and retain the friendship of the innumerable men and women whom she met in the course of her long life of eighty-nine years. Dr Johnson's advice, 'A man, sir, should keep his friendship in *constant repair*,' is seldom easy to follow.[33] It demands infinite expenditure of time, well-developed powers of adaptation, and a heavy and exacting correspondence. Hannah More not only nursed her old friendships with care, she repaired the chain with new friendships when the old links dropped out. Of few persons could it be said as it was of her in her old age, even if it was not strictly true, that she had never lost and never lacked a friend. The range and number of her extant letters, and they are but a fragment of those written by her, show that she took her correspondence seriously.

Early in her childhood she discovered to her proud but uneasy parents an ambition for learning unusual among women. Responding to her eager request to study classics and mathematics, Jacob More taught her the rudiments of Latin and sent her during her

Bristol schooldays to continue her Latin studies under James Newton, the distinguished Tutor of the Bristol Baptist Academy, thus preparing the way for Horace Walpole's encomium upon her Latin in later years.[34] But Jacob More's instruction of his daughter in mathematics came to an abrupt end when he discovered that Hannah's ability was superior to that of the schoolboys under his care. Mathematical prowess such as hers threatened to be was unfeminine and not to be encouraged.

Deprived by parental disapproval of the astringent training which mathematics is alleged to bestow, the eager child, as she grew older, gave full rein to the 'velvet studies' of history and of literature, reading omnivorously English, French, Italian, and Spanish poets, and jotting down from the age of four, if family heroics may be believed, poems and stories whenever she could beg, borrow, or steal a scrap of paper. From her early days she showed considerable skill in writing the fashionable *vers d'occasion*, with an ease and spontaneity which later delighted her fellow scribbler, David Garrick. The birthday of one pupil, the success of another, the death of a third afforded ready scope for her pen. At other times she addressed hymns to her revered friend next door, one of which was sent, presumably by him, to Dr Johnson, who learnt it by heart and recited it to her, as his opening conversational gambit, when Hannah first met him in Sir Joshua Reynolds's drawing-room in Leicester Fields. Even more prolific was her pen, as she grew older, in manufacturing epitaphs for the tombstones of departed friends, for which, in the nature of things, there was an unceasing demand. Most of them are in Johnsonian English, and are best forgotten. None of them subscribed to Burke's definition of an epitaph as 'a grave epigram'. Nevertheless, requests for lines from her pen poured in as late as the 'eighties, when 'my monumental wit had worn itself out'. 'I defy any poet', she remarked with unruffled good humour and mock despair, 'to introduce two names so peculiarly unlucky and obnoxious to puns as Fortune Little.'[35] The inscription was one of her more successful efforts. Burke, on one of his rare visits to his Bristol constituents, committed it to memory, and he, in his turn, recited it to her at an evening party in London.[36] The tablet and inscription are still to be seen in lovely St Mary Redcliffe Church.

Nor could a girl whose pen moved with such dangerous facility refrain from expressing in laudatory verse her pleasure when visitors to Bristol, such as the elder Sheridan, 'Old Bubble and Squeak', lectured on rhetoric in his exuberant way. The introduction which followed the presentation of her verses to him marked the beginning of the friendship between the Sheridans, old and young, and Hannah More, which Richard Brinsley Sheridan stamped with his approval when he wrote the prologue to Hannah's third play in 1779.

Her local fame was not confined to her success in writing facile verse. She was a good talker and held her own, even as a girl, with the several notable men who sought her acquaintance. Among them were Samuel Peach, the Bristol linen-draper, amanuensis of David Hume; and John Ford, one of the founders of the Bristol Library Society and later joint-lessee of Drury Lane Theatre. Josiah Tucker, the political economist, and James Ferguson, author of *Astronomy Explained*, demanded her help in polishing the rough edges of their MSS., regardless of her plea that economics and astronomy were beyond her comprehension. 'Pish!' said Tucker, paying her the highest compliment at his command, 'common sense will always appeal to common sense.' Conversation, which gave the Bas Bleu ladies in London so much anxious thought in their mixed assemblies, did not greatly perturb the provincial lady when she arrived in the metropolis. 'Boeotian Bristol' had trained her well.

The demands of the school were, however, responsible for her appearance as a dramatist. Henry Thornton's eldest daughter, Marianne, and Tom Macaulay have charmingly testified to her happy relations with children in her later years. She was a rare favourite with them. Gay, friendly, indulgent, sometimes too indulgent, she wrote nursery rhymes and fairy tales for her pupils, and told them 'Bible Stories of Joseph and his brothers and the wonderful adventures of the Children of Israel with such eloquence and force that I fancied she must have lived among them herself'[37]. A stimulating teacher, she used the dramatic method to modify the deadly monotony of learning by rote, the common method of her day. Religious instruction, in particular, suffered from a verbal rigidity which she urged in her later pedagogic writings could be broken down by referring, as Christ had done in his parables, to the surrounding objects and passing events which children could understand. To show 'Christ walking on the water not of Genesareth but Thames' was her desire. Her *Sacred Dramas*, 'her boldest experiment', were acted by the children in the school before they were published in 1782.[38] When they appeared, their stiff wooden verses of formal gravity provided 'Peter Pindar', Miss More's persistent critic, with an irresistible opportunity for satire upon:

> The Holy Dramas of Miss Hannah More
> Where all the Nine and little Moses snore.[39]

In her sixteenth year she turned her attention to the elder girls of the school and supplied in her pastoral drama, *The Search After Happiness*, 'a substitute for the very improper custom of allowing plays, and they not always of the purest kind, to be acted by young ladies in boarding schools'.[40] *The Search After Happiness* made the author and the Park Street school known throughout the scholastic world. The play, which provided harassed schoolmistresses with the satisfaction of a long-felt want, passed in manuscript from school to school, was first published in 1773, went into its ninth edition in 1787, and before that date had sold ten thousand copies. Patty, to whom Hannah made over the rights to all future royalties, was promised a small fortune. Mary Mitford, who acted in the play with the girls of the Abbey School, Reading, testified that it satisfied the mistresses, if not the girls.[41] The success of this highly moral little drama, only too truly described by Hannah More (who throughout her life maintained a highly critical estimate of her own work) as 'void of wit and free from love', was one of the two factors which determined her immediate future.

The second factor was her betrothal in her twenty-third year to the wealthy middle-aged squire, William Turner of Belmont, Wraxall, whose young cousins were pupils at the school. Hannah's pleasure in the beauties of his estate found its normal vent in descriptive verse:

> Where beauteous Belmont rears her modest brow
> To view Sabrina's silver waves below.

Turner, delighted with the verses, ordered them to be painted on boards and affixed to the trees, looking, said Miss Charlotte Yonge a hundred years later, exactly like notices to trespassers.[42] Equally charmed by the versifatrix, Turner proposed marriage and was accepted. Hannah gave up her share in the school and fixed the wedding day. Three times, according to Thomas de Quincey, whose mother, in later years, was a close friend of Hannah More, the bridegroom, blowing hot and cold in turns, postponed the marriage day. During these years of protracted humiliation Hannah More behaved with exemplary dignity. Twice she accepted the apologies of her laggard bridegroom, yet once again, when the bride and her friends awaited him in Clifton Church, he excused himself, sending a note of apology by his groomsman.[43]

This miserable and mortifying episode ended when the sisters and their friends, outraged by Turner's inexplicable conduct, prevailed on Hannah to break the engagement. The bridegroom still protested his affection and his desire to marry her on any day and hour she might choose, but she remained firm. Stonhouse, self-appointed guardian to the sisters, agreed, without Hannah's knowledge or consent, to Turner's urgent desire to settle an annuity upon her. It was this settlement which, when time had softened the bitterness of so humiliating an experience, gave a provincial schoolmarm the financial independence without which her literary triumphs in London and her philanthropic work in the Mendips would have been impossible. But Miss More's acceptance of Turner's money, says her biographer, was not uniformly approved. It provoked 'undeserved imputation of inconstancy or a calculating prudence'.[44]

The School in Park Street

(ii)

No explanation of Turner's extraordinary conduct was offered by Miss More's biographers, and none appears in her published correspondence. Most probably, as Miss Charlotte Yonge shrewdly suggests, 'it was a case of an elderly man growing shy'. The humiliating experience goes some way to explain Hannah More's determination to return to her first love, the drama, and, in spite of later proposals of marriage, to remain a spinster. The effects of the unhappy affair on herself it is not possible to assess. Letters and memoirs are silent on so intimate a theme. It is possible, but improbable, since the sisters were not women to wear their hearts on their sleeves, that Hannah's ballad, *The Bleeding Rock*, a Somerset legend of a forsaken maiden, published in 1775, was an open protest to her inconstant lover. In her later didactic writings there is a passage in which she condemns the reading and writing of poetry by young and sentimental girls who are too inexperienced to know that 'the exchange of sonnets is to men but the recreation of an idle hour of which they soon grow weary'.[45] All that is known is that after a period of distress of mind she found, like other courageous young women, a new and absorbing interest when she had sent William Turner away. She began to study drama in earnest, and being 'very partial to the King Street Theatre' she became during the next few years a well-known figure there. She gained considerable experience in play production and made for herself a new circle of friends among the actors and actresses she met.[46] Their pride in her later achievements was pleasingly expressed in the epigraph inscribed on the walls of the Theatre Royal: 'Boast we not a More?'[47] For William Powell, the actor-manager, and Miss Pritchard, 'the highly respected daughter' of Garrick's 'divine peerless Lady Macbeth', Miss More had warm regard. In the 'eighties Hannah More and Sarah Siddons, of blameless character, formed a lasting friendship, which in later years aroused the ribald mirth of Thomas de Quincey.

A free translation of Metastasio's *Attilio Regolo* provided Miss More with the materials for her first play, *The Inflexible Captive*.

17

She took it with her in her pocket when she went to London in the winter season of 1774. Whether she met Garrick first in London, as Roberts states, or in Bristol, where her friends Bishop Newton, Stonhouse, Powell, and Ford were his friends also, is not clear, but she knew enough of Garrick's reputation as 'the House of Lords to dramatic poets'[48] to realize that he held the key to her future. With so dazzling a prospect it was not possible to be indifferent to William Turner's annuity.

(iii)

Other incidents in the 'seventies attest the affection and admiration of Hannah More's friends and her growing reputation. John Langhorne, the Somerset poet, Rector of Blagdon, proposed marriage.[49] He and Hannah met, according to Thompson, at Weston-super-Mare, when Hannah was recovering from 'a morbid sensibility of constitution', a synonym for the modern nervous breakdown, attributable, it may be assumed, to William Turner's defection. They rode together on the shore and local tradition preserved his lament written on the sands when they failed to meet:

> Along the shore,
> Walked Hannah More.
> Waves, let the record last;
> Sooner shall ye,
> Proud earth and sea,
> Than what she writes, be past.

Miss More, dismounting demurely from the pillion behind her groom, and using her riding whip as a pen, answered:

> Some firmer basis, polished Langhorne, choose,
> To write the dictates of thy charming Muse;
> Thy strains in solid character rehearse
> And be thy tablet lasting as thy verse.

This 'amatory flirtation', when Hannah had refused Langhorne's proposal, developed into a lasting literary friendship, carried on, at least on his side, for her letters are not extant, in terms of 'great sensibility'.

18

The School in Park Street

Blow, blow, my sweetest rose,
For Hannah More will soon be here
And all that crowns the ripening year
Shall triumph where she goes.

Few things could be more consoling to a young woman morti-
fied as Hannah More had been by her unhappy betrothal than an
offer of marriage which she had no intention of accepting. It was
gratifying, too, that Langhorne's admiration extended, with obvious sincerity, to her work, for he was not only a poet but a critic
of repute. His extravagant praise played its part in building up her
reputation. The epilogue written by him for her first play, and, in
particular, his review of her poems in the *Monthly Review* for
February 1776, created a stir in London. Even if, at the back of her
mind, her critical sense threw doubt on Langhorne's praise, it was
agreeable to be told that her 'fame had reached the ends of the
earth'.[50]

Politics, too, provided new interest and made possible new
friendships in the 'seventies. The famous Bristol parliamentary
election of September 1774 brought Edmund Burke (whom Hannah had met in London) to Bristol to contest, in company with his
Bristol colleague, Henry Cruger, the seats held by the old members,
Lord Clare and Matthew Brickdale. The election, extending for
over a week, was fought primarily on the question of the taxation
of the American Colonies—a question which touched closely Bristol's colonial trade. It had already brought Burke and Josiah Tucker
into vehement and embittered controversy in the summer of 1774.
The sisters, showing a cheerful indifference to the principles at
stake and profoundly impressed by the brilliant intellectual powers
of 'the sublime and beautiful Edmund Burke', became his ardent
supporters and the house in Park Street a centre of political activity.
There Burke was a frequent visitor, and on one never-to-be-forgotten occasion Burke and Tucker, at daggers drawn, followed
by Catharine Macaulay, the historian, who had recently attacked
both of them, called upon the sisters, 'happily', said Hannah, relating the story later with enjoyment, 'not together, but in succes-

sion.' When Burke, overwhelmed by the innumerable letters attacking him in the local press, needed help, Hannah assisted him to deal with his correspondence. Some of the more important replies, says the Bristol historian, W. E. Weare, were believed to have been written by her at Burke's dictation; others 'on which it is still possible to put one's fingers' were Hannah's composition. In addition, verses in Burke's support dripped from her pen. The lines

> He is himself the great sublime he draws,
> In action faithful and in honour dear.
> Correct with spirit, elegant with ease,
> Justum et tenacem propositi virum.

were attached by the sisters to a cockade composed of the colours classified by Burke as the beautiful and sublime, and enwreathed in myrtle, bay, laurel, and ivy. It was worn by the triumphant candidate in the procession on chairing day, when Hannah's share in Burke's success was publicly acknowledged, to the sisters' lively amusement, by a cheering mob outside the school in Park Street.[51]

Burke's contact with Hannah More did not end with this entertaining incident. He was one of the few men of her London acquaintance concerned with politics. She professed no interest in them and regarded them as a man's province and unfitted for women. But her letters show that in regard to two of the three big political questions of her early London days, the struggle for the Colonies and the government of India, she was neither indifferent nor uninformed. Parliamentary reform is not mentioned. This was in keeping with the lack of public interest in the matter. On these questions of the day she could not agree with Burke. None the less few of the friendships made in her London days exercised greater influence in her life. Years before Walter Scott 'translated into the dialect of fiction Burke's basic principles', Hannah More borrowed these principles and incorporated them in her popular village tracts written for the labourers and mechanics of England in an age of threatened revolution.[52]

At the age of twenty-eight, Hannah More, accompanied by two of her sisters, paid the first of her annual visits, continued for over twenty years, to London. She had given up her share in the school on her approaching marriage and did not resume her place as an active partner in the firm. But her letters show that she spent the greater part of each year with her sisters in the Park Street school, participating in its life and anxieties, setting literary puzzles on which the young ladies 'could exercise their wit', writing plays for the children and studies in education for adults, entertaining her London friends who came to meet her family, and never forgetting her Bristol friends and patrons. To them she was indebted for the remarkable welcome London offered her. The Garricks opened their doors to a protégée of Stonhouse. Sir Joshua Reynolds, whose favourite niece, Offley Palmer, was to marry Richard Lovell Gwatkin, gave cordial greeting to Mrs Lovell Gwatkin's young friend, and Mrs Boscawen, widow of Admiral Boscawen and mother of the Duchess of Beaufort, took her under her wing and assured her a welcome from her friends among the quality and the Blue Stocking coteries. A welcome of such distinction made no small demand upon the courage and adaptability of an unfashionable, humbly bred provincial schoolmistress; equally, if not more, intimidating were 'the low minds and bad hearts' of London's dreaded literary reviewers, 'the envious Kendrick and the savage Wolcot, the asp George Steevens and the polecat John Williams' of Lord Macaulay's full-flavoured denunciation,[53] who lay in wait with sharpened pens to destroy the effusions of literary ladies.[54] But courage, always one of her leading characteristics, prevailed. Hannah More arrived in London in 1774.

PART II

LONDON

'*You are the fashion.*' Mrs Boscawen to Miss More

CHAPTER II

THE DRAMA

'Garrick's Bantling.' Kitty Clive

HANNAH MORE's earliest friends in London were David Garrick
and his wife, Eva Maria Veigel,[1] famed in her early days in Vienna
and London as a *danseuse*, 'the finest and most admired dancer in
the world' in Horace Walpole's opinion.[2] Garrick in 1774 was in his
fifty-seventh year. His great days on the stage were over. As the
town wags pointed out in allusive couplets,

> I'm on the edge of nigh three score,
> 'Tis really time to give it o'er.[3]

But to a provincial who had not known him in his prime his
Lear, the first play in which Hannah More saw him act, possibly in
1774, was an overwhelming experience. 'It is literally true', she
wrote, after attending his farewell performance of *Lear* in 1776,
'that my spirits have not yet recovered from the shock they sustained. I generally think the last part I see him in, the greatest, but
in regard to that night it was the universal opinion that it was one of
the greatest scenes ever exhibited. I called today in Leicester Fields,
and Sir Joshua declared that it was full three days before he got the
better of it. The eagerness of the people to see him is beyond anything you can have an idea of.' Writing to Stonhouse in the same
year, she told him, 'I have, at last, had the entire satisfaction to see
Garrick in *Hamlet*. I would not wrong him myself so much as to
tell you what I think of it: it is sufficient that you have seen him; I
pity those who have not. Posterity will never be able to form the
slightest idea of his pretensions.' A few nights later she told the sisters she had seen him as Abel Drugger in Ben Jonson's *Alchemist*,
'and had I not seen him in both parts I should have thought it as

possible for Milton to have written *Hudibras* and Butler *Paradise Lost* as for one man to have played *Hamlet* and *Drugger* with such excellence.'⁴ Kitty Clive, most engaging of comedians and Garrick's old 'friend-enemy', expressed the same opinion in a more vivid, if less cultivated, phrase. 'Damn him, I believe he could act a gridiron.'⁵

Garrick's attitude towards the stage appealed to Hannah More no whit less than his genius as actor and manager. Her dramatic standards, intelligent as they were, were inextricably mixed up with her moral standards. Not for her the doctrine 'Art for art's sake'. The theatre to her was an instrument of the good life and the actor's profession was not, of necessity, identified with the flagrant immorality usually associated with it. Tragedy, her favourite mode of dramatic expression, she regarded clearly as a purgation of the emotions, and Garrick, not without reason, as a wholesome and cleansing force. 'Who shall now hold the master key to the human heart,' she wrote to the sisters after his retirement from the stage in 1776, 'who direct the passions with more than magic power? Who purify the stage, and who in short shall direct and nurse my dramatic muse?'⁶ Extravagant adulation, which only her obvious sincerity can excuse, marked her letter to Garrick of the same date:

Whatever reputation the world may ascribe to you, I, who have had the happy privilege of knowing you intimately, shall always think you derived your greatest glory from the temperance with which you enjoyed it, and the true greatness of mind with which you lay it down. Surely to have suppressed your talents in the moment of your highest capacity for exerting them, does as much honour to your heart as the exertion itself did to your dramatic character; but I cannot trust myself with this subject because I am writing to the man himself; yet I ought to be indulged, for is not the recollection of my pleasures all that is left me of them? Have I not seen in one season that man act seven and twenty times, and rise each time in excellence, and shall I be silent? Have I not spent three months under the roof of that man and his dear charming lady and received from them favours that would take me another three months to tell over and shall I be silent? ⁷

Hannah More's ingenuous, unaffected, and uncritical enthusiasm was responsible, in no small degree, for the affection which the Garricks lavished upon her. It won their hearts. Garrick's gargantuan appetite for praise had not diminished with the years, nor had Mrs Garrick's vicarious enjoyment in 'dear Davy's' happiness lessened one iota in the twenty-five years of their married life. In Hannah More Mrs Garrick, whose elegance, perfect manners, and irreproachable private life made her as acceptable a guest as her husband in the houses of the condescending quality, found a congenial and age-long friend. In the 'seventies the Garricks welcomed her and her sisters, who in the early days accompanied her to London, to their town house, No. 5 the Adelphi, and to their villa at Hampton; introduced her to Mrs Elizabeth Montagu and other friends among the *literati* and the quality, nicknamed her 'Nine' because they held she was the personification of the Nine Muses, and made it possible for her to satisfy her passion for the stage. Sometimes in company with Sally or Patty, sometimes alone in the pit, sometimes 'sitting in the best place', with the best company in the house, or near her friends Edmund and Richard Burke, Warton, Sheridan,[8] she attended performances at Covent .Garden, Drury Lane, and the Hay. Though Roberts is silent on so distasteful a theme, her stage experience in London was not confined to the auditorium. An ambitious playwright, who had helped Powell produce in Bristol and was part producer of her own play at Bath in 1775, would not have been content to remain merely a spectator. Part of the rigorous training to which Garrick 'subjected her muse' was the experience she acquired behind the scenes.[9] The greenroom at the Lane saw Hannah and her sisters in Garrick's company, and buzzed with excitement. 'Pray what is the meaning of a hundred Miss Mores purring about you with their poems and plays and romances?' wrote Kitty Clive to Garrick. 'Send them back to Bristol with a flea in their ears.'[10] Her advice was not followed. Instead, the Garricks insisted in 1776 that Hannah should leave her lodgings in Henrietta Street and stay with them for the London Season. This was the first of her annual visits to the Adelphi and Hampton. 'It is not possible', she told the sisters, 'for anything on earth to be more agreeable to my taste than my present manner of living. I am so much at my ease, have a great many hours at my disposal to read my own books and see my own friends, and whenever I please may join in the most polished and delightful society in the world.'[11] Any incongruity between 'my own books' and her new environment escaped her. 'I have read through all the Epistles three times since I have been here,' she wrote to Mrs Gwatkin, 'the ordinary translation, Locke's Paraphrase, and a third put into very elegant English (I know not by whom) in which St Paul's obscurities are elucidated and Harwood's pomp of words avoided. I am also reading West on the Resurrection; in my poor judgement a most excellent thing, calculated to confound all the cavils of the infidel and to confirm all the hopes of the believer.'[12]

Innumerable incidents attesting the generous tempers of Garrick and his wife related by Hannah More to her sisters help to modify the often malicious portraits of Garrick's detractors. As 'Dictator of the London Stage' he was a favourite target of abuse from less successful members of the profession. His privileged social position did not make things easier for him. No actor of his time was welcome, as he was, in the houses of great families, or entertained the quality as he did in his own home. Mrs Garrick confided to Sir Joshua Reynolds that the malignant diatribes of Thady Fitzpatrick and Samuel Foote were a very real trouble to David and herself.[13] He had the misfortune to live in an age which employed calumny and vituperation with pen and pencil, not to build up, but to destroy established reputations.[14] Nor did his friends spare him. Dr Johnson's studied rudeness and Goldsmith's famous thirty-two lines of disparagement were not calculated to encourage confidence in any man.[15] Hannah More was not ignorant of the steady stream of belittlement. A young woman of independent opinions, it aroused her anger. Why, she asked Garrick indignantly, was Dr Johnson so often harsh and unkind in his speeches both to and of him, and Garrick's mild answer, 'Why, Nine, is it not to be expected that I who have so much less merit than he should have had so much greater success?' did not cool her anger.[16] She was highly critical of Goldsmith's estimate of Garrick's acting, and she dealt faithfully with one of Garrick's detractors, Frances Brooke, the dramatist, in the *Monthly Review* for August 1777. Johnson had advised Mrs Brooke to consign her play, *The Siege of Sinope*, to the fire; Garrick had refused more than once to produce it. Mrs Brooke 'indulged her spleen' by a vilification of Garrick in her novel, *The Excursion*. Hannah More seized her opportunity. With satisfaction and considerable effect she chastised *The Excursion* in the *Review*.[17]

Hannah More's letters are of interest for the light they throw on Garrick as a man rather than as a national institution. She is a witness, were one needed, to the devoted affection of Garrick and his wife and to the 'decorum and propriety and regularity' of their married life.[18] His care for the comfort and happiness of a provincial schoolmistress bears witness to the generosity of a man whose petty economies were a favourite theme of his contemporaries. Writing from her rooms in Gerrard Street to the sisters, avid for detail, she tells them:

Mrs Garrick came to me this morning and wished me to go to the Adelphi, which I declined, being so ill. She would have gone herself to fetch me a physician, and insisted on sending me my dinner which I refused; but at 6 this evening when Garrick came to the Turk's Head [in Gerrard Street] to dine, there accompanied him in the coach a minced chicken in the stew-pan, a canister of her fine tea and a pot of cream. Were there ever such people? Tell it not in Epic, or in Lyric, that the great Roscius rode with a stew-pan . . . in the coach for my dinner![19]

The letters reveal, too, Garrick's respect for religion and the Church. To the serious More sisters he made known his desire 'to study the more important duties of life' and his ardent wish to bring his *domestique* under such regulation of order and sobriety as should be a credit and example to his profession.[20] Garrick, Hannah noticed, took pains to keep his home life free from contamination with the actors and actresses of his business life, a policy which did nothing to endear him to them. 'I never even met except in one instance', she told the sisters, 'a person of his own profession at his table.'[21] She paid his new gravity a charming but disconcerting compliment when she asked him to read and criticize a slim volume of moral essays 'on matters peculiarly feminine' which she had completed between her bouts of play-writing.[22] And he protected her from the embarrassments in which her sabbatarian principles not infrequently enmeshed her. Taken by the Garricks to spend a weekend at Farnborough Place with Wilmot, 'who lived like a prince', she was alarmed by the preparations for a concert on Sunday evening, 'but before I had time to feel uneasy Garrick turned round and said, "Nine, you are a Sunday woman: retire to your room and I will recall you when the music is over." '[23]

Not the least of the unfailing kindnesses of Mrs Garrick to her provincial friend was her care of Hannah More's dress and appearance in the new world of fashion. Miss More informed her sisters, with the exaggerated indifference of the unfashionable to sartorial art, that she had 'just escaped from the hands of one of the most fashionable disfigurers. I charged him to dress me with the greatest simplicity and to have only a very distant eye upon the fashion, just enough to avoid the pride of singularity, without running into excess.'[24] Comparison of Miss Reynolds's portrait of Hannah More, painted in 1780, with Opie's portrait of her in 1786 bears pleasing testimony to Mrs Garrick's good taste. It fortified Miss More, dressed by Mrs Garrick for an assembly at Mrs Ord's, to meet an embarrassing situation with the poise of the well-dressed. 'When I came into the drawing rooms I found them full of company,' wrote Hannah to the sisters. 'Every human creature in deep mourning, and I, poor I, all gorgeous in scarlet. I never recollected that the mourning for some foreign Wilhelmina Jacquelina was not over. However I got over it as well as I could, made my apology . . . and I hope this false step of mine will be buried in oblivion. . . Even Jacobite Johnson', she added, satirically, 'was in deep mourning.'[25]

At the Adelphi and at Hampton the Garricks found in her the perfect guest. She shared Mrs Garrick's admiration for dear Davy and David's admiration for his wife. She waxed enthusiastic about their ménage. Their breakfast parties were 'little literary societies'.

The Drama

Their dinner parties 'as all good dinner parties should be were small and carefully selected'. With her sprightly conversation she helped them to entertain their innumerable guests, 'the great Doctor Burney', Richard Brinsley Sheridan and his lovely wife, 'unaffected and sensible', Burke, Gibbon, the Bunburys, Richard Rigby, Sir William Forbes among them, and a host of French guests who arrived in 1776 to take a last look at the 'great dramatic sun before he sets'. On these occasions 'We had not one English sentence the whole day.'[26] It was at the Garricks that Hannah More established a warm friendship with Monsieur and Madame Jacques Necker, and through them became acquainted later with their famous daughter, Madame de Stäel.[27]

Garrick's jocosities which passed for wit she found exactly to her taste. She had a robust sense of humour and was enchanted by his pleasantries and his amazing gift of mimicry. 'Roscius', wrote Hannah in 1777, telling of a dinner party at Hampton, with Sheridan, Lord Palmerston, a noisy and exuberant talker, and the Norfolk Windham, 'surpassed himself, and literally kept the table in a roar of laughter for hours. He told his famous story of Jack Pocklington in a manner so entirely new and so infinitely witty that the company have done nothing but talk about it since. I have often heard of this story: it is of a person who came to offer himself for the stage, with an impediment in his speech.' It did not derogate from Miss More's enjoyment that Garrick gave the character 'in as strong a manner as Fielding could have done'.[28] 'Garrick', she writes again after she had entertained him and his wife, Dr Johnson, Dean Tucker, and Mrs Boscawen at her first *petite assemblée*, 'was the very soul of the company, and I never saw Johnson in such perfect good humour. Sally knows that we have often heard that one can never properly enjoy the company of these two unless they are together. There is a great truth in this remark... Johnson and Garrick began a close encounter telling old stories, "e'en from their boyhood days", at Lichfield. We all stood round them above an hour, laughing in defiance of decorum and Chesterfield. I believe that we should not have thought of sitting down or of parting had not an

31

impertinent watchman been saucily vociferous. . . Johnson out-
staid them all and sat with me half an hour.'[29]

When there were no guests to be entertained, she and Davy,
who shared her passion for writing *vers d'occasion*, read aloud to each
other their more successful efforts and even enveigled Mrs Garrick
to try her hand. Or David would read aloud to the two ladies, and
on one never-to-be-forgotten occasion, soon after the publication
of her ballad *Sir Eldred of the Bower*, which according to Miss Reynolds was 'the theme of conversation in all polite circles', Garrick
picked up the current number of the *Monthly Review* and read
aloud the poem to his wife and guests. Modelled on the ballads collected by Dr Percy, it began:

> There was a young and valiant knight,
> Sir Eldred was his name,
> And never did a worthier knight
> The rank of knighthood claim.

The story, based on the old ballad of Gil Morice, anticipated the
catastrophe of *Rokeby* and elicited the moral:

> The deadliest wounds with which we bleed
> Our crimes inflict alone.
> Man's mercies from God's hands proceed
> His miseries from his own.

As he finished, his guest disgraced herself by bursting into tears. 'I
was never so ashamed of myself in my life,' she wrote to the sisters, 'but he read it so superlatively that I cried like a child. I could
have beaten myself for it looked as if I thought it very moving,
which I can truly say', she adds with her usual disarming criticism
of her own work, 'is far from being the case.'[30]

As early as 1775 Garrick had decided to try out her classical
drama, *The Inflexible Captive*, in the provinces.[31] The Roman hero,
Marcus Attilius Regulus, taken captive by the Carthaginians, was
sent by them to Rome to propose an 'accommodation' under oath to
return if he were unsuccessful. Through five long, immobile acts
he harangued his countrymen in dignified and sententious declama-
tion to refuse the terms proposed by the enemy, and returned to Car-
thage, apostrophizing glory and honour, to suffer a horrible death:

The Drama

Glory exalts, enlarges, dignifies,
Absorbs the selfish in the social claim.
And renders man a blessing to mankind.
It is this principle, this spark of deity
Rescues debased humanity from guilt
And elevates it by her strong excitements.
It takes off sensibility from pain,
From peril fear, plucks out the sting from death
And teaches man to imitate the gods.

The Bath Theatre Royal, most famous of the provincial theatres, which shared a repertory company with the Bristol Theatre Royal, arranged to produce the play. Family and friends combined to give the play a good send-off. Langhorne wrote the Prologue, Garrick the Epilogue. His decision to produce the play in person aroused great local interest, not least among the fashionable world which crowded to the waters. In April Hannah joined him and Mrs Garrick in Bath for a rigorous week's rehearsing of this 'famous Bath *Première*' billed for 18 April, which is completely ignored by Roberts in the *Memoirs*. Happily Sally More's ecstatic letter to Mrs Lovell Gwatkin provides an entertaining account of the production. The four sisters, with a party of supporting friends, slipped over from Bristol and sat in agonized excitement to see Hannah's first play. Hannah, 'author-like', had a place behind the scenes, where she forgot her own anxiety in endeavouring 'to exhilarate the spirits of the actors', who were overcome, not only by 'the most Brilliant Audience that ever were assembled', but by the unnerving presence of Garrick and the author. John Henderson, later known as 'the Bath Roscius', played the hero, Miss Mansel the heroine. 'Never were mortals in such trepidation. . . All the world of Dukes, Lords, and Barons were there who expressed their highest approbation. Never was a piece represented there known to have received so much applause. A shout continued for some minutes after the curtain dropt, which is the highest mark of distinction that can be paid an author.'[32] Indeed so cordial was the response that Garrick played with the idea of carrying *The Captive* to Drury Lane. Hannah, showing her strong common sense where her own work was concerned, demurred. The play, she held, was 'not

33

sufficiently bustling and dramatic for representation'.[33] It owed its warm reception, she knew well, not to its dramatic merits, nor, as did most later eighteenth-century successes, to the actors, but to the skill and popularity of its producer. She had her way, and London waited two years for her masterpiece, *Percy*.

In 1777 the remarkable success of her new tragedy at Covent Garden repaid in some measure the care Garrick had lavished on her muse. The play was planned by them in London in the spring of 1777. From Bristol she sent the acts of the play, as they were written, to Garrick and awaited his appraisement and criticism. These she received in full measure. He was a hard critic, Mrs Garrick no less severe. 'She will criticize you to the bone,' he wrote. 'A German commentator (Montaigne says) will suck an author dry.'[34] 'I tremble for my fifth act,' wrote Hannah, 'but I am afraid that I shall never make other people tremble.'[35] 'Let your fifth act be worthy of you', he chided, 'and tear the heart to pieces, or woe betide you. I shall not pass over any scenes or parts of scenes that are merely written to make up a certain number of lines. Such doings, Madam Nine, will neither do for you nor me.'[36] The play was accepted by Harris of Covent Garden and was billed to appear in December 1777. Miss More came up from Bristol for the rehearsals, but no letters to her sisters telling of her experiences appear in the collected correspondence. The 'dreadful news' of the surrender at Saratoga, which had just reached England, made it, in her opinion, an unsuitable time to bring out a play. 'If the country had the least spark of virtue remaining, not a creature would think of going to it,' she said. Garrick, for his part, could think of nothing, write of nothing, talk of nothing but *Percy*.[37] The 'Garden' was to enjoy the triumph of the season. He put all his magnificent stagecraft, stage patronage, and stage propaganda at her disposal; wrote both Prologue and Epilogue; and peremptorily refused to grant to 'several very great personages' their customary privileges of hearing the play read before its first performance. *Percy* was played to crowded and enthusiastic houses, keyed up to concert pitch by these devices, in December 1777 and January 1778.[38]

The Drama

The play, founded on the twelfth-century story of Eudes de Faiel, was a Border drama of the great houses of Douglas and Northumberland. The heroine, Elwina, played by Mrs Barry, loved Percy, and was married by her obdurate father, Earl Raby, to Douglas. Her husband, madly jealous, challenged Percy to a duel, and instructed his wife, should he be slain, to drink a cup of poison which he had provided for her. She, hearing incorrectly of his death, drank the poison. The play ends with the death of Douglas, who stabbed himself when he saw that his wife was dead.

It would be possible to make a great play out of material far less promising than this. Taken out of cold storage after 170 years, it is difficult to believe, even when allowance is made for eighteenth-century conventions and standards, that *Percy* could have aroused to enthusiasm an eighteenth-century audience, for it is entirely lacking in dramatic quality. There is no interrelation of character and action, no surprise or suspense in any situation, no variety of tone or pitch, no light or shade, no contrasts of any kind. It begins and ends on the same monotonous note. Yet there is this to be said for it: that in spite of Shakespearian echoes, poetic diction, and insipid characterization, Miss More has a sense of the language of her age, so that, though often ridiculous, it is somehow never undignified. More than this, it was, says a modern critic, an attempt to present ethical problems which were of lively interest in her day: 'what a woman owes to her father, her husband and her own good name ... the regard for decorum which a "person of quality" should observe, even in moments of high emotion'.[39] The inevitable recoil of revenge on the head of the avenger, the moral of the play, found expression in Earl Raby's closing words:

> With impious pride I snatched
> The bolt of vengeance from the hand of heav'n.
> My soul submissive bows. A righteous God
> Has made my cause become my chastisement
> And pulled these miseries on my guilty head
> I would have drawn on others. O! 'tis just,
> 'Tis righteous retribution! I submit!

Negatively the play was no worse than dozens of other plays of a lean period. It bears comparison with Home's *Alfred* and Cumberland's *Battle of Hastings*. Kitty Clive, no friend of the Mores, and a good judge of drama, considered that it was 'by much the best modern tragedy' that had been written in her life-time,[40] and Tom Davies, Garrick's earliest biographer, 'prognosticated to the English State a rising genius in tragedy who would in time produce scenes not inferior to the best of Otway and Southerne, without that mixture of licentiousness and vulgarity which disgraces the productions of these excellent writers'.[41] To Hannah More's contemporaries the 'combination of emotion, action and theory' of her play was considered 'a revelation'.[42]

It is difficult to read with becoming gravity the history of the next few weeks. The play was received with bursts of applause; strong men shed tears, as Hannah noticed with satisfaction 'sitting well back in a snug corner with Mrs Garrick' in the stage box. The gallery, disliking Douglas, expressed its disapproval. Mrs Montagu, who seldom appeared at the theatre, 'overcome by the universal plaudits of the first night' ordered a box for the third, sixth, and ninth performances; the 'bad Lord Lyttleton' attended every night for seven nights; the Duke of Northumberland and his son Earl Percy sent Dr Percy of the *Reliques* to convey their appreciation of the honour which Miss More had done to their house, and their regrets that gout had prevented their appearance at the play. Countess Bathurst, the Lord Chancellor's lady, refused to make any engagement for a fortnight but on condition that she should be at liberty to break it for *Percy*; the sisters came up from Bristol to see the 'bantling' and reported that the theatre 'overflowed prodigiously', notwithstanding that Their Majesties were attending the *School for Scandal* at the 'other house'. The critics, meeting, as was the custom, at the Bedford after a new play, pronounced warmly in its favour; the press with few exceptions was uniformly favourable. Laurels crowned the elated authoress and congratulations were showered upon her. 'May you ever be the pride of your friends', wrote Mrs Montagu, 'and wear your bays with pleasure.' 'An elegant morçeau' with an elegant ring came from Mrs

Boscawen. Berenger, Master of the King's Horse, wrote from Paris begging that the fair author should not be crowned, but covered with laurels. 'I have had so much flattery', wrote Hannah inelegantly to her sisters, 'that I might, if I would, choke myself with my own pap.'[43] The play was a triumphant success. It was performed for twenty-one nights, an almost unprecedented occurrence in an age of repertoire. The author's rights amounted to £600, and her publisher Cadell paid her £150 for the play; 4,000 copies were sold by March 1778, and a second edition was almost exhausted. *Percy* retained its popularity throughout the eighteenth century. It was several times revived. In 1787, with Mrs Siddons as *Elwina*, it was again the talk of the town. She played it with 'such exquisite grace', reported Edmund Burke and Sir Joshua Reynolds to Hannah, that tears ran down the cheeks of Charles James Fox, who had attended the play with them.[44] It was performed in Vienna in 1779 and was translated into French by no less a personage than M. de Calonne. So warm was French appreciation of the play that in 1784 Miss More was made a member of the Rouen Academy of Arts, Sciences and Letters.[45]

Except for an adverse criticism by Richard Cumberland, a characteristic sneer by 'Peter Pindar', a cool appraisement by Horace Walpole, and an acid remark by Mrs Thrale that 'if Fanny Burney could not get more from her publishers than Hannah More had got from her foolish play, she deserved to be whipt,' and Miss More's own judgematical remark, 'It happened rather luckily for *Percy* that so many unsuccessful plays were brought out this Winter,' nothing but praise was heard.[46]

Encouraged by Garrick and by her amazing success, Hannah set to work on her third play, *The Fatal Falsehood*. The first four acts were read by Garrick and the fifth act was ready for his approval when he died suddenly in January 1779. So eager was Harris of Covent Garden to secure the play that Miss More reluctantly allowed him to produce it late in the season of 1779. Hannah, 'ill and overcome with grief, seems mightily indifferent about the matter', wrote the sisters in London to the sisters in Bristol. She could not be persuaded to interest herself in its production. Her friends rallied around her. R. B. Sheridan wrote the Epilogue and Mrs Boscawen took the unnecessary precaution of sending a party of men armed with thick staves to sit in the pit and lead the applause at the first performance. 'In a very full house there was not one dissenting voice.' Yet the play, described as 'a perfect triumph', had a run of three nights only.[47]

Read side by side with *Percy* there is little in the text to explain the success of the one or the failure of the other. *The Fatal Falsehood* showed to what crimes unscrupulous love may lead. Like *Percy* it is uninteresting and undramatic. It was produced, it is true, when most of the polite and learned were out of town, and when some of the leading actors were not available. But the explanation of its failure is clear. In 1779 there was no Garrick to nurse the bantling, no Garrick to boost the play, no Garrick, with ebullient temper, to keep at fever heat the expectations of his vast clientèle. Hannah More, who throughout the greater part of her life was able, in spite of overwhelming adulation, to keep her judgment in repair, was aware of this. She knew, none better, what she owed to Garrick. *The Fatal Falsehood* was her last play.

It is possible, but for an embarrassing incident on the second night of the play, followed by an unseemly wrangle in the press in the summer of 1779, that Hannah More's break with the stage would have been less abrupt and final. A rival playwright, Hannah Cowley, fainted in her box on the second night of *The Fatal Falsehood* after shouting loudly 'at one of the finest parts' of the play 'That's mine! That's mine!' She and her friends followed up this attack in the morning papers. They charged Miss More with stealing the plot of her tragedy from Mrs Cowley's *Albina*, a play read and refused by Garrick some years earlier. A paper war, carried on with the virulence and lack of restraint characteristic of the age, followed. 'By some wonderful coincidence', wrote Mrs Cowley unpleasantly, 'Miss More and I have one common flock of ideas between us.'[48] Hannah More, too well trained to object to public criticism of her writings, took strong objection to the attack on her character, and as Garrick could not answer her detractors, she took up her pen to defend herself. 'Repugnant' as she found it 'to my own feelings and to the delicacy of my sex' to answer these charges in the public press, 'I am under the necessity of solemnly asserting that I never saw, or heard, or read a single line of Mrs Cowley's tragedy, nor did I even hear she had written a tragedy till after *The Fatal Falsehood* came out at Covent Garden.'[49] So angry was Miss More that she was barely restrained from making an affidavit against Mrs Cowley.

This unfortunate incident explains, in part, Hannah More's break with the stage. A vulgar wrangle in the press offended her sense of propriety. But it was the discovery, as her *Historiomastic*, written twenty years later, affirmed, that even high tragic dramas, 'the least blameable of stage plays', suffered from an 'essential radical defect' which determined her withdrawal. For honour, 'the religion of tragedy', was opposed to the religion of Christianity. Love, jealousy, hatred, ambition, pride, revenge elevated to the rank of splendid virtues formed 'a dazzling system of worldly morality in direct opposition to the spirit of a religion whose characteristics are charity, meekness, peaceableness, long-suffering and gentleness'.[50] This discovery, rather than Garrick's death or Mrs Cowley's attack, explains her recoil from the stage.

Garrick's death cemented still more firmly the friendship of Eva Garrick and Hannah More. A woman of many acquaintances and few friends, it was to Hannah More that Mrs Garrick turned for comfort when Garrick died. Hannah stayed with her during the greater part of her period of mourning, visited her for over twenty successive winter seasons and corresponded with her for forty years. 'Here', she wrote on January 1780, telling the sisters of the harmony of the years of seclusion at Hampton, 'we never see a human face but each other's. . . We dress like a couple of Scara-mouches, dispute like a couple of Jesuits, eat like a couple of Alder-men, walk like a couple of porters, and read as much as any two doctors of either University.'[51] At Hampton Miss More, in defer-ence to Mrs Garrick's request, took over the moral and spiritual care of the servants. 'In the evening I read a sermon and prayers to the family which Mrs Garrick much likes,'[52] and as chaplain, said Boswell, who dined with them in April 1781, she sat at the foot of the table when they had guests.[53] When the period of mourning was over, the two ladies again visited their friends and entertained them at Hampton and the Adelphi. Not until the late 'nineties, when Hannah More was absorbed in her tracts and her schools, and Mrs Garrick's multitudinous German relatives over-ran her house and monopolized her attention, did their friendship, never drained of affection, lapse. Mrs Garrick died in her ninety-ninth year in October 1822.

CHAPTER III

THE *LITERATI*

'She is the most powerful versificatrix in the English Language.'
Dr Johnson on Hannah More

'I think Hannah More is the cleverest of all us female wits.'
Mrs Thrale

(i)

THE London to which Hannah More had the entrée in the middle
'seventies was a little London of elderly and middle-aged men and
women. Samuel Johnson was over sixty-five; Soame Jenyns was
seventy; David Garrick was sixty-two when he died in 1779;
Joshua Reynolds was in the early fifties, and the Blue Stocking ladies
of her acquaintance, Mrs Montagu, Mrs Vesey, Mrs Carter, Mrs
Chapone, were by many years the seniors of the young woman
from Bristol.[1] The eager interest and enthusiasm of an intelligent
and good-looking young woman was not unwelcome to the distinguished men and women who opened their doors to her. To her
they were not only arbiters of literature and the arts, but of morals.
Brought up from their childhood on the *Spectator*, Hannah More
and her sisters, in common with thousands of their countrymen be-
longing to the rapidly increasing, uncouth and unlettered middling
classes, were profoundly influenced by the standards of practical
morality presented so attractively by Addison.[2] Johnson's Essays in
the *Rambler* and the *Idler*, his grave *Prince of Abyssinia* and his pious
Irene, and the echoes of his conversation listened to in Bristol, enlarged their horizons and those of their fellows by new and lofty
conceptions of the principles of morality. To meet the Great Moralist in the flesh, to hear him discourse with men and women whose
names were household words, offered delights almost incredible to

41

a provincial whose ambition it was to contribute through the medium of literature to the improvement of literary culture and standards of social decency.

An introduction, presumably from Mrs Lovell Gwatkin, to the kindly and eccentric Miss Reynolds, sister to Sir Joshua, brought Miss More at once into the large and distinguished circle of his acquaintance. He invited Hannah and her sister to drink tea and sup with 'a brilliant circle of both sexes . . . and would not suffer us to come away until one'. 'Our first visit', Miss More reported in 1775, 'was to Sir Joshua's, where we were received with all the kindness imaginable.' She met Sir Joshua at the magnificent dinner parties given by Mrs Montagu and Bishop Shipley, and visited him later at his Richmond home, in company with the Garricks, to meet a select company of Gibbon, the three Burkes, Lord Mahon, and Mr Eliot, 'an *embarras de richesse*, a party much too large to please me'. She and her sisters found a '*parti-quarrée*' with Sir Joshua more to their taste: it allowed him to sparkle as he could not in a large assembly, because of his deafness. He sought Hannah at Mrs Ord's assembly, 'when I had Sir Joshua, Cambridge and Mr Smelt all to myself'. They shared an interest in each other's work. She read and admired his *Discourses* on Art, hailing the Fourth Discourse as 'a masterpiece'. He read aloud to his friends her poem *Dragon*—an ode to Garrick's dog.[3] It was to Sir Joshua that she owed the introduction, so eagerly desired, to Samuel Johnson. Prepared by her host, as he handed her up the stairs, to find Johnson in 'one of his moods of sadness and silence',[4] she was surprised and elated when, with Sir Joshua's macaw on his wrist, the Doctor shambled across the room to meet her, reciting aloud a verse from her *Morning Hymn*, and in the same pleasant humour 'continued the whole evening'. The most amiable and obliging of women, Miss Reynolds, a week later took the excited sisters, Hannah and Sally, to call on Dr Johnson, 'Abyssinia's Johnson! Dictionary Johnson! Rambler's, Idler's, and Irene's Johnson! at his very own house. Can you picture to yourselves the palpitation of our hearts', wrote Sally rapturously to the sisters at Bristol, 'as we approached his mansion. . . When our visit was ended he called for his hat (as it rained) to attend us down a very long entry to our coach, and not Rasselas could have acquitted himself more *en cavalier*. We are engaged with him, at Sir Joshua's, Wednesday evening.' Then with a hoot of joy she asks 'What do you think of us?'

Dr Johnson, whose opinion of Hannah More has for long been a subject of controversy, confided to Miss Reynolds how much he had been touched by Hannah's genuine and unaffected enthusiasm,[6] and there is ample evidence in Sally's letters to the sisters at home to attest his enjoyment of Hannah's company.

[Tuesday evening wrote Sally in 1775] 'we drank tea at Sir Joshua's with Dr Johnson. Hannah is certainly a great favourite. She was placed next him and they had the entire conversation to themselves. They were both in remarkably high spirits; it was certainly her lucky night! I never heard her say so many good things. The old genius was extremely jocular and the young one very pleasant. You would have imagined that we had been at some comedy had you heard our peals of laughter. They, indeed, tried which could "pepper the highest".'

and it was Sally's opinion that Hannah beat Johnson at his own game. The lexicographer, she held, was not really the highest seasoner.

Again, writing late in 1776, Sally reported:

If a wedding should take place before our return don't be surprised—between the mother of *Sir Eldred* and the father of my much-loved *Irene*; nay, Mrs Montagu says if tender words are the precursors of connubial engagements we may expect great things, for it is nothing but 'child', 'little fool', 'love', and 'dearest'. . . If Hannah's head stands proof against all the adulation and kindness of the great folks here, why then I will venture to say that nothing of this kind will hurt her hereafter. . . Dr Johnson and Hannah last night had a violent quarrel, till at length laughter ran so high on all sides, that argument was confounded in noise; the gallant youth, at one in the morning, set us down at our lodgings.[7]

These diverting interludes occurred in the early years of Hannah's acquaintance with the Great Panjandrum. Clearly the two excited young women enjoyed themselves prodigiously and believed, not without reason, that he was equally entertained. But Mrs Piozzi in 1786 and Boswell in 1791, in the *Anecdotes* and the *Life* respectively, published different versions of a story which did much to discredit Miss More in her lifetime and after her death. Without attempting to date the incident, or to put it in the setting which Sally provides, Mrs Thrale, anxious to illustrate the roughness of Johnson's manner, reports that the doctor 'once bade a very celebrated lady [identified by Fanny Burney as Miss More] who praised him with too much zeal perhaps, or perhaps too strong an emphasis (which always offended him), consider what her flattery was worth before she choaked *him* with it'.[8] Amended five years later by Boswell in the *Life*, this outrageous remark takes on an equally boorish if less sharp tone: 'At Sir Joshua Reynolds's one evening, this same lady', referred to as a person, '*then* just come to London from an obscure situation in the country', met Dr Johnson.

She very soon began to pay her court to him in the most fulsome strain. 'Spare me, I beseech you, dear madam', was his reply. She still *laid it on*. 'Pray, madam, let us have no more of this,' he rejoined. Not paying any attention to these warnings she continued still her eulogy. At length, provoked by this indelicate and *vain* obtrusion of compliment, he exclaimed: 'Dearest lady, consider with yourself what your flattery is worth before you bestow it so freely.'[9]

'I was obliged', said Dr Johnson, referring to Miss More's blandiloquence, 'to speak to Miss Reynolds to let her [Miss More] know that I desired she would not flatter me so much.'[10]

Whichever version is accepted, and accepted the substance must be, it is curiously out of keeping with Johnson's attitude to Hannah More. Possibly, as Miss More's apologists suggest, the remark was made in fun and was misrepresented by those who heard it.[11] But it is more probable that, in one of his testy humours, Johnson found her adulation, which he usually enjoyed, unpalatable, as he not infrequently did that of others of his admirers. That he was, according to Mrs Thrale, sorry afterwards for the offensive speech he had made supports this view. The social conventions of the age expected, indeed demanded, a spate of cajolery, deserved or undeserved. No one indulged more freely when the mood seized him than Dr Johnson; no one, with the possible exception of Garrick among his contemporaries, worked harder to deserve the encomium bestowed on him. Hannah More, according to Miss Reynolds, perhaps inspired him with 'an unusual ardour to shine'.[12] It was his fault, not hers, if in the fashionable game of paying compliments she peppered too high.

Far more in keeping with Johnson's regard for her was his mild remonstrance on her uncritical enthusiasm for men and books. Writing to Mary Hamilton in 1783, Hannah says:

Dr Johnson tells me that among my faults vehemence of praise is one of the greatest. If this be true it invalidates my credit as a critic, and, to tell you the truth, I do not find in myself much of the stuff out of which critics are made. Very transcendent genius in any book or persons excites in me pleasures even to rapture.[13]

With the exception of Johnson's one harsh remark, all available evidence shows the doctor's appreciation of her and her work. Cadell, the publisher, delighted with his new client, offered her for her ballads as much as Goldsmith had been paid for *The Deserted Village*, and the doctor invited himself to tea, 'that we may read *Sir Eldred* together', an intimidating occasion for Miss More, since Johnson had loudly advertised his contempt for the genuine ballads discovered by Dr Percy. When he arrived, wrote Hannah to Patty, and had had his fill of tea, 'we then fell upon *Sir Eldred*.' The doctor read both poems through, approved of *The Bleeding Rock*, and did not alter a word. He suggested some little alterations in *Sir Eldred*, and 'did me the honour to write one whole stanza:

> My scorn has oft the dart repelled
> Which guileful beauty threw;
> But goodness heard, and grace beheld,
> Must every heart subdue.'[14]

Posterity, remembering the manner in which Dr Johnson was capable of amending verses submitted to him,[15] might tremble for Miss More's ballad, but his emendation, while adding no distinction to an indifferent poem, did it little harm. 'I shall not tell you what he said of it,' she wrote in great delight, 'but to me the best part of his flattery was that he repeats all the best stanzas by heart with the energy, though not with the grace of a Garrick.' To Hannah More, wedged in a corner with him at Mrs Ord's assembly, Dr Johnson confided King George's injunction, made to him that morning, to add Spenser to the *Lives of the Poets*. When Miss Reynolds painted Hannah's portrait, Dr Johnson called 'and staid the whole time, and said good things by way of making me look well'. They argued vigorously when they discussed literature. She did not always accept his estimate of men and books, and held her own with spirit. 'I was very bold', she wrote, 'in combatting some of his darling prejudices; nay, I ventured to defend one or two of the Puritans whom I forced him to allow to be good men and good writers.'

An ardent lover of Milton and an admirer of the brothers Warton, she was in sympathy with their efforts to revive interest in Milton's works, and had the courage to accuse Johnson 'of not having done justice' to the *Allegro* and *Penseroso*.

He spoke disparagingly of both. I praised *Lycidas*, which he absolutely abused, adding 'if Milton had not written the *Paradise Lost* he would have only ranked among the minor poets; he was a Phydias that could cut a Colossus out of a rock, but could not cut heads out of cherry stones.'

He reproved me [she wrote again] with pretended sharpness for reading *Les Pensées de Pascal*, or any of the Port Royal authors; alleging that as a good Protestant, I ought to abstain from books written by Catholics. I was beginning to stand up on my defence when he took me with both hands and with a tear running down his cheek, 'Child,' said he, with the most affecting earnestness, 'I am heartily glad you read pious books, by whomsoever they may be written.'

I never [she wrote in 1780] saw Johnson really angry with me but once; and his displeasure did him so much honour that I loved him the better for it. I alluded, rather flippantly, I fear, to some witty passage in *Tom Jones*: he replied 'I am shocked to hear you quote from so vicious a book. I am sorry to hear you have read it; a confession no modest lady should ever make. I scarcely know a more corrupt work.' I thanked him for his correction.[16]

The visit of Hannah More and Dr Johnson to Oxford in June 1782 is one of the best, but seldom remembered, stories in *Johnsoniana*. Mrs Kennicott, a new friend of Hannah's, and wife to the Professor of Hebrew, invited her to Oxford. Dr Johnson arranged to be there at the same time, to act as her *cicerone*. 'We do so gallant it about,' she wrote gaily to the sisters, tickled as every woman would have been by his immense seriousness in showing his university and his college. 'You cannot imagine with what delight he showed me every part of his own college [Pembroke]. He would let no one show it me but himself. "This was my room, this Shenstone's." Then, after pointing out all the rooms of the poets who had been of his college, "In short," said he, "we were a nest of singing-birds." ' A distinguished company was invited to meet her. 'There are', she wrote to the sisters, in mock gravity, 'three Canons, three *Heads*, three Ladies, one Dean, one Student and *one* Professor awaiting me in the next room.' She dined at Jesus to meet the most learned and famous in the University, and the wits of Oxford commemorated her visit by gallant compliments, one of which has survived:

> Muses Nine we had before,
> But Kennicott has given us More.

The visit was crowned by 'a very pretty piece of gallantry' contrived by the Master of Pembroke. 'When we came into the common room at Pembroke we spied a fine large print of Johnson, framed and hung up that very morning with this motto "*And is not Johnson ours, himself an host.*" Under which stared you in the face, "From *Miss More's Sensibility*".'[17]

Dr Johnson's commendation of Hannah More's literary work provides an amusing illustration of the doctor in the rôle he had denounced for Miss More. Her flattery was a poor thing compared with his. 'Hush! Hush!' said he, when someone mentioned poetry at Bishop Porteus's dinner party, 'It is dangerous to say a word about poetry before her . . . it is talking of the art of war before Hannibal.' To this elephantine flattery he added the indelicate regret that she had not married her fellow townsman Chatterton, 'that posterity might have seen a propagation of poets'.[18] Her *Bas Bleu*, a description of the Blue Stocking assemblies, written in 1782, passed from hand to hand in MS., and enraptured London society. It drew from Johnson the most extravagant praise. 'All the flattery I ever received from everybody together would not make up the sum,' she wrote with pardonable jubilation. 'He said (but I insist that you do not tell anybody, for I am ashamed of writing it even to you) he said that there was no name in poetry that might not be glad to own it.' When she told him that she was delighted with his approbation, he replied, quite characteristically, 'And so you may be, for I give you the opinion of a man who does not rate his judgement very low in these things.'[19] 'Miss More', he wrote to Mrs Thrale, 'has written a poem called *Bas Bleu*, which in my opinion is a very great performance.' 'Johnson told me with great solemnity', reported James Beattie, 'that she was the most powerful versificatrix in the English language.'[20] This was praise indeed. Nevertheless the feminine noun used by him discounts it heavily. His standards of judgement were not the same for women as for men. A woman poet, it may safely be assumed, resembled Boswell's hypothetical woman preacher, who was like a dog walking on his hind legs. 'It was not well done, but you are surprised to find it done at all.'[21]

Burke, Garrick, Reynolds, Johnson, and, later, Horace Walpole were Hannah More's friends and admirers. She responded to their interest and esteem with warm affection and enthusiastic admiration. But for one man of transcendent genius, who stood head and shoulders above his fellow *literati* in the almost perfect achievement of a colossal task, she was incapable of appreciation. In 1782, when all the world was reading Volumes II and III of Edward Gibbon's *Decline and Fall of the Roman Empire*, Miss More conscientiously read aloud to Mrs Garrick every day between dinner and tea in the autumn months, 'this fine but insidious narrative of a dull period'. She had no liking for 'that dear middle age these noodles praise', and she detested the skill of the 'malignant painter' who took a profane delight in making hideous a depraved Christianity. 'In the two last volumes', she wrote, discussing them in a letter to her sister, 'he has taken some pains to hide the cloven foot, but whenever a Christian emperor, or Bishop of established reputation is brought forward, his encomiums have so much coldness, and his praises so much sneer that you cannot help discovering contempt where he professes panegyric.' Six years later, when the last volumes appeared and she was an established literary critic, she attacked both matter and style. Her strong disapproval was no longer confined to Gibbon's interpretation of a dull period of history. 'I have almost waded through that mass òf impiety and bad taste,' she wrote to William Weller Pepys in 1788. 'I protest . . . if this work were to become the standard of style and religion, Christianity and the English language would decay pretty nearly together, and the same period would witness the downfall of sound principles and true taste. I have seldom met with more affectation or less perspicuity. The instances of false English are many; and of false taste endless. In numberless passages he is so obscure that the fashionable phrase of the *luminous* pages of Gibbon seems to be as diametrically opposite to the truth. . . That you may not think by all this criticism', she added, 'that I am blinded by prejudice, I will own that *par ci et par là* I have been well amused, particularly with Justinian, Belisarius and the accounts of the pastoral nations.'[22]

(ii)

Equally gratifying to the newcomer was the welcome extended to her by members of the curious and diverting Blue Stocking coteries, attenuated London models of the famous Paris salons. The number of English women of social position interested in literature and the arts in the last quarter of the eighteenth century was a new phenomenon. It cannot be claimed for them that their contribution to art or literature was of any outstanding merit. Their influence, such as it was, was social rather than literary. To them may be ascribed a share in the reform of manners and social behaviour which distinguishes the England of Jane Austen from the England of Fielding; they played a part in transforming the hitherto anomalous social position of men and women of letters by bringing them into personal contact with the quality; they held a watching brief for the discovery of genius, and they lit a flickering candle on behalf of the emancipation of women.[23]

'A drum, a rout, a racquet, a hurricane, where every chance of conversation was driven away by that foe to human society, whist,' was Elizabeth Carter's pungent description of London parties in the 'seventies.[24] In the 'sixties and 'seventies a dozen or more ladies, better educated than the rank and file of their sex, led by Mrs Elizabeth Montagu and Mrs Agmondesham Vesey, arrived almost simultaneously at the idea of providing mixed conversation parties as a counter-attraction to the popular and omnipresent card-table. Hannah More, greatly impressed, told the sisters that the sole purpose of the Bas Bleu assemblies was conversation. 'They differed in no respect from other parties except that the company did not play cards.'[25] This civilized alternative to the card-table had provoked 'rancour and scorn', 'bitter reproach', and much contemptuous amusement.[26] Women chattered, they did not converse. Moreover they had no learning wherewith to lace their conversation. The few who had rashly acquired learning were warned that it destroyed their matrimonial chances much in the same way, said Lady Mary Wortley Montagu in the 'sixties, as would the handicap of a crooked body or a game leg, and this view, in spite of the 'enlightened 'sixties' and the even more enlightened 'seventies, still maintained. 'Keep your knowledge of Latin a dead secret,' said Sir William Hamilton to his niece, Mary, when he launched her into London Society in 1784. 'A lady's being learned is commonly looked upon as a great fault, even by the learned.'[27]

But the Blue Stocking hostesses, Mrs Montagu, Mrs Vesey, Mrs Walsingham 'who had had a man's education', Lady Rothes, Lady Crewe, Mrs Ord, Miss Monckton, Mrs Thrale among them, lacked neither courage nor confidence. Most of them were already married. The threat of celibacy did not alarm them. Nor did they wilt under the squibs and satires which met their efforts. They had the support of a select body of *literati* and a large enough clientèle of men of affairs and women of quality to make their assemblies not only attractive but popular. According to Wraxall, the most brilliant period of the London salons was the years 1770 to 1785.[28] It is not without significance that Hannah More was introduced to Mrs Montagu, the 'Queen of the Blues', in the middle 'seventies, and that by 1785 she was the acknowledged poet of the Blues. She arrived in London when the most distinguished of the learned ladies were elderly women. They welcomed a budding genius, whose

PLATE I

THE NINE LIVING MUSES OF GREAT BRITAIN

By Richard Samuel. Miss Carter, Mrs Barbauld, Mrs Angelica Kauffman, on the right hand; Mrs Sheridan in the middle; Mrs Lenox, Mrs Macaulay, Hannah More, Mrs Montague and Mrs Griffith, on the left hand.

ready wit was combined with a reforming spirit in sympathy with theirs. She justified their patronage. Her plays and ballads and essays on education, published in the 'seventies, her poems, *Bas Bleu*, *Sensibility*, *Florio*, *Bishop Bonner's Ghost*, in the 'eighties, advertised the learned ladies and their assemblies in an easy and pleasing manner. She popularized the Blues, as Mrs Montagu with her tedious Essay on Shakespeare, or Mrs Carter with *Epictetus*, or Mrs Chapone with her persistent echoes of Addison, could not do. The classical pseudonyms, 'Maro' or 'Lelius', which veiled the personalities mentioned in her verses, aroused the curiosity of the court and the *beau monde* and the encomium of the *literati*. To gratify King George's request for a copy of her *Bas Bleu*, Miss More sat up one night in April 1784 to make one for him.[29]

Compared with Fanny Burney's dynamic representations of the same society in the same environment, Hannah More's figures take on a static character. She had no gift as a reporter of living speech. She was aware of this. 'You do not, I presume, expect that I should send you a transcript of the conversations,' she wrote to the sisters, after a *petite* assembly at Mrs Boscawen's. 'I have told you the interlocutors, but you are not to expect the dialogue. Patty says if she had such rich subjects she could make a better hand of them. I believe her; my outlines are perhaps more just, but she beats me all to nothing in the colouring.'[30] The art of James Boswell and Fanny Burney was outside her range; nevertheless there is much vivid characterization and shrewd comment on the *literati* and the quality which make her letters of considerable interest to students of social history of the later eighteenth century.

In this new and curious world, compounded of learning and fashion, three women played parts of especial importance in Hannah More's life: Mrs Montagu, 'the Maecenas of Hill Street', and later of Portman Square, Mrs Carter, usually considered the most learned woman of her time, who won Dr Johnson's heart because she could make a pudding as well as translate Epictetus, and Mrs Boscawen, the Admiral's widow, 'of whom', said James Boswell, 'if it be not presumptuous in me to praise her, I would say that her manners are the most agreeable and her conversation the best of any lady with whom I ever had the happiness to be acquainted'.[31] These three women were Hannah More's warm friends through life. Her letters discover 'the high character for piety, sterling sense and edifying conversation' of this group of Bas Bleu ladies. Indeed, bidden by Mrs Montagu to a Sunday party, Miss More forgot her sabbatarian principles and was called to order by a 'seasonable admonition' from Dr Stonhouse. 'I *did* think', she answered him, 'of the alarming call, "What doest thou here, Elijah?" ' But on the following Sunday she dined out again, and justified her conduct: 'I have been at Mrs Boscawen's. Mrs Montagu, Mrs Carter, Mrs Chapone and myself only were admitted. We spent the time, not as wits, but as reasonable creatures; better characters I trow. The conversation was sprightly but serious. I have not enjoyed an afternoon so much since I have been in town,' and though she deplored Sunday visiting, she added courageously, that 'it was a day spent without any uneasy sensations.'[32] Her new friends, amused and tolerant, refrained, it would seem, from subjecting her conscience again to so severe a test.

Mrs Montagu, 'who made each rising wit her care', took Hannah More under her wing and invited her in the winter of 1775 to her first assembly. Mrs Montagu's critics, and they were many, agreed in general with Lady Louisa Stuart that she was a woman of great vivacity, no small share of wit, a competent portion of learning, considerable fame as a critic, a large fortune, a fine house, and an excellent cook. 'Observe the climax,' said Lady Louisa unkindly, 'it is not unintentional.'[33]

The inability of this kind and incurably pedantic woman to promote conversation, the most intimate and informal of the arts, among the heterogeneous collection of wits, *beau monde*, sycophants, dabblers in literature, fops and coxcombs seated at her magnificent assemblies in a vast semi-circle which, says Fanny Burney, 'retained throughout the whole evening its unbroken form with the precision of a Brobdingnagian compass', provided her critical and malicious contemporaries with unfailing opportunity for raillery. 'It needed courage', the venerable and sophisticated Mrs Delany observed, 'to exchange more than a *whisper* with Mrs Boscawen, another with Lady Bute, and a *wink* with the Duchess of Portland.'[34]

Hannah More, whose instinct it was to admire and not to disparage, told the sisters with breathless excitement of her first assembly:

Mrs Montagu received me with the most encouraging kindness; she is not only the finest genius but the finest lady I ever saw; she lives in the highest style of magnificence; her apartments and table are in the most splendid taste. But what baubles are these in speaking of a Montagu!

The dinner party which preceded the assembly consisted of:

Mrs Carter, Dr Johnson, Solander, Maty, Miss Reynolds, Sir Joshua (the idol of every company), and some other persons of high rank and less wit, and your humble servant, a party that would not have disgraced the table of a Lelius or Atticus. I felt myself a worm...

After dinner the company adjourned to the vast salon, where the plethora of literary suns stealing each other's brilliance made the newcomer long, regretfully, for 'fewer luminaries' and 'a clearer, steadier and more beneficent light'.

Miss More passed her first assembly with flying colours. Dr Johnson, whose devastating silences were warranted to destroy the most promising of parties, addressed a question to her:

He asked me how I liked the new tragedy of *Braganza*. I was afraid to speak before them all, as I knew a diversity of opinion prevailed among the company: however, as I thought it a less evil to dissent from the opinion of a fellow-creature than to tell a falsity, I ventured to give my sentiments.

Virtue was rewarded. 'You are right, Madam,' said Dr Johnson.[35]

After this promising beginning Miss More was a frequent guest at Hill Street, and later at Portman Square. Unsophisticated as she was, she did not lack, as her verses and letters testify, either Fanny Burney's powers of observation or Lady Louisa Stuart's gift of satire. She was quick to see that Mrs Montagu's initial mistake lay in collecting half the wits of the age together at the same time, and she noted with amusement on the rare occasions when the Brobdingnagian circle was broken up into smaller groups, how instead of a happy fusion of rank and talent 'the people of sentiment singled out each other', and the fine ladies and pretty gentlemen 'slid into each other's society'.[36]

When she became the fashion in the 'eighties, she had acquired a reputation for wit and was listened to instead of listening. Lady Louisa Stuart, then one of the younger set, bears unwilling witness —for she did not like or approve of Miss More—to her reputation. When she spoke, the inattentive young were called to order by a twitch of the sleeve and a murmur, 'My dear, did you listen? Did you mark? Mrs Montagu said—Mr Harris said—Miss Hannah More said—'[37]

Mrs Montagu's patronage did not end with the issue of coveted invitations to her dinner parties and assemblies. She was a warm admirer of Hannah More's ballads and plays and essays. She introduced her to her friends among the quality and carried her off time and again to Sandleford Priory, 'gothic without being gloomy', where Miss More's friend Capability Brown spread the pox of the picturesque 'by beckoning the distant hills to come into the prospect'.[38] She visited Hannah More in Bristol, to meet her family, and later, impressed by Hannah's discovery of the Bristol poetess, Ann Yearsley, acted with her as patron and joint-trustee in the unhappy affair of the Bristol milk-woman. Her letters testify to her pleasure in Hannah More's company and, incidentally, to Miss More's popularity among the Great.

Much has been written [wrote Mrs Montagu] on the fallaciousness of hope, but no one was ever so seriously enraged at it as I have been ever since I received your letter of the 24th. What, having indulged with such sensibility the hope of having you here in June, then in July and then August, and now you would put me off to the 15th of September, and, when hope deferred has made the heart sick, instead of the cordial of several weeks of your charming society you talk of one single week! Oh, my dear Madam, for pity's sake come as soon as you can get your trunks packed up and stay here to the last week in October.[39]

And their friendship stood the test of time, and of Hannah More's changed conception of life. She was received with flattering attention in later years, whenever she called on Mrs Montagu, and corresponded with her till her death in 1800. 'With Mrs Montagu's faults', she wrote in 1808, 'I have nothing to do. Her fine qualities were many.'

Elizabeth Carter, the friend of Mrs Montagu and Hannah More, was that rare bird among women—a Greek scholar of distinction. Her long delayed translation of Epictetus, published with an introductory essay in 1751, had established her reputation in England and on the Continent. Unlike Mrs Montagu she carried her learning lightly. There was nothing of *la femme savante* about her. She was reserved in manner and conversation—too reserved, in Dr Johnson's opinion, for a woman of her eminence. Fanny Burney, who loved her, described her as a 'really noble-looking woman'. A good conversationalist, she nevertheless enjoyed a game of cards, read modern novels, and thoroughly appreciated *Tom Jones*. In a society of literary pretension and petty social rivalries she epitomized serenity, balance, and solid worth. She saw life steadily. Hannah More, who possessed in a marked degree the power of establishing warm and lasting friendships, quickly broke through Mrs Carter's reserve. They discovered in one another a passionate love of poetry and a religious piety, different in form, but similar in essentials. Mrs Carter was Hannah's father confessor when conscience pulled one way and the world the other.

I do assure you, my dear Mrs Carter, with all the truth of sincere friendship, that one of my deepest causes of uneasiness is lest I should deceive others, and especially myself as to the motives of my own action. It is so easy to practise a creditable degree of seeming virtue and so difficult to purify and direct the affections of the heart that I feel myself in continual danger of appearing better than I am.

She told Alexander Knox in later years of her friendship with Mrs Carter adding, 'She was my zealous and attached friend for near thirty years. I loved dearly her honest, correct heart and cultivated mind. We differed just enough in our religious views for the exercise of mutual charity.'[40]

Describing her new friends to her sisters in 1775, Hannah wrote, 'I do not like one of them better than Mrs Boscawen. She is at once polite, learned, judicious and humble.' Nothing could have been kinder than Mrs Boscawen's affectionate welcome to Hannah More. That she was interested in her family may be assumed, but her interest does not explain the warm friendship which sprang up between the middle-aged lady of quality and the middling-class provincial. 'Others', said Mrs Boscawen in 1788, 'who may appear equally fond of you love you because you are the fashion. . . I love you for yourself.'[41]

Mrs Boscawen's stockings were blue, but they were not the royal blue of Mrs Montagu's, or the 'mazarin blue' of Lady Lucan's. She was not a learned lady. She was a sensible and unusually well-read woman, and her letters, which Hannah extravagantly compared with Madame de Sévigné's, have in common with hers a 'happy and becoming negligence'. As a leading London hostess she did not forget her duty to entertain the low-brows as well as the high-brows of London society, and as the low-brows preferred cards to conversation she provided at her assemblies card-tables in the outer drawing-room, which, said Miss More approvingly, 'weeded the company of some of the great and all the dull'. The grace and tact of this great lady enchanted Hannah. She tells the enthralled sisterhood of Mrs Boscawen's 'splendid assembly' of 'above forty people, most of them of the first quality', when 'our hostess was in every place at once, and so attentive to every individual that I dare say everybody, when they got home, thought as I did, that they alone had been the immediate object of her attention.'

From none of her new friends did Hannah More receive the extravagant praise which Mrs Boscawen, a highly intelligent woman, lavished upon her and her work. 'Your charming *Dragon* delighted me.' Tears stopped her voice when she read *Percy* aloud to her daughters, the Duchess of Beaufort and Mrs Leveson. She devoured 'the sweet poem' *Sensibility* which Miss More addressed to her. *Bas Bleu*, she held, was 'incomparable'; *Florio* she 'loved prodigiously'. And her affection for Hannah did not lag behind her appreciation of her 'genius'. Miss More was continually bidden à deux to Mrs Boscawen's town house in Audley Street, to her country villas in Kent and Surrey, and was taken by her to visit the Duchess of Beaufort at Badminton to meet the family, and to Stoke to visit the Dowager Duchess, who had 'long wished to meet her'. Mrs Boscawen called on her in her lodgings, presented her with Mason's life of Gray, for whose poetry they shared 'the eagerness of a glutton'; she purchased all the writings of the Gentlemen of Port Royal which they read together. She commissioned Opie, 'the Cornish Boy', to paint Hannah's portrait that she might have it as a perpetual reminder of her dear friend. 'I have taken down his Days and Hours of Leisure,' wrote Mrs Boscawen, 'and humbly submit them to your choice. I will call for you and attend you and read to you there, to cheat the weary hours.'[42] In 1776 Mrs Boscawen persuaded Mrs Delany, who, as interpreted by Lady Llanover, was a Queen of Snobs, to meet Miss More at dinner. Miss More again passed muster. 'She has invited me to visit her,' she told the sisters, 'a singular favour from one of her years and character.' In 1780 Miss More was bidden to one of the old lady's 'very select dinner parties', never exceeding eight in number, to meet her inseparable friend the Dowager Duchess of Portland (Prior's 'noble lovely little Peggy'), the Countess of Bute, the Dowager Lady Leicester, Lady Wallingford, Mrs Boscawen 'and my friend Horace Walpole, son to the minister of that name'.[43] This was the highlight of Hannah More's social career. From it may be dated her friendship with Horace Walpole and the invitations to visit the Duchess of Portland at Bulstrode.

The patronage of Mrs Montagu and Mrs Boscawen and her growing reputation, when her dramas were played and her verses published, opened the doors of other Bas Bleu coteries, and of many of the great houses of the London squares. She made friends with the most unexpected persons. Mrs Walsingham, the brilliant daughter of Sir John Hanbury-Williams and 'a wit from birth', who was reported by Fanny Burney to be 'civil only to people of wealth or fame and extremely insolent to others',[44] did not live up to her reputation when she met Hannah More. She liked and approved of her at once, regretting only that she was not a stronger feminist; invited her to her exclusive assemblies, and carried her off for week-ends to the house she was building and decorating at Thames Ditton. She begged to be allowed to copy Opie's portrait of Miss More, that she might hang it in her library. At Mrs Ord's and Lady Rothe's Hannah More was a frequent visitor, and Mrs Vesey, in her younger days the most popular of Bas Bleu hostesses, now old and mentally unstable, invited her to her famous Tuesday evenings, where, in alternate weeks, the distinguished members of the Literary Club, after dining at the Turk's Head, finished the evening at her crowded assemblies. 'Here', wrote Hannah, 'everything that is witty and everything learned is to be found,'[45] for the hostess collected 'all the graduates and candidates for fame'.[46] Her almost unique power of putting her guests at their ease, the elaborate informality of her salons, and the calculated simplicity of her cake and lemonade put her assemblies in a class by themselves. To Mrs Vesey Hannah More addressed her masterpiece of fugitive verse, *Bas Bleu*, eulogizing her as the 'Enchantress', who by the disordered order of her salons had succeeded, where Mrs Montagu had failed, in 'squaring the circle'. Mrs Vesey, in a characteristically inconsequent letter, thanked 'her polished and delightful friend' for 'the place you have given me in your charming poem'.[47]

> Vesey! of Verse the Judge and Friend,
> Awhile my idle strain attend:
>
> . . . .
> Long was Society o'er-run
> By Whist, that desolating Hun;
> Long did Quadrille despotic sit,
> That Vandal of colloquial wit;
> And Conversation's setting light
> Lay half-obscur'd in Gothic night;
> At length the mental shades decline,
> Colloquial wit begins to shine;
> Genius prevails, and Conversation
> Emerges into *Reformation*.
> The vanquish'd triple crown to you,
> Boscawen sage, bright Montagu,
> Divided, fell—your cares in haste
> Rescued the ravag'd realms of Taste;
> And Lyttleton's accomplish'd name,
> And witty Pulteney shar'd the fame;
> The men, not bound by pedant rules,

The 'Literati'

Nor Ladies, *précieuses ridicules*:
For polish'd Walpole shew'd the way,
How wits may be both learn'd and gay;
And Carter taught the female train,
The deeply wise are never vain;
And she, who Shakespeare's wrongs redrest,
Prov'd that the brightest are the best.
This just deduction still they drew,
And well they practised what they knew;
Nor taste, nor wit, deserves applause,
Unless still true to Critic laws;
Good sense, of faculties the best,
Inspire and regulate the rest.

. . . .

Here sober Duchesses are seen,
Chaste Wits, and Critics void of Spleen;
Physicians, fraught with real science,
And Whigs and Tories in alliance;
Poets, fulfilling Christian duties,
Just Lawyers, reasonable Beauties;
Bishops who preach, and Peers who pay,
And Countesses who seldom play;
Learn'd Antiquaries, who, from college,
Reject the rust, and bring the knowledge;
And, hear it, *age*, believe it, *youth*,
Polemics, really seeking truth;
And travellers of that rare tribe,
Who've seen the countries they describe;
Who studied there, so strange their plan,
Not plants nor herbs alone, but man!
While travellers, of other notions,
Scale mountain tops, and traverse oceans;
As if, so much these themes engross,
The study of mankind—was moss.

In the seemingly endless paean of praise and appreciation several discordant voices may be heard. Some of her new acquaintances were highly critical of Miss More's conspicuous sabbatarian piety; others disliked her habit of extravagant adulation. Her published work did not escape the 'dread reviewers', and the meteoric rise of a young woman who came from an 'obscure situation in the country' was not uniformly pleasing to all the literary ladies. With Mrs Thrale of Streatham, Miss More was not on terms of easy friendship. Mrs Thrale hunted the same literary lions as did Mrs Montagu or Mrs Walsingham, and had the advantage of 'domesticating' two of them, Dr Johnson and Miss Burney, on the premises, but in society the circles, though they cut, did not coincide. Mrs Delany refused to meet Mrs Thrale; Mrs Walsingham and Lady Louisa Stuart never frequented the Streatham assemblies. Miss More, a nobody by birth and social position, was a *persona grata* in the most exclusive circles of the Blues. Until 1780 Mrs Thrale, who had disposed of *Percy* as 'a foolish play', ignored Miss More; then, paying her 'particular attention' at Mrs Ord's assembly in the winter of 1780, 'desired that we should meet'.[49] Mrs Thrale's recognition of Hannah More's existence, cool and tardy as it was, proved a good investment to her. In the astonishing outburst of disgusting vituperation which greeted Mrs Thrale's marriage with Signor Piozzi, Hannah More, seldom censorious, took no part. Moreover she and her sisters received the Piozzis when later they settled in Bath, a gesture of friendship which implied, according to Mrs Piozzi, that 'everything is forgiven'. Miss More henceforward, by the transmutation of time, became 'a kind soul', 'a glorious creature,' whose health was 'a public concern' and whose cottage in the Mendips acquired sanctity as a 'half-sacred roof'. But in the 'eighties 'nobody', said Mrs Thrale, 'liked Miss More at Streatham'. In the diverting *Table of Characters* which Hester Thrale drew up for her own amusement to assess the characters of her friends and acquaintances, three of the six marks she allotted to Hannah More are curiously at variance with other contemporary estimates.[50]

Worth of Heart	$\frac{20}{20}$
Conversational Power	$\frac{7}{20}$
Person, Mien and Manner	$\frac{0}{20}$
Good Humour	$\frac{10}{20}$
Useful Knowledge	$\frac{20}{20}$
Ornamental Knowledge	$\frac{20}{20}$

Clearly Mrs Thrale did not then care for Miss More.

The 'Literati'

In Fanny Burney's detailed and meticulous *Diary* Hannah's name appears but seldom, never with enthusiasm. Miss Burney relates without comment the opinion of her 'gay, flighty, entertaining' friend Mrs George Cholmondeley [Peg Woffington's sister] on Hannah More. 'I do not like her at all, in fact I detest her. She does nothing but flatter and fawn, and then she thinks ill of nobody.' 'Don't you', she asked 'hate a person who thinks ill of nobody?' Miss Burney did not commit herself.[51] Miss More for her part refers but seldom to that 'extraordinary girl', who has picked up, no one knows where, 'her knowledge of nature and low life'.[52] She devoted two lines to her in *Bas Bleu*, which neatly characterized the socially shy young woman:

> Mute angel yes, thy looks dispense
> The silence of intelligence.

A greater contrast between the silent Miss Burney, always unsure of herself, and the sprightly Miss More, whose presence anxious hosts and hostesses hastened to secure so as to make their dinner parties a success, could not easily be found. It was left to Dr Johnson to bestow equal praise upon the two young women. 'I dined yesterday', he said, 'at Mrs Garrick's with Mrs Carter, Miss Hannah More, and Miss Fanny Burney. Three such women are not to be found.' And then he spoilt his compliment by adding meditatively, 'I know not where I could find a fourth, except Mrs Lennox, who is superior to them all.'[53]

In the 'eighties, when Miss More was at the height of her fame, the range of her friendships was remarkable. She was on terms of friendship not only with the giants, but also with the less distinguished *literati* and with a steadily increasing number of men distinguished in the world of affairs and women of rank and fortune. She introduced them to her sisters in her letters, sometimes with lively characterization, sometimes adding a brief opinion on them and their work. Laetitia Barbauld, whose charming verses are not yet forgotten, was an early and remained a late friend in spite of their antipathetic religious views. Soame Jenyns, 'gay, gallant and young as ever at the age of eighty' she thought delectable'. 'There is', she said discerningly, 'a fine simplicity about him and a wit in the Addison manner,' but on the Christian religion she wrote him down as a 'sucking child'. The elderly Scots Lord Monboddo, who, according to John Harford, proposed marriage to her in Mrs Garrick's garden at Hampton, and received 'a positive refusal', she found highly entertaining. 'In his valuable third volume of the *Origin and Progress of Language* he entertained some opinions so absurd that they would hardly be credible if he did not deliver them himself. . . He is so wedded to system that as Lord Barrington said to me the other day, rather than sacrifice his favourite opinion that men were born with tails he would be content to wear one himself.' Richard Owen Cambridge, who later compared her political tracts with those of Swift, 'talked dactyls and spondees till midnight', when he called on her. Henry Mackenzie, the *Man of Feeling*, became a life-long correspondent after he had wept when reading *Percy*. Of William Mason's poems and his life of Gray she was an ardent admirer. 'Never was there a more generous editor or more faithful friend.' Out of friendship for her he sent several poems for publication in her tracts in later years. Corsican Boswell she considered 'a very agreeable good-natured man', until the unfortunate incident at Bishop Shipley's dinner party when Boswell 'much disordered with wine addressed me in a manner that drew from me a sharp rebuke which I fancy he will not easily forgive me'. 'Mythology' Bryant was a very special friend. 'He is not only a remarkable, but a pious man and has devoted his pagan learning to truly Christian purposes.' Allan Ramsay, the artist, held her opinion in such respect that he convened a small party of wits that she might hear his *Essay on the Harmony of Numbers* read aloud. 'He denies Pope to have been an excellent harmonist which I will never allow.' 'Two of my great friends' were the Warton brothers—'Joseph of Winton and Thomas of Oxenford'. Their efforts to re-establish Spenser and Milton won her complete sympathy. Barnard, the witty Provost of Eton, was an extravagant admirer; 'he paid me a thousand attentions.' Leonard Smelt, 'the King's Friend', appointed because of his 'incomparable virtue' tutor to the unpleasing cub, the Heir Apparent, was 'an old acquaintance but a new friend'. Their friendship too stood the test of time. Berenger, Master of the King's Horse, poured out compliments with Gallic extravagance. Greatly amused, she described him with truth and economy as 'all chivalry, and blank verse and anecdote'. Bathurst, damned by Wraxall as the least able lawyer to whom the Great Seal was confided in the eighteenth century, was her admiring friend. He offered her anything she cared to have from his fine collection of original letters, and gave her a standing invitation to dine with him whenever he could get away from a Cabinet meeting, but forbade her to come when he had an engagement and could not be at home.[54] Almost the only young man among these elderly admirers was William Weller Pepys, later Master-in-Chancery. When Hannah met him he was a gay young man-about-town and a prime favourite with the literary ladies. He had, said Mrs Thrale, 'an unremitting ardour for literary talk' and, as his forty years correspondence with Hannah More testifies, an equally unremitting ardour for literary letter-writing. 'I believe', she wrote gaily in the middle of the Great War, 'that we are the only existing correspondents who write letters of nine pages without using the words "Bullion", "Portugal", "Wellington".' He paid her marked attentions and never failed in his warm appreciation of her writings. 'I begin to take an interest, and that rather a warm one, in whatever you do,' he wrote in 1783. 'Pray come either to London, or near it ... and give me an opportunity of telling you as soon as may be in person how much I am yours.'[55]

Men famous in the world of action and affairs found her equally attractive. They poured out their confidences to her in snug corners at the great assemblies or in the buzz of conversation at big dinner parties. General Howe, home again in 1779 from his unsuccessful campaign in America, complained bitterly to her that it was a little hard after a man had devoted his whole time and talents to the service of his country that 'he should be held up as a public criminal for not doing what could not be done'. Warren Hastings she met in 1786 and liked immediately. 'He is', she wrote, 'a man of remarkable simplicity of manner and dress and deportment, full of admirable good sense. Nothing of the Nabob about him.' Two years later, escorted by Lord and Lady Amherst, she attended his trial on the day 'of my friend Edmund Burke's splendid and powerful oration'.

It was abusive and vehement beyond all conception; I never felt such indignation as when Burke, with Sheridan on one side and Fox on the other, said, 'Vice incapacitates a man from all public duty; it withers the powers of his understanding and makes his mind paralytic.' I looked at his two neighbours and saw that they were quite free from any symptom of palsy.

'Lord Macartney', she told Patty, 'is one of the most agreeable men I know, of political mind and fine taste, besides the rare merit he possesses of having brought clean hands and a pure fame out of India.' Introduced to Miss More in 1782, General Paoli, the romantic Corsican patriot, then on a visit to England, 'became at once my chief beau and flirt'. She rubbed up her Italian—'I have not spoken seven sentences in seven years'—to converse with him. 'We talk whole hours . . . he is extremely lively when set a-going.' For General Oglethorpe she shared Pope's enthusiasm. She regarded him as the most remarkable man of his time. He responded with warm admiration. 'We flirt together prodigiously.' Burke, joining them at Mrs Vesey's assembly, told Oglethorpe, she relates, that he looked upon him as a more extraordinary person than any he had read of, 'for that he had founded the Province of Georgia; had absolutely called it into existence and had lived to see it severed from the empire that created it and become an independent state. I could have added', wrote Hannah, ' "and whose wicked eloquence was it that helped to bring about this mighty revolution?" And by his looks I believe the venerable Nestor had the same thought.'[56]

Except for Burke, whom in her early days she met frequently, statesmen and politicians seldom crossed her path. Sheridan's political career and his intemperate habits brought their early friendship to an end. Pitt, for whom in later years she expressed extravagant admiration as 'the Pilot that weathered the Storm', she does not appear to have met. Fox, anathema to reforming hostesses bent on abolishing the card-tables, did not, for obvious reasons, frequent the 'Bas Bleu Babels'. She saw him for the first time during the Westminster Election of 1784. 'He looked so sensible and agreeable', she wrote to Patty, 'that if I had not turned my eyes another way I believe it would have been all over with me.' Lord North, 'delightfully entertaining', asked her at an evening party to initiate him in 'the mysterious game' of Twenty Questions. She did not find him very intelligent. His questions were exhausted before he had guessed the Earthen Lamp of Epictetus. 'I am quite provoked at my own stupidity,' said his lordship, 'for I quoted that very lamp last night in the House of Commons.' The renowned John Wilkes she met in his regenerate days. Carefully choosing his conversation to suit her taste, he gave her an amusing specimen of the bad French his daughter learned at her school. When the child's escort arrived to accompany her home from school she said to her governess 'Je suis venu pour.' Miss More found him 'very entertaining'.[57]

Leading ecclesiastics did not lag behind the laity in their admiration of a woman whose wit and charm marched side by side with religious orthodoxy and genuine piety. Shipley of St Asaph invited her to his monstrous assemblies, which were not to her taste;[58] Watson of Llandaff corresponded with her; Horsley of Rochester knew her well enough to treat with contempt the extraordinary charges made against her in 1801. Lowth of London, scholar and wit, was her warm admirer. The stately Horne, Dean of Canterbury and later Bishop of Norwich, was an old friend. He sent his daughter to the Park Street school because of his admiration for Hannah and her sisters, and later incited her to write her didactic essay on 'The Manners of the Great'. Shute Barrington, whose speedy progress up the ladder of preferment is remembered when his blameless character and unaffected piety are forgotten, regarded her with lively affection and esteem. When Beilby Porteus, a man of vision and liberal sympathies, was translated from Chester to London in 1787, he and Hannah More, whose minds travelled on the same lines, formed a lasting friendship. To a pious woman who enjoyed the flesh-pots of Egypt and the compliments showered upon her, the friendship and admiration of these distinguished servants of the Church was a peculiar pleasure. 'I have lately', she wrote with elation to the sisters, in the winter of 1782, 'had three sprightly copies of verses from three of the gravest men in England, who posterity will never believe to have written epigrams.' Lowth's neatly turned Latin verse, addressed to *Hannae Morae, virgini piae eruditae, eleganti, ingenio, facundia et sapientia pariter illustri*, was the talk of the town; Horne slipped four lines of verse into her hand when an accident at the dinner table despoiled her gown without despoiling her temper; Porteus, whose poem 'Death' was apostrophized by Miss More in *Sensibility*, addressed a quatrain to her in return. Fifty years later, when the *Memoirs* were published, these pleasant compliments received rough treatment in the *Quarterly Review*. 'Bishops', it said, 'shoot their ambrosial curls at her footstool and some of them indited encomiastic twaddle in heathen language which the *pia virgo* could not understand.'[59] But in the 'eighties these epigrams were repeated with delight in social and literary circles, and no one would have dreamed of questioning her latinity.

(iii)

The most interesting and diverting of Hannah More's friendships was her friendship, late in her London days, with Horace Walpole. To students of eighteenth-century history brought up on Macaulay's diatribe on Walpole as 'the most eccentric, the most fastidious, the most capricious of men . . . to whom serious things were trifles and trifles serious things',[60] no two persons could have appeared more incompatible. Miss More's biographer found it impossible to understand her friendship with this 'loose light-minded person'; it required, he admitted regretfully, 'explanation and perhaps apology'.[61]

A modern estimate of Walpole, which shows him to have been 'a kindlier, wiser, more consistent, and more straightforward man' than his critics were prepared to allow, is curiously similar to that of Hannah More.[62] It was not from her that Tom Macaulay, whose familiarity with eighteenth-century personalities has sometimes been ascribed to her vivid descriptive powers, drew his portrait of Horace Walpole.

Their friendship took some time to mature. Neither, it may be hazarded, found the other attractive on hearsay, or was prepared to be appreciative. A provincial schoolmistress who advertised her precisianism by her ridiculous Sunday observance was not the type of woman he cared about. Her introductions to London celebrities did not include one to him. She was a protegée of Garrick, whom he disliked, and of Johnson, whose manners he detested, and whose *Life* of his friend Thomas Gray he never forgave. He was not, like the rest of the world, prepared to acclaim *Percy* a masterpiece, though he admitted that it was not without its good points. Nor could he have failed to hear, in so small a society as the London of his age, that this young woman from Bristol, completely ignorant of scholarship, had refused to accept the findings of the Pundits, Warton, Johnson, Percy, and himself, on the alleged authenticity of Rowley's poems, and on sentimental grounds alone was convinced of Chatterton's ascription. She, for her part, moving in London's literary circles, could not have been ignorant of Walpole's reputation as historian, antiquarian, novelist, and *virtuoso*. But his main interests lay outside her line of country; she was not interested in them. 'I have not', she said, 'a spark of *virtù* in my composition.'[63] His play *The Mysterious Mother* could not have been any less detestable to her than it was to Fanny Burney, and it would seem that she followed Catcott and Broughton and other of her Bristol contemporaries in holding him in part responsible for Chatterton's suicide. Nor was it likely that Walpole's religious scepticism, and his much admired persiflage, would appeal to a woman of her principles.

It was Walpole's friendship with the more select of the *Bas Bleu* hostesses, and in particular with Mrs Vesey, for whom he and Hannah shared a very real affection, which gave them the opportunity to know and like one another. She found in his gentleness and he in her goodness much to appreciate. She told him so in a letter written from Cowslip Green in June 1787.

Cowslip Green, June, 1787

Dear Sir,

It is no encouragement to be good, when it is so profitable to do evil: and I shall grow wicked upon principle, and ungrateful by system. If I thought that not answering one letter would always procure me two such, I would be as silent as ingratitude, bad taste, and an unfeeling heart, can cause the most undeserving to be. I did, indeed, receive your first obliging letter, and intended, in the true spirit of a Bristol trader, to have sent you some of my worthless beads, and bits of glass, in exchange for your ivory and gold dust, but a very tedious nervous headache has made me less than ever qualified to traffic with you in this dishonest way, and I have been so little accustomed to connect your idea with that of pain and uneasiness, that I know not how to set about the strange association; but I am now better, and would not have named being sick at all, if there were any other apology in the world that would have justified my not writing. Mrs Carter and I, have a thousand times agreed that your wit was by no means the cause of our esteem for you; because you cannot *help* having it if you would: and I never in my life could be attached to any one for their wit, if wit was the best thing they had. It is an established maxim with me, that the truest objects of warm attachment are the small parts of great characters. I never considered the patriotic Brutus with any delight as the assertor of freedom, and as 'refulgent from the stroke of Caesar's fate;' no, it is the gentle, compassionate Brutus that engages my affection, who refused to disturb the slumbers of the poor boy who attended him in that anxious night, when he destroyed himself, and so much needed his services. So when I sit in a little hermitage I have built in my garden, *not to be melancholy in*, but to think upon my friends, and to read their works, and their letters, Mr Walpole seldomer presents himself to my mind as the man of wit, than, as the tender-hearted and humane friend of my dear infirm, broken-spirited Mrs Vesey. One only admires talents, and admiration is a cold sentiment, with which affection has commonly nothing to do, but one does more than admire them when they are devoted to such gentle purposes. My very heart is softened when I consider that she is now out of the way of your kind attentions, and I fear that nothing else on earth gives her the smallest pleasure. But I shall make you sad, and myself too, if I talk any longer in this strain, for I do love her with a tender affection, and cannot but take a warm interest in every thing that is either useful or pleasant to her. Even in this affecting decay of her sweet mind, her heart retains all its unimpaired amiableness. Her purity rather resembles that innocence which is the ignorance of evil, than that virtue which is the conquest over it. But I am running on just as if you did not know and love her as well as I do; I hope she is gone to Tunbridge, which will amuse her a little, though it can do her no good.

I am become a perfect outlaw from all civil society and orderly life. I spend almost my whole time in my little garden, 'which mocks my scant manuring.' From 'morn to noon, from noon to dewy eve,' I am employed in raising dejected pinks, and reforming disorderly honeysuckles.

Yours, dear sir, very faithfully,

H. M.

Walpole was sixty-two when Hannah More met him in 1780. In the later years of his life, when illness and boredom pressed hard upon him, he was always happiest among his women friends. His distaste for the 'Babels' of the learned ladies did not prevent him from an occasional attendance at the more select of their assemblies, where he was assured of a warm welcome from the delighted ladies he honoured by his presence. Miss More began by appreciating his wit; she ended with an affection for himself.

The frequent references to Walpole in Hannah More's letters for the next seventeen years show this remarkable friendship in process of formation. She began by modifying her attitude in the 'Chattertonian Controversy', after reading Mr Walpole's 'sensible, temperate and humane pamphlet'. When they met at Bishop Shipley's in 1781 she enjoyed 'a vast deal of snug chat' with Mr Walpole. At Mrs Vesey's grand assembly she found in one corner 'the pleasantest group in the world'. It included Mr Walpole. 'The conversation was quite in my way, and in a great measure within my reach; it related chiefly to poetry and criticism.' Her modest deference was gradually replaced by 'pleasant wrangles' with Mr Walpole about poets, 'he abusing all my favourites, and I all his; he reprobating Akenside, Thomson, and all my bards of the *blank song* and I all his odes and lyrics. I told him (rather lightly I fear) that David has expressed my notion of the obscurity of lyric poetry when he said "I will utter my dark speech upon the harp."' And so close a guard did he keep on his tongue in her presence that she asseverated she had never heard a sentence from him which 'savoured of infidelity'. 'I never', she wrote, when she called to see him after his long illness in 1786, 'knew a man suffer pain with such entire patience. This

F

submission is certainly a most valuable part of religion, and yet, alas, he is not religious!'[64] That he found her personally attractive becomes clear in their correspondence. Her charm, her wit, her probity compensated for the lack of high breeding which he had required from his women friends in his younger days. He enjoyed talking to her. He made 'assignations' with her. He developed a very real interest in her light verse, the only kind of poetry he cared about. He admired her *Florio*, dedicated to himself, and complimented her on the admirable ingenuity with which she had introduced very difficult rhymes in her *Bas Bleu*, a poem which combined learning with 'all the air of negligence instead of that of pedantry'.[65] He paid her ballad *Bishop Bonner's Ghost* the highest compliment, insisting that she should allow him to print it on his superlative printing press at Strawberry Hill, and eulogized it in a letter to Miss Mary Berry as 'most beautiful'. 'Every stanza of *Bonner's Ghost* furnishes you with a theme of ideas. I have read them twenty times and every time they improve on me.'[66]

Early in their acquaintance he invited her to Strawberry Hill. From a man who had declared 'it is few people I ask to come hither, and, if possible, still fewer that I wish to see here' the invitation, as Miss More remarked to her sisters with justifiable pride, was 'a great compliment'. 'We passed', she wrote later, 'as delightful a day as elegant literature, high breeding and lively wit can afford. As I was the greatest stranger Mr Walpole devoted himself to my amusement, with great politeness, but I have so little virtû and antiquarianism about me that I really felt quite unworthy of all the trouble he took for me.' This rare compliment, repeated by him, was followed by one even more unusual when Walpole begged to be allowed to furnish part of a shelf in her cottage at Cowslip Green with his published works.[67]

Far more remarkable than these charming courtesies were the letters written by Horace Walpole to Hannah More, during the last decade of his life. In the vast corpus of his letters, which the Yale edition of his correspondence will make available, those written to Hannah More are but a fraction of the whole. What is astonishing is not that they are few in number, but that they should have been written at all. A recent life of Walpole provides an illuminating explanation. It suggests that Walpole's correspondence, the main foundation of his future fame, was planned deliberately to provide future generations with a picture of his age, as it appeared to him, 'so that posterity might know all about it'. It supplemented his political *Memoirs* of the reigns of George II and George III 'with the subtleties and undertones, the anecdotes and manners and social trivialities which formed the background to the march of great events'. And his 'key' correspondents, Horace Mann, George Montagu, William Mason, William Cole, the Countess of Upper Ossory, perhaps even Mary and Agnes Berry, and certainly Hannah More, representing in themselves his different interests in life, were carefully selected to this end.[68] When he began his correspondence with Hannah More he was an old man. He wanted a correspondent who shared his elderly interests and prejudices when the world he knew was in process of disintegration before his eyes. They shared an interest in literature and a love of Thomas Gray's works; they disliked the new 'poetasters'. She disapproved, as he did, of the new woman. They detested the new 'philosophizing serpents', 'the Paines, the Tookes, and the Wollstonecrafts'. She shared his horror of the new type of revolution in France, described so vividly by him to her, and his perturbation that the new kind of war, unlike the old wars, 'was not a war of nation and nation' but 'the cause of everything dear and sacred to civilized men'. And, though he teased her gently for her Puritanism, he admired her goodness; was interested in the philanthropic ploys which were beginning to occupy so big a place in her life, her 'black-manity' and her village schools, and occasionally he untied his purse-strings to assist her. In the 'disgusting subject' of the Bristol milk-woman his sympathies were wholly on Hannah's side. Perhaps when he defended her against the strictures of Ann Yearsley and her supporters he was unconsciously defending himself against the strictures of the Chattertonians, with an eye on the 'undutiful urchin Posterity'.[69]

The 'Literati'

But on one point they disagreed vehemently. He was not a religious man. He had a rooted distaste for religious enthusiasm of
any kind, and Hannah More's precisianism appeared to him to be
dangerously akin to the 'new Puritanism' of the age. As early as
1786 he had teased her, she told the sisters, 'for what he calls over-
strictness'. 'Mr Walpole', she writes again, 'pursues his persecution
of me about Puritanism.' He scolded her for her 'monstrously
severe' doctrines for the rich, and rallied her upon the 'ill-natured
strictness' of her tracts for the poor.[70] He addressed her mockingly
as 'Holy Hannah' and 'my dear Saint Hannah', and then withdrew
the sting by an appeasing postscript: 'He forgot to say that the
warmth of his heart towards those he loves and esteems has not
suffered the least diminution and consequently he is as fervently as
ever Saint Hannah's most sincere friend and humble servant.'[71]
But she was deeply concerned by his lack of religion, and grasping
her courage 'never flinched from any of his ridicule or attacks, or
suffered them to pass without rebuke'.

She paid her last visit to him before his death in April 1795, when
he again rallied her on her sabbatarianism and she responded by
urging him to read Law's *Serious Call to a Devout and Holy Life*.
His was the last word. He sent her shortly afterwards a copy of
Bishop Wilson's Bible inscribed as follows:

To his excellent friend
Miss Hannah More
This book,
which he knows to be the dearest object of her study,
and by which
to the great comfort and relief
of numberless afflicted and distressed individuals
she has profited beyond any person with whom he is acquainted,
is offered
as a mark of his esteem and gratitude
by her sincere
and obliged humble servant
Horace, Earl of Orford
1795.

He died on 2 March 1797. 'I could not help mourning for him',

72

she wrote to Martha More, 'as if I had not expected it. But twenty years' unclouded kindness and pleasant correspondence cannot be given up without emotion.'[72]

(iv)

When Hannah More was at the height of her literary and social fame in London, fate delivered a blow which was as painful as it was unexpected. Patronage of genius, particularly of female genius, was regarded by the Bas Bleu ladies as their duty and privilege. Miss More was herself an outstanding illustration of this patronage. Her Bristol connection introduced her in the years 1784–5 to 'a poetic genius' to whom she in her turn could play the patron. Verses written by an unlettered and wretchedly poor Bristol milkwoman, with a family of five small children and a husband of 'little capacity', were shown to Miss More when she returned to Bristol in the autumn of 1784, after a visit to Mrs Montagu. The poems of this 'uneducated poet' were treated critically and sympathetically by her Bristol contemporary Robert Southey. 'Very few passages', he held, 'can be extracted from her writings which would have any other value than as indicating power which the possessor knew not how to employ,'[73] and it is doubtful, remarkable as some of the verses are, if more can be said in their praise. But Hannah More, with her easily aroused and uncritical enthusiasm, was immensely impressed. 'The verses', she wrote to Mrs Montagu, 'excited my attention, for, though incorrect, they breathed the genuine spirit of poetry and were rendered the more interesting by a certain natural and strong expression of misery, which seemed to fill the heart and mind of the author.' She made diligent inquiry into Ann Yearsley's history and character, and, convinced that she was not only a genius, 'buried in obscurity' but also a deserving case, 'active and industrious in no common degree . . . without the least affectation and pretension of any kind', she decided to raise a subscription from her literary and aristocratic friends for the publication of Ann Yearsley's verses and for the relief of her estate. Filled with philanthropic ardour and literary enthusiasm 'for one

73

who did not know a single rule of grammar and who had never seen a dictionary', she assured her friends, whose opinion on the proper station of the inferior orders she shared, that it was not intended to place Mrs Yearsley in such a state of independence 'as might seduce her to devote her time to the idleness of poetry, or indispose her for the laborious employment of her humble condition', and, acting upon these set principles, she devoted the greater part of the next thirteen months to teaching Ann Yearsley the common rules of composition, to translating and correcting her poems, and to writing more than a thousand pages of letters appealing for subscriptions. The list of over a thousand names, headed by nine duchesses, attests both the scope of Miss More's efforts on behalf of Mrs Yearsley and her own popularity with the great. Nor did the interest of the fashionable world end in subscriptions. Mrs Yearsley was bidden by command invitation to visit the Duchesses of Beaufort and Rutland, Countess Spencer, and Mrs Montagu. She was the recipient of books from the Duchess of Devonshire, and of gifts from other ladies in money and kind. Mrs Montagu consented to be co-trustee with Miss More of the funds raised for Mrs Yearsley, but rather uneasily warned Hannah that in her experience 'a legion of little demons, vanity, luxury, idleness and pride might enter the cottage the moment poverty vanished.'[74]

Mrs Yearsley's first volume of poems, abounding in eulogies of Miss More as 'the Bright Instructress and Soother of the Soul', was published with a prefatory letter to Mrs Montagu in 1784.[75] It aroused some interest in London, and enthusiasm in Bristol, so proud of its literary reputation. All might have gone well had not the mammon of unrighteousness entered in. Mrs Yearsley expected, not without reason, that the subscriptions—'the produce of her poems'—would be handed to her. The trustees, anxious to safeguard the capital sum of £360 and ensure a permanent income for Mrs Yearsley, thought otherwise. They invested the money in 3 per cent stock and, taking powers under the Trust Deed 'to expend, apply and dispose of principal and interest in such way and manner as they shall think fit for the benefit and advantage of Ann Yearsley and her children', sent it to Bristol for her and her husband's signature. Mrs Yearsley's fierce pride—her outstanding trait, as her poems manifest—was at once up in arms. 'I felt', she wrote in her account of the bitter dispute with Miss More, 'as a mother deemed unworthy of the tuition and care of her family.'[76] She carried her objections to Mary and Elizabeth More in Hannah's absence in London, and was by them persuaded to sign the deed. When Miss More returned to Bristol in the summer of 1785 the two women met. 'Angry recriminations', says Southey, ensued. Mrs Yearsley demanded the return of her MSS. Miss More, embarrassed, informed her that they had been burnt at the printers. Unforgivable words were spoken on both sides, and Hannah More, obstinately refusing to modify the deed and admit Mrs Yearsley as joint-trustee, resigned from the Trust and refused further communication with her.

The affair did not end with the cancellation of the Trust. Friends and supporters hurried to aid the protagonists. Press and publicists took up the cry. Bristol opinion was divided, as it had been in the Chatterton controversy. Mrs Yearsley, emotionally uncontrolled, lost no opportunity in speech and writing to deride the character of her benefactor, making even the ridiculous statement that Miss More intended to misappropriate the subscriptions to buy herself a house in the country. Later, lacking all decent restraint, she disinterred the story of Hannah's broken engagement, twenty years before, and triumphed over 'the slighted prude' of her imagination.[77] Hannah More, to whom the vulgar publicity was profoundly distasteful, behaved in public with her usual dignity and restraint. She made no answer to Mrs Yearsley's manifestos; she ignored the allusions in her later volume of poems.[78] But her letters to her friends provide ample proof of her anger and humiliation. Ingratitude quite vanquished her. She could not leave the 'odious tale' alone. She bored her closest friends with its repeated recital. Mrs Montagu could barely restrain a polite 'I told you so', and Mrs Garrick, whose temper did not grow sweeter as she grew older, expressed the hope that Miss More would 'shut up her feelings and throw the writing of the Trust at Mrs Yearsley's head and have done with it'.[79] Hannah More struggled hard with her resentment and assured herself that she had put it under control, but when Mrs Yearsley's friends urged a reconciliation she remained inexorable. Nothing had happened, she declared, to alter her opinion of the milk-woman.

This unhappy incident defines the limitation of Hannah More's mind and sympathies, and marks the assimilation of her social ideas to those of her class and her age. Gratitude and submission were the due returns of the lower orders for the beneficence of their superiors. Hannah More's conscience was clear. Her intentions were generous and philanthropic. Mrs Yearsley's proud intransigeance angered and puzzled her. With considerable hesitation—for the explanation, she realized was Methodistical, and she disliked Methodism—she found the answer in an excess of human pride undisciplined by the influence of religion.[80]

CHAPTER IV

THE SAINTS[1]

'If to be an anti-slavist is to be a Saint, Saintship for me.'
                                                            Bentham

'These Evangelical Saints of his are Saints indeed, but they are very human, and it may fall out that the spices wherewith he embalmed them will preserve their lineaments when the holy men of a newer dispensation are the merest skeletons.'

F. W. Maitland, *Life of Leslie Stephen* (1906), referring to
Sir James Stephen and his essay on 'The Clapham Sect'

(i)

THE second half of Hannah More's life was in manifest contrast to that of her earlier years. Her interest in literature and the stage was replaced by an interest in philanthropy and an absorption in religion, which posterity and many of her contemporaries condemned by the opprobrious term of 'enthusiasm'. Her changing interests appear to have perplexed William Roberts and her later biographers. They ascribe it to an out-crop of the puritanism of her grandparents, or to the death of three men dear to her, or to 'the wickedness of London'.[2] It may be accepted that there was a puritan strain in her make-up; it is possible that in an age of morbid concern with the charnel house and the tomb—a morbidity which she shared—the death, in rapid succession, of Garrick, Johnson, and her father, was a potent reminder that in the midst of life we are in death; and it is certain that the ungodliness of London, more blatant and less evasive than that of Bristol, was a matter of concern to her. Facts such as these played their part in the readjustment of her life, but they fail adequately to relate the reaction of a pious and essentially practical woman to the Evangelical revival within the Church of England in the last decade of the century, which left an

77

The Saints

indelible mark on English religious, social, and political history far into the nineteenth century.

Though Hannah More and her sisters lived in a city which was 'the cradle of Methodism', they appear to have had no contact and no sympathy with the Methodist movement. Their piety may have derived from the Puritanism of their paternal grandparents, or from the High Anglicanism which their father professed. It did not derive directly from the Methodism of Wesley and Whitefield. Nor were their clerical mentors sympathetic to Methodism. Josiah Tucker had been a highly critical opponent from the November day in 1739 when two Anglican clergymen, John Wesley and George Whitefield, both deeply attached to the Church, using Bristol as a centre, began their efforts to regenerate the Church by teaching and preaching with magnetic power the venerable doctrine of the Justification by Faith in Jesus Christ. Stonhouse, an early convert to Methodism, had dissociated himself from the movement because, said Lady Huntingdon, of his incurable dread of being called a Methodist.[3] His devotional piety, though it owed something to Whitefield, owed as much, it would seem, to his friendship with Philip Doddridge and to classical Nonconformity. His interest in the stage and his encouragement of Hannah More's dramatic genius derived neither from Dissent nor from Methodism.

As far as evidence is available, it seems clear that the sisters were not intimate with John Wesley, though his neat precise figure was well known in Bristol streets and Bristol homes; nor with Charles Wesley, who lived for twenty years as local superintendent of the Movement at Stoke's Croft; nor with Whitefield, who was only less well-known in Bristol than in the neighbouring city of Bath. There is no reference to them in Hannah More's published correspondence; there is no reference to Hannah More and her sisters in Wesley's detailed and meticulous *Journal* or in his *Letters* until 1790, when, in response to an invitation to visit the sisters, he demurred, pleading other interests and doubting whether his conversation would suit the Miss Mores.[4] It is significant that, when Wilberforce desired to meet Charles Wesley, Hannah More arranged a meeting not in her own house but in that of a friend.[5] Never, according to her own statement, had she attended Lady Huntingdon's Chapel in Bath, 'or the tabernacles of Wesley and Whitefield in London or the country'.[6] Indeed, if it were not for her remark that John Wesley had sent a message by Betty More urging Hannah to continue her work in reforming the rich, 'for they will not let *us* come nigh them', it would appear that there was no contact between the leaders of the Methodist movement in the eighteenth century and the woman who was a recognized leader of Evangelicalism in the nineteenth century.

Social considerations in part accounted for the lack of contact. Methodism was a lower-class movement. Methodists were not gentlemen, and the Mores were endeavouring, with the help of their patrons, to build up connections for a high-class school. But this is not an adequate explanation. The sisters, it would seem, felt no need of a spiritual revival in their own lives, and doubted the wisdom of a revival on Methodist lines for others. And this, not because they were indifferent to religion—far from it—but because the Anglican Church, as they knew it, provided them with the spiritual piety and spiritual unity they required. In sympathy with other quiet Christians of their age they found in the loving Fatherhood of God, which Church teaching stressed, a principle on which to rely. Strictly brought up on orthodox lines, they were sound Anglicans, accepting the doctrines of the Church as commonly interpreted, submitting to its order and its discipline, and paying to it, in Hannah More's words, 'an affection entire, cordial and inviolable'.[8] They regularly attended their parish Church, never frequented conventicles, and kept holy the sabbath day.

Nor was there lacking a practical side to their religion. Their benevolence was wide and generous. The *Memoirs and Correspondence* and the letters of their friends are strewn with references to their charity. And they taught their pupils, using, it may safely be asserted, the *Whole Duty of Man*, to care for the widows and the fatherless and 'to live neighbourly and godly in the present world'. Tolerant of classical Nonconformity, they were not sympathetic

to Methodism, whose followers they, in common with Churchmen of their type, regarded as fanatical zealots. 'Enthusiasm', a
term which its critics in the eighteenth century identified with
fanaticism, not zeal, they deplored; religious controversy of any
kind they abhorred. 'We', said Sally tersely, 'are of the *Christian*
faction.'[9]

Until the 'eighties Hannah More was seemingly unaware of the
spirit of inertia which, even if it has been exaggerated, was a
characteristic feature of the Anglican Church in the eighteenth
century. Possibly her close friendship with two unusual eighteenth-
century clerics was in part responsible for her attitude. Whichever
estimate of Josiah Tucker be accepted, that of Bishop Warburton
or that of Bishop Newton, one thing is certain. He did not suffer
from inertia, either as preacher or parish priest. Rather was he the
catfish of the fisherman's haul, lashing lethargic mankind into
acceptance of his liberal and humane, social, moral and religious
views.[10]

Stonhouse, too, was not typical of the inert eighteenth-century
cleric. His association with Doddridge and Whitefield had opened
his mind to spiritual things. When he 'dropped' Methodism, apprehensive of the religious and social opprobrium which attached
to it, he settled down as a parish priest of the Evangelical persuasion,
though 'very near the border line', said Jay of Bath, without am-
biguity, 'which separates them from others'; and as Lecturer at All
Saints Church, Clifton, he was one of the earliest Evangelical
preachers in the city. But his mild and cautious Evangelicalism, 'the
skim-milk of the Gospel', was not rich enough to upset Hannah
More and her sisters.[11] Nor did either of their spiritual directors
suffer from the semi-Socinianism of the eighteenth century. The
sisters had little fault to find in their Bristol days with a Church
which numbers of earnest men and women in the eighteenth century, and an even greater number in the nineteenth century who
saw it through the eyes of the Oxford Movement, united in condemning.

It is conceivable that had Hannah not spent part of each year in

London she would have remained unaware of the difference between the steady piety and habitual philanthropy of herself and her sisters, and the religious indifference and lazy charity of all but a few of her London friends and acquaintances. For in Bristol, 'a city no whit better than London', she was not conspicuous. Her precisianism was there regarded as the appropriate accompaniment of her profession. In London, on the contrary, the piety of a writer of plays and a devotee of the theatre met sometimes with ridicule, sometimes with amused tolerance. No one, she found, not even the Bas Bleu ladies of high character for piety, thought fit to keep holy the sabbath day. Men and women of social and intellectual distinction laced their conversation with expletives; attendance at Church was perfunctory; serious reading was at a discount, and she found it difficult to interest the most obliging of her dinner partners in the recent books of divinity which she read assiduously, even at the height of the London Season. 'There are so few people', she remarked lugubriously to the sisters, 'to whom one can venture to recommend sermons.'

Her slow and tentative approach to Evangelicalism was made by way of her new humanitarian interests. It would be a misreading of history to ascribe the humanitarian movement at the end of the eighteenth century to religion alone. Rationalistic theories throughout played a part of no small importance, and at the end of the century French philosophy treating of 'pure disinterested goodness acting for its own end'[13] was a formidable rival to Christian charity. It is none the less true that the religious revivals, by stressing the sense of individual responsibility, changed a trickle of private and semi-private benevolence into a spate of organized philanthropy. It was not difficult for Charles Middleton, then a half-pay naval captain, to arouse the enthusiasm of a woman whose quick responsiveness was a leading characteristic, in his absorbing humanitarian interests. Meeting him first at a dinner party in 1776 she told the sisters later of her new friendship with the 'stern and simple captain' whose character would delight them; his wife 'made up of feeling and compassion', and her friend Mrs Bouverie, 'whose charities are boundless' and with whom the Middletons lived in 'the heavenly paradise of Teston'.[14] Hannah discovered when she knew them intimately that this pious and philanthropic trio shared a passionate desire to abolish the West Indian Slave Trade. At Teston she heard in the 'eighties of its Rector, James Ramsay, one of the earliest and most able of the Abolitionists, who, as Rector of St Kitts in the West Indies for twenty-seven years, had seen the trade in the raw. His recital of its abominations aroused in Mrs Middleton, the importance of whose share in the movement is seldom remembered and sometimes disputed, 'an ardour for reform'.[15] She persuaded Ramsay to publish his famous *Essay on the Treatment of Slaves* in 1782; she supported him against the merciless attack of platform and press in 1784-5; and she prevailed upon her friends to find 'a fit and willing protagonist to lead a Crusade against the Trade in the House'. When their choice fell upon Wilberforce, a young man already deeply interested in the Trade, 'a powerful advocate of truth and virtue', M.P. for Hull and an intimate friend of the Prime Minister, William Pitt, she persuaded her husband to approach the young man and invite him to Teston to consult with the family. Three years later, after associating himself with the Quaker opponents of the Trade, with Granville Sharp and other members of the newly formed Committee for its Abolition, and with their agent Thomas Clarkson, he agreed to take up the cause in Parliament. The fight was on and at Teston Court, Battersea Rise, and Palace Yard, where Wilberforce's crowded ante-rooms 'provok'd the wit of Mrs Hannah More to liken it to Noah's Ark full of beasts clean and unclean', Wilberforce and his 'white negroes' slaved for the slaves.

There is no evidence in the *Correspondence* to show that Hannah More, a native of Bristol, whose sugar-refining industry was one of the most important in the kingdom and where evidence of the Trade was visible in the city's streets and docks, was interested in the anti-Slave Trade movement until she knew the ardent Middletons. But a reader of Richard Baxter's works, a friend of Josiah Tucker, and a resident of Bristol when Wesley, after some initial hesitation, forcibly condemned the Slave Trade and enlisted the help of Christians against it, could not have been indifferent or unmoved. 'Everyone', said Clarkson, after visiting Bristol in the summer of 1787, 'execrated the Trade, but no one thought of its abolition.'[16] For the Trade had been regarded throughout the greater part of the eighteenth century as a reputable trade, authorized by Scripture and carried on by respectable persons, some of whom were the parents of pupils at the Park Street school. It was, moreover, an integral part of the West Indian trade monopoly, which Englishmen almost uniformly regarded as the principle and foundation of British trade.[17] The disparate efforts of a few harebrained poets, or of an occasional Christian minister, or of some, but not all, of the Quakers, could make little headway against a policy so well entrenched. Nor, it may be hazarded, without derogating from the impassioned piety and humanitarianism of the Abolitionists, would their efforts have been crowned with success had not the West Indian monopoly gone the way of all monopolies under the impact of free trade.[18] Economics and humanitarianism began to pull in the same direction after 1783, and their combination made possible the triumph of the West Indian anti-Slave Trade movement.

Hannah More's lively letters, after she was swept by the enthusiastic Middletons into the storm-centre of reform, describe some of the unremembered preliminary efforts to launch one of the earliest propaganda campaigns for social reform in English history. They tell of the dinner parties in London, the careful selection of guests at Teston, and the steady canvass of possible supporters by letter and personal contact. During the months in each year which she spent in 'my savage city Bristol' she kept her London friends and colleagues informed of the heroic labours of the impetuous Clarkson, engaged in his dangerous search for evidence in Bristol docks. She knew him and sympathized with his difficulties and disillusionment, and she reported to the Middletons his urgent desire that the London Committee should appeal to 'the popular affections in this slave business',[19] a suggestion which Wilberforce, who preferred parliamentary action and distrusted 'systematic agitation', was slow to approve.

Hannah More proved herself a valuable recruit. She was keen and competent. She knew and was listened to by men of weight and distinction. She was ingenious in devising new methods of propaganda, selling prints of Mrs Bouverie's portrait in oils of a negro boy, urging her friends, as early as 1788, to taboo the use of West Indian sugar in their tea. She carried about with her a copy of Clarkson's famous plan of an African slave ship, and showed it to interested and horrified guests at evening parties.[20] She made the suggestion, surprising in one who had recently abjured the stage, that Southerne's affecting tragedy, *Oroonoko, or the Royal Slave*,[21] should be played at Drury Lane, 'for so many go to a play who will never go to church'; and she recommended with some acerbity that Sheridan, whom she had heard talk for five and a half hours on the oppression of two Begums, should be asked to write 'an affecting prologue' to the play.[22] A letter to Elizabeth Carter, begging her 'to canvass everybody who has a heart', records the sanguine expectations of the Abolitionists when Beilby Porteus was translated from Chester to London, where his ecclesiastical jurisdiction, extending to the West Indies, 'will make him of infinite usefulness'.[23] In January 1788, at the urgent request of her fellow Abolitionists, who considered that a last-minute demonstration was imperative before Wilberforce presented to Parliament his resolutions binding the House to consider the slave trade, she wrote at break-neck speed her poem on the trade. It was not, as with her usual acumen she realized, a 'good' poem, 'but, good or bad,' she told the sisters, 'if it does not come out at this particular moment, when the discussion comes on in Parliament, it will not be worth a straw. . . Time is everything.'[24] As a last-minute demonstration it came out four months too soon; the bill was held up until May 1788, when Pitt, in Wilberforce's absence through illness, moved and carried a resolution binding the House to consider the Slave Trade in the following session of Parliament.

The story of the long drawn-out efforts in what Wilberforce

called 'the first round' in the twenty years' struggle to persuade Parliament to abolish the trade is well known.[25] The hopes and fears of the Abolitionists are reflected in Hannah's letters from London to the sisters in Bristol in the spring and summer of 1789. She writes jubilantly of 'the glorious and most promising opening of the great cause', when the Report of the Privy Council Committee, appointed by the Prime Minister in 1788 to inquire into the conditions of British trade with Africa, was presented to Parliament, and the support of Pitt and Fox assured. 'The Douglas and the Percy both together', she quotes, 'are confident against the world in arms.' When Tarleton, 'the Liverpool delegate who is come up to defend slavery against humanity', arrived in London she was less confident. A dinner party of men at Lord Ossory's still further depressed her spirits. 'There was not a friend to that humane bill among them.' Later, hearing from Mrs Middleton that 'Wilberforce and his myrmidons and the whole Junta of Abolitionists were locked up at Teston, slaving till 2 o'clock every morning on the Committee's Report,' her spirits rose again, for there was more evidence against the trade than for it. 'Teston', she tells her sisters, 'will be the Runnymede of the negroes.' 'The great Charter of African liberty' would there be completed.[26]

The confident hopes of speedy success were not realized. In April 1789 the Report of the Privy Council Committee was presented to Parliament, and the debate opened on 12 May. In spite of an impressive oration by Wilberforce and the support of Pitt, Fox, and Burke, there was a demand for further inquiry and consideration of the evidence, and the question was adjourned. In June 1790 the General Election again postponed action. It was not until the spring of 1791 that Wilberforce moved for leave to bring in a bill to prevent the further importation of slaves to the West Indies. After a two-days debate the motion was rejected, by 163 votes to 88. 'Alas,' wrote Miss More to Mrs Kennicott, 'we have lost that cause for the present.'[27]

Two revolutions, one across the Channel, the other in the West Indies, played into the hands of the opponents of Abolition.

The Saints

Interest in the country began to flag when the French Revolutionary wars distracted attention. French Revolutionary principles dismayed the timid and French interest in the abolition of slavery smirched English efforts with the taint of Jacobinism. Perpetual delays, public indifference, and open hostility to an issue regarded as unimportant at a time of national danger made it difficult for the small body of the 'Saints' to carry on. Only two meetings of the Abolition Committee were held from 1794 to 1797, and from 1797 until 1804, when once again success appeared possible, they ceased altogether. In 1794 even the indomitable Clarkson, worn out by his ceaseless efforts, retired from the struggle.

(ii)

The campaign against the slave trade brought Hannah More, when she was at the height of her literary and social fame, into contact with men and women whose interest lay not in literature and conversation but in philanthropy based on a deep and vital sense of religion. Though Quakers, Dissenters, Methodists, and 'formal' churchmen were among the advance guard of later eighteenth-century philanthropy, it drew its recruits, in the main, from a growing body of Anglicans to whom, in later years, the term Evangelical Party was given. The legal recognition of the Countess of Huntingdon's chapels as Dissenting Conventicles in 1782, Wesley's break with the church in 1784, the registration of his chapels as Dissenting chapels in 1787, and, in 1791, after Wesley's death, the extension of the circuit system throughout the country, in direct contradistinction to the ancient parochial system, provided tests which helped to define the position of Methodists and 'Church' Evangelicals. 'We have the character of Methodism complete,' wrote Jones of Nayland in a phrase which helped to lay bare the difference between it and Church Evangelicalism. 'It is christian godliness without christian order.'[28] Owing, in part, to the commanding influence of Charles Simeon, a strong churchman, whose sway over the Church was, in Lord Macaulay's opinion, greater than that of any primate,[29] Evangelicals were dissuaded from leaving the Church as the Methodists had done, and with the financial help of Evangelical laymen, such as John Thornton, advowsons were provided for the continuity of Evangelical teaching within the Church. The combination of ordered piety and ordered discipline attracted a number of earnest men and women to Evangelicalism in the last decades of the eighteenth century. Its influence in the half-century 1780–1830 upon the upper and middle classes of society, though not as spectacular as that of Methodism upon the lower orders, was not less remarkable. It may be argued that, as much as any other single factor in the pre-Victorian Age, it moulded the Victorian era.

In the 'eighties, when Hannah More, profoundly impressed by the 'vital religion' and passionate philanthropy of her fellow workers for Abolition, began to set her spiritual house in order, the lines of demarcation between 'Methodist' and 'Evangelical' were still blurred. The opprobrious terms 'Methodist' and 'Enthusiast' were applied indifferently to all those within and without the Church who were moved by a profound desire for holiness. During the war years, when the Established Church gathered strength as a bulwark of loyalty, law, and order against Jacobin influences, the position of Dissenters, Methodists, and Evangelicals did not, as Hannah More was to discover, grow easier. Any deviation from the established order in doctrine or practice was anathema. When to religious disapprobation was added the social stigma which attached to Methodism, it needed some courage for a woman brought up on orthodox Church lines and enjoying the friendship of members of the governing classes to associate herself with the Evangelicals. She knew that they were an unpopular party—how unpopular she was to learn by bitter experience.

As early as 1780 she had read John Newton's once famous book *Cardiphonia*. 'I like it prodigiously,' she wrote to its donor, Mrs Boscawen. 'It is full of vital experimental religion. Who is the author?'[30] Newton of Olney is, by the general consent of his admirers and detractors, one of the dynamic Evangelical figures of the late eighteenth century. In the opinion of Sir George Trevelyan he was the real founder of the Evangelical School in the Church of England. His extraordinary career as sailor, planter, master of a slaver, curate of Olney, and, when Hannah More met him, Rector of the City church of St Mary Woolnoth, was known to all. Equally extraordinary were his spiritual adventures. After years of infidelity and militant atheism he was ordained by the Bishop of Lincoln and, through the patronage of Lord Dartmouth, Cowper's 'Peer who wears a Coronet and prays', was appointed curate at Olney. In 1780 he was, with the exception of William Romaine, Rector of St Ann's, Blackfriars, the only Evangelical incumbent of the Established Church in the metropolis. Influential as spiritual adviser to men and women who sought his advice rather than as theologian or popular preacher, his influence found its vent in his voluminous correspondence. In his desultory letters to Hannah More he appears less as the 'pushing, impelling, compelling', converting engine of Walter Bagehot's denunciation[31] than as the transparently honest and robust-minded good man, of excellent common sense, humour and patience, of Dr Cairns's recent estimate.[32] From Newton Hannah More gained first-hand knowledge of the African Slave Trade. 'My account', he said drily, 'has the merit of being true,'[33] and from him she learned the meaning of the evangel which inspired his life and that of his fellow saints.

The doctrines which he taught were not new to her. For over two hundred years the Anglican Church of the Reformation settlement had taught the doctrines of the Trinity, the fall of man, his redemption through Jesus Christ and the obligation of holiness. All these things she had known and accepted from her youth up. What was new to her, as her correspondence with Newton illustrates, was the deep and abiding consciousness of the reality of God which filled the minds and hearts of the Evangelicals, and the supreme importance which they attached to conversion—the spiritual encounter between God and man, when God in his own good time brought the individual into direct personal contact with himself. Their 'robust Christianity' moved her profoundly, a

'Christianity practical and pure which teaches holiness, humility, repentance and faith in Christ, and which, after summing up all the Evangelical graces, declares that the greatest of these is charity.'[34]

Deeply impressed, she set herself with characteristic determination to study the faith of the Evangelicals and to examine her powers of resolution and consistency to practise a religion which, in the opinion of at least one vociferous contemporary, made impossible demands on human nature.[35] Her decision involved a long and vacillating struggle between a conception of life which permitted 'quiet worldliness'[36] and one which demanded the undivided allegiance of the individual; between a conception of religion as *an* essential of life and a conception of religion as *the* essential of life.

Her protracted indecision is reflected in her correspondence. Letters to the sisters, telling them that she had been into the city 'to hear good Mr Newton preach, and afterwards sat an hour with him and came home with two pockets full of sermons', alternate with others describing with undisguised enjoyment a 'magnificent assembly at Lady Amherst's' at which the Prince of Wales, 'all gaiety and gracefulness', did not arrive 'till near mid-night and did me the honour to ask for me, to tell me that he had often wished to see me... I may', she wrote in strong self-criticism, 'cry out with Wolsey, "Vain pomp and glory of the world, I hate ye." He did not however renounce it while he could keep it and I', she adds, 'am in much the same way.'[37]

The same despair of herself informs her correspondence with Newton. 'The deceitful favour' and 'insinuating applause of the world', the friendship and kindness of individuals whom she dearly loved, interfered with her efforts to know and love God as she desired to know and love him. Solitude in the country, 'where the world is wiped out of my memory', did not help as she had confidently hoped. Nor did Newton's constant reminder 'that God must be waited *on* and waited *for*', until 'he who has taught you what to desire will in his own best time do everything for you,' comfort her. 'I am fully persuaded', she wrote to him as late as 1791, 'that all things work together for good to them that love God. My only fear is that I do not love him cordially, effectually, entirely.'[38] And as the few pages of her diary, found after her death, show, the assurance she desired with increasing fervour was long delayed.[39]

During the early years of her friendship with Newton Hannah More met and knew his friends, the saintly Richard Cecil, William Bull, Congregational Minister at Newport Pagnell, and William Cowper, in whom she discovered a poet after her own heart. 'I have found what I have been looking for all my life, a poet whom I can read on Sunday,' she wrote to Mrs Bouverie; 'I am enchanted with this poet.'[40] Her enthusiasm for Cowper was in keeping with the opinion of her day. 'The most popular poet of his time'[41] was not in her eyes the 'poor Cowper' whose alleged effeminacy repelled the sympathy of a later generation, but a virile poet who discovered to his generation things they had passed a hundred times and failed to see. For the poet of domesticity was also the poet of humanitarianism and Evangelical piety.[42] Though Cowper and Miss More do not appear to have met or corresponded, their common friends, John Newton and Lady Hesketh, made them well known to one another. Admiration of each other's work cemented a curious and unusual friendship. '*Slavery*', he said, 'I admired as I do all that Miss More writes, for energy of expression as for the tendency of the design. I have never yet seen any production of her pen that has not recommended itself by both these qualifications.' His poems, informed with pity, aroused her compassion. It was not a mere coincidence that her untiring work for the infant and adult poor at home, for 'poor Africans' and ignorant pagans abroad, or her sympathy with the efforts of Pulteney and Wilberforce in Parliament to prohibit the barbarous sport of bull-baiting, followed so closely the 'humane sentiment and genuine Christianity of this original and philosophic thinker'.[43] Hannah More owed much to William Cowper.

Of greater influence than Newton or Cowper in the readjustment of her life was William Wilberforce, who, when Hannah met him in Bath in the autumn of 1787, was in his twenty-eighth year. A warm friendship sprang up between the young man and the middle-aged lady whose lives and characters were so curiously similar. He too was a favourite of London society. His conversational powers rivalled hers. He was gay, intelligent, entertaining and witty, 'with as much wit', wrote Hannah divertingly to her sisters, 'as if he had no piety' [44] He possessed, as contemporary opinion was almost unanimous in agreeing, a personal charm which left few who met him unaffected. His army of friends were agreed in prophesying for him a great political career. A famous book, Doddridge's *Rise and Progress of Religion*, had aroused his interest in religion, as Newton's *Cardiphonia* had aroused hers. From John Newton, to whom they had independently turned for help, they had received the same advice—to work for God by participation in and not by detachment from the world; and like her, but with a speed which left her halting spirit far behind, he made known his determination to devote himself 'for whatever might be the term of my future life to the service of my God and my Saviour'.[45] That a young, successful and liberally gifted man should be willing to sacrifice some of the great prizes of political ambition, even if, as Lecky observed, the self-sacrifice seems to have been exaggerated, much impressed Hannah More. 'That young gentleman's character', she reported to the sisters in 1787, 'is one of the most extraordinary I have ever known for talent, virtue, and piety. It is difficult not to grow better and wiser every time one converses with him.'[46]

Identity of outlook cemented their liking for one another. Impassioned champions of the African slave, they kept the anti-Slave Trade movement alive during the years of hope deferred, when political activity was at a minimum and committees ceased to function, by their efforts to make the black man known to the white man. Among Hannah More's *Cheap Repository Tracts* of the 'nineties are to be found Tales and Ballads and Sunday Readings on 'This Slave Business' which kept the question before tens of thousands of readers at a time when the Abolition Committee had abandoned its efforts to distribute literature.[47] The same identity of outlook expressed itself in their religious views. Wilberforce's approach was dominated, as was hers, by 'the awful consequence arising from the prevailing easy confidence in the loving-kindness of God'. Only by a complete surrender of soul and body to the will and service of man and God could man, 'an apostate creature fallen from his high original', hope for salvation.[48]

With his deep and abiding concern for the blatant immorality of the age she was in close agreement, and as their religious convictions grew, they developed a passion for moral reform based on Christian standards. The schools set up for the poor in the Mendips were their joint affair. Wilberforce supplied the greater part of the required funds and Hannah More organized the work in a manner pronounced by him as 'truly magnificent'.[49]

In her old age she expressed, indirectly, in her essay *Candidus* her indebtedness to him as the pattern *par excellence* of the consistent Christian, unswerving in his piety, rigid in his principles, distrusting enthusiasm and venerating the offices, liturgy, and government of the Church of England, 'in whose formularies he found truth, as it were, preserved, and perpetuated'.[50] His gay unruffled temper, his lively conversation, made him in her eyes the living example of her cherished belief that religion did not forbid the cheerful enjoyment of life or impose a life of hard austerity and pining abstinence on its disciples.

(iii)

To Wilberforce Hannah More owed her introduction in the 'nineties to the remarkable group of 'consistent Christians' called, incorrectly but not inappropriately, the 'Clapham Sect'. The strength and extent of Evangelicalism in the last decades of the eighteenth century are, apparently, not ascertainable. Modern scholarship corrects the exaggerated estimate of earlier writers and holds that there was but a small and 'calumniated' minority of Evangelical clergy and laymen throughout the country. In the 'nineties, when Evangelical clerics were in short supply and Evangelical laymen existed in unorganized groups, two centres were conspicuous as fulfilling the Evangelical tradition of Christian fellowship. With the Cambridge Evangelicals Hannah More appears to have had little contact. She knew and admired Dean Milner, President of Queens' College, the 'Doctor Johnson of Evangelicalism'. 'There never was', she wrote to Alexander Knox years later, 'a more genuine Christian.'[51] Simeon is not mentioned in her published letters, but it is hardly conceivable that she did not meet him when he and Milner, 'habitual associates and zealous allies of the Sect', visited their Clapham friends, nor is it likely that she lacked sympathy and admiration for his courage and his work. But Clapham was her spiritual home. There, with the goodly fellowship of the saints, embalmed for all time by the inimitable skill of a young contemporary, she found 'a hardy, serviceable, fruit-bearing and patrimonial religion'[52] after her own heart. There, religion was applied to everyday life by a notable group of Christian neighbours—public-spirited, influential, highly respected, well-to-do business and professional men, their wives and families, living comfortable lives in comfortable homes[53] under the pastoral care of their spiritual guide, the wise and good father of the Society, John Venn, Vicar of Clapham.[54] One and all were marked by unswerving devotion to the Anglican Church, whose framework and organization they took for granted; strict adherence to Christian piety; a strong sense of personal responsibility; and, as the outcome of their religious commitments, an ordered and generous charity and severe self-discipline, which called for the renunciation of certain specified diversions of the world. Not only convinced of the reality of God, but conscious of his guidance in all things great and small, they condemned as displeasing to him 'worldly pleasures' such as cards, dancing, plays, and novel reading, of which they disapproved. Living together in a close community seeking divine guidance on every occasion, they were exposed, as Dean Milner reminded Wilberforce, to the great danger of conceit, spiritual pride, and a cold and critical spirit.[55] They did not always lack censoriousness in their judgements of others.

Hannah More's generous appreciation was proof against any cold and critical spirit manifested by her new acquaintances in the 'holy village of Claphâm', as Sydney Smith sardonically called it.[56] She shared their personal piety, their distaste for 'enthusiasm, cant and sectarian phrase',[57] and adopted their severe self-discipline and fine humanitarianism. She found in them the most devoted of her friends.

When Henry Thornton, banker and Member of Parliament for Southwark, bought the estate of Battersea Rise in 1794[58] and invited his friend William Wilberforce to share his house with him, the two young men, like William Law before them, but without his transcendent mystical power, worked out a 'system' for living the Christian life, and drew into their orbit men and women who were of one mind with them. 'I am surprised', wrote Thornton, 'to find how much religion everybody seems to have when they get into our house. They all seem to submit to and acknowledge the advantage of a religious life'; and he added drily, 'We are not all queer, or guilty of carrying things too far. I am in hopes that some good may come of our Clapham system.'[59]

From Battersea Rise it was but a stone's throw to Broomfield, where Wilberforce lived after his marriage in 1796. Glenelg, on the Thornton estate, was built by Charles Grant, a notable man in his day, M.P. for Inverness-shire and 'Director of Directors of the East India Company and real Ruler of the East'. James Stephen, Master-in-Chancery, sometime M.P. for Tralee and East Grinstead, had a house across the Green. In the High Street from 1802 to 1810 lived the Mores' much-loved pupil and sometime successor at the Park Street school, Selina Mills, with her husband Zachary Macaulay, editor from 1804 to 1810 of the *Christian Observer*, the organ of the sect, and her son, young Tom Macaulay. Charles Grant's intimate friend, Lord Teignmouth, when he retired from the Governor-Generalship of India in 1802, conformed to the adage, 'Seek a neighbour before you seek a house,' and settled in old John Thornton's house nearby.

Hannah More was one of the earliest guests of the joint hosts at Battersea Rise. She told the sisters in one of her lively letters of the attentions the 'two masters' showered upon her, adding appreciatively 'There's politeness for you.'[60] After Thornton's marriage she was for years an annual guest at Battersea Rise, where she met his friends and neighbours and discussed with them their religious and philanthropic activities. And there she met the country allies of the Sect, John Babington, sometime M.P. for Leicestershire, and Thomas Gisborne, Perpetual Curate of Netherwood, among them, and Saints who were not Church Evangelicals: the aged Granville Sharp, resolute champion of the African slave, who lived on the Common, John Bowdler the younger, a strict High Churchman, Joseph Hughes, Baptist Minister at Battersea, formerly Classical Tutor at the Bristol Baptist Academy and a friend of Hannah More, and his fellow Baptist, the quaint Rebecca Wilkinson, schoolmistress in Clapham village, who spent her life in rescuing children from vicious environments. Her case-book, it has been suggested, subsequently provided Hannah More with material for her tracts.[61] It is likely, too, that she came into contact at Clapham with the philanthropic William Smith, the Unitarian M.P. for Northampton, and with Methodist philanthropists such as Joseph Butterworth, M.P. for Coventry, and his friend Thomas Thompson, M.P. for Wendover,[62] who were well known to members of the Sect; for the Sect, though they disapproved of Methodism and Dissent, willingly co-operated with all those who shared their benevolent interests. One and all regarded Hannah More with admiration and respect. Her sound common sense, her 'alacrity, and decision' impressed them;[63] her literary reputation and her important connections were of no small value to men whose work depended for success on public response.

Faith, works, environment, and intermarriage[64] held the Sect together long enough to allow them, individually or corporately, to act as the vanguard in the series of remarkable religious and humanitarian activities associated with Evangelicalism: the abolition of the West Indian Slave Trade; the establishment of the great voluntary societies, the Sunday School Society, the British and Foreign Bible Society, the Church Missionary Society, the African Institution, the Sierra Leone Trading Society, the Society for

Bettering the Condition and Improving the Comforts of the Poor; and a multitude of unorganized personal charities so unobtrusive that the right hand was ignorant of the behaviour of the left. The exceptional organizing powers of the group marked them out for administrative office. Untiring in their practical piety, they supplied in the nineteenth century chairmen, secretaries, and treasurers to the new associated efforts, which, it has been said not without reason, 'moved the world'.

From none of her Clapham friends did Hannah More receive a warmer welcome when she came up from Somerset than from Thornton at Battersea Rise. She had a special affection for the able, reserved, high-minded man whose character seen through the eyes of his friends was a study in integrity. To her he was not only the most attached and faithful friend, but the 'most wise and consistently virtuous of men'. 'It is not for doctrine I esteem him', she told Mrs Bouverie, 'but for living, while in the hurry of the world, in that heroic self-denial and close communion with God which makes him the most impressive example I ever saw.'[65] Life in his household introduced her to Evangelicalism as 'the religion of the home'.[66] Careful religious instruction of children and servants in the 'Gospel Plan' and family prayers at morning and night were the established order. The quiet, dignified ritual was not new to her, but family prayers she found difficult and embarrassing when she introduced them into her own home. At the request of his friends Thornton published a *Manual of Family Prayers*. Its use, said G. W. E. Russell a hundred years later, became 'the distinctive mark of the true Evangelical'.[67]

The delightful *Recollections* of Henry Thornton's daughter Marianne, the long series of letters written by the Thorntons, parents and children, to Hannah More and her letters to them, her visits to Battersea Rise and theirs to her at Cowslip Green and Barley Wood provide material for a much-needed corrective to the portrait of the austere and sanctimonious precisian of Roberts's creation. 'She was', wrote Miss Thornton in her old age, 'my father's nearest associate and most confidential friend before his marriage, and the nearest and dearest friend my mother had outside her own family.' The letters of the two women bear witness to their friendship. As for the children, they awaited her visits with undisguised impatience, for she had 'the rare gift of knowing how to live with both old and young'.[68] 'May is coming and Hannah More will soon be here was one of the earliest hopes of my childhood, and when she did arrive I always felt that I had a fresh companion just of my own age.' When severe weather prevented the delicate middle-aged lady and the Thornton children from attending Church, they sat on her bed as she told them Bible stories. 'At other times she would hear me my lessons, which would consist in telling me story tales, and, good woman as she was, she taught me to believe in Tom Thumb nearly as implicitly as in Joseph and his brethren.'[69]

(iv)

It has been said that although Hannah More associated herself with Evangelicals she did not completely identify herself with the Evangelical Party within the Church.[70] The accuracy of the statement would be easier to assess had Evangelicalism been distinguished by a more systematic theology and Evangelicals by less individuality. With the vital piety characteristic of Evangelicals Hannah More was in close and complete sympathy. Religion to her, as to them, was a matter of unceasing practice in living the Christian life to the glory of God and the good of mankind. But in doctrinal matters Church Evangelicals, who, as a whole, were Calvinistic in their beliefs, appeared to lack the uniformity characteristic of their piety. Basing their stand on the Anglican settlement, some of them read into its formularies an extreme form of Calvinism; others accepted 'a more balanced and reserved form of Calvinism', such as the Evangelicalism of John Newton and John Venn.[71] Unhappily the growing tendency, as the *Christian Observer* later lamented, was to give or to assume names as descriptive of religious opinion which imposed a rigidity of belief where it did not exist. 'No opinion was allowed to be Calvinistic but such as precisely agrees with the peculiar doctrines to be found in the writings of John Calvin.'[72] Well versed in Christian devotion and Christian evidence, Hannah More was unversed in Christian doctrine and detested Christian controversy, and her approximation to a party within the Church whose interpretation of the Articles of Belief was Calvinistic perturbed her. She cannot have been ignorant that no small part of Calvin's teaching 'belonged to our common Christianity', as wise Bishop Horsley reminded the clergy of his diocese in 1800, 'when it was the fashion to abuse Calvinism',[73] but she could not accept the 'peculiar doctrines', in particular those on Election and Reprobation, according to which God had destined some men to everlasting life and others to eternal damnation. She lived, as Newton reminded her, 'among fashionable people who uniformly decry Calvinism',[74] and it is not without significance that in her Bristol days she counted among her friends Charles Daubeny, later Vicar of Christchurch, Bath, and Archdeacon of Sarum, who, as his writings testify, held vehemently that Calvinism was incompatible with true Churchmanship. Hannah More wanted an assurance, her correspondence with Newton reveals, that her association with Evangelicals would not involve her in acceptance of Calvin's peculiar doctrines. She could not reconcile them with the Book which she read assiduously.

Viewed philosophically, the problem she faced was the insoluble problem of God's sovereignty versus man's free will; the choice in strict logic between limited and unlimited salvation. She found that her Evangelical friends were not strictly logical, nor did they seem to be troubled by their lack of logic. The majority of Evangelicals, it is said, had learned the lesson of the Calvinistic Controversy that to certain metaphysical questions there can be no logical answer.[75] Those who called themselves, or were called, High Calvinists presumably accepted all 'the five points of Calvinism';[76] others were referred to as 'moderate Calvinists', an elastic and nebulous term which, in the opinion of Daubeny and his school, was a contradiction in terms. To them Calvin's doctrines did not admit of a moderate interpretation.[77] Newton, to whom Hannah

More turned confidently for assistance, was of little help. He was no theologian. He spoke of himself as an 'avowed Calvinist', a term which might seem to embrace all the 'five points', yet in his letters to her he admitted that there were 'schemes of Calvinism of which he disapproved', and that 'the talk of some reputed Calvinists was no more musical in my ears than the mewing of a cat.'[78] He told her that she was herself a Calvinist though she was unaware of it. In spite of her respect for him he did not convince her. 'I hate Calvinism,' she asserted bluntly, and her detestation of its peculiar doctrines remained a constant factor in her life.[79]

Wilberforce, whose advice she sought, was the friend and admirer of John Wesley and, like him, was Arminian in his doctrinal affinities. Though convinced of the radical corruption of human nature, he too repudiated what he called, but did not define as, 'rigid Calvinistic principles', and declared in later years, 'every year I live I become more and more impressed by the unscriptural character of the Calvinist system.'[80] Dean Milner, whose 'high-toned morality and scrutinizing spirit of holiness' rejoiced Hannah More, was reputed to be a High Calvinist, yet, when she read the two stout volumes of his sermons, she could find no trace of the 'peculiar doctrines'. 'I defy any critic', she wrote with her customary vigour to Hart-Davis, 'to find one sentiment peculiar to Calvinism throughout the two volumes.'[81] Simeon, with his 'deep and honest loyalty to scripture',[82] sought doctrinal truth in the polarity of the extremes of Calvinism and Arminianism. Not so Hannah More: 'How I hate the little narrowing names of Arminian and Calvinist.'[83] Henry Thornton, her closest friend, revealed, to the surprise of his Evangelical friends, in his private papers read after his death that he was a Calvinist.[84] Gisborne, the publication of whose sermons were red-letter days in her life, was confessedly non-Calvinist,[85] and level-headed James Stephen confessed to Wilberforce in later years that he was more than half a Roman Catholic.[86]

It was not easy for a woman ignorant in matters of Christian doctrine and resolutely opposed to Christian controversy to find her bearings in so uncharted a sea. Only very gradually, when she found that, confusing as were their labels, Evangelicals did not as a body accept Calvin's grim and immoral logic, did she slowly identify herself with Evangelical doctrine which, while insisting on the total corruption of human nature, magnified God's love in Redemption. Accepting the sacrifice of the Cross as the punishment of the innocent for the guilty, it did not insist that it availed only for the Elect but for all who would accept it. It was therefore the bounden duty of Evangelicals, and it is this fact which justifies the name by which they were known, to constrain men by unceasing prayer and untiring zeal to accept the good tidings of salvation through Jesus Christ.

So slowly did her convictions move that it was not until 1799 that Hannah More ventured to publish her doctrinal views. They became immediately the object of vehement censure from High Calvinists on the one hand and High Churchmen on the other. It is possible to argue, as Hannah More's clerical biographer Henry Thompson argued, that had she been less ignorant of Christian doctrine and Christian controversy she might have averted the attack upon her doctrinal position which later overwhelmed her.[87]

Her attitude to the Anglican Church, as the visible Church of Christ, does not appear identical with that commonly ascribed to Evangelicals. In matters of Church polity Hannah More remained throughout her life an orthodox Churchwoman. She regarded the Establishment with a reverence not commonly expressed in her day. None of the indifference to the Church as a divine institution, often and unfairly ascribed to Evangelicals, characterized her attitude. 'Perhaps', she wrote in 1791, 'there has not been since the time of the Apostles a Church upon earth in which public worship was so solemn, so cheerful, so simple and so sublime: so full of fervour and yet at the same time so free from enthusiasm, so rich in the gold of antiquity, yet so astonishingly free from its dross.'[88] Nor was she indifferent, as some at least of the Evangelicals were, to the Church principle of Episcopacy. She had 'a genuine attachment to apostolical order',[89] an attachment matched by the range and warmth of her episcopal friendships. If on these points she did not identify herself with the Evangelicals, she fell short, Henry Thompson admits regretfully, on two counts required from orthodox members of the Anglican Church. In her writings she has little to say on the sacraments and ordinances of the church, an omission which did not escape criticism from High Churchmen of the nineteenth century, and on the sacrament of Baptism she held opinions which were 'the negation of sacramental efficiency'.[90] To her, the sacrament was a sign of grace already given, and not a means by which grace was acquired. This error Thompson ascribed to her ignorance of Anglican doctrine. She forgot that a sacrament consists of two parts, the outward visible sign and the inward spiritual grace, and that 'to deny the reality of the latter is in truth to deprive the sacrament of its essence.'[91]

Less excusable, Thompson insists, was her association with Dissent, not only in matters philanthropic, but in 'religious objects' such as attendance at Dissenting places of worship. The effects of the early years of the war, he quoted from the historian Osler, had been to combine all parties for defence against the common enemy, until every difference seemed to be forgotten. 'Thus Dissent became exalted by the direct sanction and almost equality conferred upon it: while Church principles, sunk to obtain the union, were at length scarcely remembered.'[92] Hannah More's attitude to Dissent goes some way to attest the truth of this sweeping statement. From her early Bristol days she had friends among the Dissenters; she was well read in Nonconformist devotional classics, and in the 'nineties she welcomed the approximation of Church and Dissent, and appeared to be conscious of no derogation of Church principles in attending, 'in common with a number of strict Church people',[93] the Dissenting Meeting-House of William Jay at Bath. Thus, says Thompson apologetically, she encouraged Dissent and weakened the great repository of religion—the Church.

Seen in retrospect, it is difficult to insist that Hannah More's principles and conduct in these years would have completely satisfied either a good orthodox or a good Evangelical Churchman. She emerges from the religious controversies of the late years of the eighteenth century as a woman of considerable independence of mind. She decided for herself the relation of 'christian godliness' to 'christian order'.

CHAPTER V

THE GREAT AND THE GAY

'Tell her to live in the world; there is the sphere of her usefulness;
they will not let us come nigh them.'

John Wesley: message to Hannah More

(i)

HANNAH MORE'S association with the Saints and their religious
and philanthropic activities did not involve her in an immediate
breach with the Great and Gay world. Not all her friends among
the quality were unsympathetic to the abolition of the Slave Trade
even when they deplored her slow approximation to a religion
termed by them indifferently 'Methodism' or 'enthusiasm'. But in
the 'nineties their affection and respect for her were severely tried.
The Saints had provided her with a basis of comparison between
their vital religion and ardent humanitarianism and the religious
indifference and lazy charity of the fashionable world. When the
anti-Slave Trade movement was thrust into the background by
the war a new interest captured her imagination. She was by upbringing a pedagogue, and in every pedagogue, it has been said,
there is a moralist.[1] Perhaps this is why the reformation of manners
remained to the end of her life her absorbing interest.[2] The idea of
moral reform, sponsored by Wilberforce, was in the air. The open
blatant immorality of the age was his chief concern when Hannah
More met him in 1787, and it is unlikely that they did not discuss it
when discussing the abolition of the Slave Trade. Convinced that
'God has set before me as my object the reformation of [my country's] manners,'[3] he, and friends of his way of thinking, secured
in 1787 the promise of a Royal Proclamation against vice and
immorality, defined as neglect of Sunday observance, excessive
drinking, blasphemy, profane swearing, immoral and disorderly

practices, the keeping of public gaming houses, and the sale of loose, licentious, indecent, and blasphemous publications. They established a powerful voluntary society which, acting 'as the ancient censor of the religion and morals of the country', would, they believed, secure the execution of the Proclamation.[4]

It is not possible to estimate with any degree of accuracy the importance of the new Society for the Reformation of Manners in correcting the morals of the age. Probably, like earlier and later efforts to restrain vice by vigilance, it had no immediate effect. 'Big flies escaped,' said Defoe in 1725.[5] 'The gambling houses of St James's remain untouched,' said Sydney Smith, referring to the Society for the Suppression of Vice in 1808.[6] But if it exerted little effective moral pressure on individuals powerful enough to ignore it, the Royal Proclamation which initiated reform, the body of high ecclesiastics and eminent laymen who supported it, and the interest the Society evoked are not without significance as a sign of growing public concern in questions of morals and religion which marked the later decades of the eighteenth century.

Hannah More's approach to the problem differed from that of the Society for the Reformation of Manners. She applied 'stricture', not law and punishment; she addressed the rich only; she attempted to deal with faults 'which were generally overlooked', because 'they were not censurable.' Early in 1786 she had asked the opinion of her friends Dean Horne, of Canterbury, and Bishop Porteus, of London, upon a didactic essay she had written on 'The Manners of the Great', and had secured their warm approval. 'You make me extremely happy', wrote Horne, 'by a sight of any production of yours calculated for the benefit of the great and the gay.'[7] 'It is a most delicious morsel,' wrote Porteus. 'It will be an excellent precursor to our Society, and will do half its business beforehand.'[8]

Two years later there appeared a slim volume entitled *Thoughts on the Importance of the Manners of the Great to General Society*, which became overnight a best seller. Seven large editions were sold in a few months, the second in little more than a week, the third in four hours after publication, and a fifth edition, said Cadell, the publisher, who had regrettably miscalculated the response of the public, 'must be put to press immediately'.[9] The essay was addressed 'not to persons of eminent virtue, nor to men of flagitious wickedness', but to the bulk of the higher orders whom Miss More described as well disposed to religion and morality, 'many of them persons of the tenderest humanity'. Though published anonymously, it was quickly and correctly ascribed to Hannah More.

There is little in this essay, accurately described by the author as 'a collection of loose and immethodical hints', which explains its remarkable circulation or the importance attached to it by contemporaries. It makes no contribution to moral or religious principles. It is not informed by religious or moral passion. It has no grace of structure or of style. It is a valiant but naïve challenge to the higher orders to amend their ways and set an example to their inferiors. Reform, Miss More urged, 'must begin with the great or it will never be effectual'.

It is characteristic of Hannah More's work as a moral reformer that the sins for which she reserved her sharpest condemnation were not those of the flesh but of the spirit. Not seldom did she show unexpected sympathy with the loose morals and conduct of the lower orders, but, as in this essay, the sins of omission—sins peculiar to the upper and middle classes—never failed to arouse her indignation. Her friends among the quality were decorous men and women in whose houses the grosser sins were not conspicuous,[10] but with the sins of 'inconsideration' and 'carelessness' she found that 'even good kind people contrive to live on excellent terms'. Servants, she noted, were the chief victims of these sins of the spirit. That they had souls to be saved was ignored in the great houses she visited. Elaborate Sunday hair-dressing kept the *coiffeurs* at work on the sabbath and prevented their attendance at church; the lie 'Not at home' which masters for their own convenience imposed upon their servants trained them to utter falsehoods; Sunday entertainments, even Sunday concerts of sacred music, which might, she admitted, be neither good nor bad in themselves, were attended with every possible moral danger to minds less enlightened. 'Will not the common people,' she asked pertinently, 'when they are already abridged of the diversions of the public house and the gaming-yard on Sunday evenings, think it a little inequitable when they shall know that many houses of the first nobility are on that evening crowded by company?' Sunday observance by the Great and the Gay held first place in her plan for the reformation of religion and manners.

> Sundaies the pillars are
> On which heaven's palace archèd lies

sang George Herbert. Sunday observance to Hannah More was 'the Palladium of Christianity'. 'As this day is neglected or observed, Christianity will stand or fall.'

Equally reprehensible was careless conversation in the presence of the younger generation. Serious conversation she had found conspicuously absent in the houses of even good people. 'Polite conversation', in her opinion the most alarming symptom of the degeneracy of present-day morals, had almost swept away the distinction between right and wrong. 'The most grave offences are often named with cool indifference, the most shameful profligacy with toleration.' It was responsible for diminishing the horror of vice in the younger generation. 'Believe and forgive me,' she wrote to their elders, 'you are the people who lower religion in the eyes of its enemies. The openly profane, the avowed enemies of God and goodness, serve but to confirm the truth they meant to oppose, but you, like the inadequate and faithless prop, overthrow the edifice you pretend to support.' The 'cold prudential caution', which impeded the well-disposed young in the progress of religion, was no less deplorable. 'Be not righteous over-much' was the excuse offered for their indifference, but she could find 'no very imminent danger that enthusiasm would lead the Great to dangerous and inconvenient excesses'. In all earthly things zeal was extolled as exhibiting marks of a sprightly temper and vigorous mind. 'Strange, that to be fervent in spirit should only be dishonourable.'

No one remembering the date when this essay was written can deny that it was a courageous little book. Few persons of her time, lay or clerical, would have had the temerity to write it. Rank had its privileges. It enjoyed a general immunity from criticism and used its weapon of social exclusiveness to punish those who transgressed. Miss More was aware of this. She knew too that her public criticism of the Great who had opened their doors to her was not consonant with accepted standards of good taste. 'When the author is discovered', she wrote to her sisters, admitting that the book with its 'resounding title' frightened her, 'I shall expect to find almost every door shut against me.'[11]

The reverse was the case. Except for rumour of malevolence exerted in some quarters, the book appeared to make no difference to the friendship of her aristocratic friends. 'I am astonished', she wrote with relief to the sisters, 'by the unexpected and undeserved popularity of the *Manners*; it is in the houses of all the Great.'[12] Her ecclesiastical friends, the Bishops of London, Salisbury, Lincoln, and Llandaff, were warm in their eulogies. 'For where', said Porteus, anticipating John Wesley's words, 'can we find anyone but yourself that can make the fashionable world read books of morality and religion?'[13]

The reception of this slight essay, so contrary to Hannah More's anticipations and to Cadell's estimate, is a fact of some significance which it is easy to miss in the social history of the period. Some part of its success may be attributed to Miss More's fame as a writer, which was well established by 1788; some to her inside knowledge of the stately homes of England, which titillated the palate of the middling classes who had not the entrée and entertained those who had. But it is clear from the sale of the book and of her subsequent essays that Hannah More had tapped a new reading public among the Great and the Gay. 'There is a circle by which what you write will be read . . . and which will hardly read anything of a religious kind that is not written by you,'[14] wrote Newton, and Hannah More's ever-enlarging acquaintance in the gay and meretricious 'eighties with serious ladies of quality who read her works and sought her friendship establishes the truth of his statement. When Johnson died in 1785, and the royal and mazarine blues slowly faded, moral and philanthropic and even religious interests gradually replaced the literary enthusiasms of the earlier decades. Hannah More's London friends in the 'seventies had quickly recognized in her not only a wit and a 'literary genius', but a young woman who took life *au sérieux*. It had amused them. But when the alarming rumours of social unrest in France crossed the Channel, and the more responsible among them held the conviction that the English aristocracy would do well to set its own house in order, they gravitated almost automatically to Miss More, with whom they discussed and deplored the morals of the day. Among them the Countess Spencer, remarkable in any age for her liberal views, strong sense of *noblesse oblige*, and philanthropic activities, was conspicuous. In Lady Charlotte Wentworth, Lord Rockingham's sister, Miss More discovered 'the best divine for a woman of quality I have ever met'. Lady Mount-Edgecombe, Lady Tryphena Bathurst, Lady Charlotte Finch, Lady Juliana Penn, and the pious and gentle Lady Cremorne visited her, corresponded with her, and invited her to their London and country houses. Other ladies of quality, whose names are discreetly omitted or disguised, called upon her to ask for religious direction. Some of them she found 'utterly unacquainted with the Bible'. She enjoined them to read it. To others she recommended her unfailing panacea for religious ignorance, Doddridge's *Rise and Progress of Religion in the Soul*.

Miss — [she wrote to her sisters] has been also with me several times—beautiful and accomplished; surrounded with flatterers, and sunk in dissipation. I asked her why she continued to live so much below, not only her principles, but her understanding—what pleasure she derived from crowds of persons so inferior to herself—did it make her happy? Happy! she said, no; she was miserable. She despised the society she lived in, and had no enjoyment of the pleasures in which her life was consumed; but what could she do? She could not be singular—she must do as her acquaintance did.[15]

Hannah More supplied the needs of some at least of her upper-class clientèle. In religion and morals this reading public was but a sucking child. It required simple pabulum. Hannah More's essay was simple stuff. Her public read what she wrote and waited for

more, and, if contemporaries may be believed, it adopted some at
least of her hints for practical reform. Queen Charlotte, an omni-
vorous reader of Hannah More's writings, set the example by dis-
missing her Sunday hairdresser. Only Horace Walpole among her
friends, she told the sisters, took her to task 'for having exhibited
such monstrously severe doctrines'.

... it was a most ridiculous conversation. He defended (and that was the joke)
religion against me, and said he would do so against the whole bench of
Bishops; and that the Fourth Commandment was the most amiable, and
merciful law that ever was promulgated, as it entirely considers the ease and
comfort of the hard-labouring poor, and beasts of burden; but that it never was
intended for persons of fashion, who have no occasion to rest, as they never do
anything on the other days; and indeed at the time the law was made there
were no people of fashion. He really pretended to be in earnest, and we parted
mutually unconverted; he lamenting that I am fallen into the heresy of *puri-
tanical strictness*, and I lamenting that he is a person of fashion, for whom the
Ten Commandments were not made.[16]

It is perhaps not surprising that Hannah's letters to her sisters reveal some pride in the eager friendship of these aristocratic neo-
phytes of serious things. She had the eighteenth century's robust
and unashamed respect for rank and position. The adulation paid
to her as moral and spiritual guide to ladies of quality threatened to
smirch a modest and unassuming Blue Stocking, always conscious
of her literary short-comings, with a touch of self-complacency:

Lady Spencer came herself to prevail on me to go to St Albans, but I could not
resolve on prolonging my stay from home...
Lady Mount-Edgcombe repeated her invitation for the Mount Edgcombe visit
next summer with the most urgent politeness. I gave her to understand that I
was afraid it must be left for another year...
I was engaged the last four days to Lady Bathurst, Lady Amherst, with whom
I am very friendly, Lady Cremorne, Lady Mount-Edgcombe. I hope my engagements are now drawing to a close...[17]

(ii)

Two years later, when alarm caused by the French Revolution
was running high, Hannah More developed her thesis on *The
Manners of the Great* in her *Estimate of the Religion of the Fashionable*

109

World.[18] This time she made no apology to her readers for a frontal attack on their 'practical irreligion'. The French Revolution had made religion fashionable in England. It offered a prophylactic, should the poison of 'French wickedness' spread, but it was a religion 'in which there was so little left of Christ that, like the women at the Sepulchre, one might say "They have taken away my Lord and I know not where they have laid him."' Religion, she held, was no longer in peril, as it had been in former times, from the attack of infidelity. The contempt of wits and philosophers was out of fashion. 'The cobwebs are as seldom brushed from Hobbes as from Hooker.' Today Christianity was in danger from those who accepted the Bible as their guide, but made no effort to understand its principles. Some among them, under the mask of enlightened philosophy, followed Voltaire in their toleration of sin. To them all errors were innocent and undeserving of punishment. Hell, and the existence of an evil spirit, they considered as merely abstract ideas, alluded to periphrastically, or ignored, not because they were terrible, but because they were 'too vulgar for the polished, too illiberal for the learned, and as savouring too much of credulity for the enlightened'. The distinguishing peculiarities of Christianity were evaded and a deadly blow was struck at religion. Others among the polite and fashionable, influenced by the benevolence of an age superior to that of any other age in its munificent liberality, and ignorant of the principles of Christianity, identified religion with benevolence. They substituted charity, 'the most lovely offspring of religion', for religion itself, and confined 'the wide and comprehensive idea of Christianity into the slender compass of a little pecuniary relief'. 'Religion', she made bold to assert, was 'not an act or a performance or a sentiment'. It was 'a turning the whole mind to God; a concentration of all the powers and affections of the soul into one steady point, an uniform desire to please him'. Benevolence might be evidence of Christianity. It was not a substitute for it. Works without faith could not achieve salvation.

No less trenchant was her denunciation of those of the Fashionable World who 'with prudence and discretion' steered a middle course and identified religion with morality. Miss More would have none of this. Christianity was more than a system of ethics. It must be embraced as a whole if it be received at all. 'There can be no separation of morality and piety.' Her most forceful invective was reserved for the growing number of the Great and the Gay who professed Christianity as a matter of faith and ignored it as a rule of conduct. Men and women who attended consecrated places, performed hallowed ceremonies, proclaimed themselves to be miserable sinners and professed a religion in which humility and unworldliness were distinctions, yet whose conduct was worldly, dissipated, and entirely lacking in seriousness, were reminded that 'Be not conformed to this world' was a leading principle of the Book they acknowledged as their guide. Yet 'the whole law of God does not exhibit a single precept which is more expressly and steadily and more uniformly rejected by the Fashionable World.'

She followed her remonstrance with an analysis of the impiety of the Great and the Gay. She attributed it to the notorious neglect of religious instruction in home and school. Family religion, she held with her contemporary Richard Cecil, was of unspeakable importance.[19] In the 'last age' parents had not accepted the fashionable maxim that religious instruction should be deferred till a child was capable of choosing for himself. Public schools were then places no less of Christian than of classical education. The omission of religious worship, public or private, was then a censurable fault. But today the Fashionable World, professing a religion which required from them a solemn vow that their children should be brought up in the nurture and admonition of the Lord, deliberately obstructed their progress. Family and public worship was neglected, boys of school age frequented race-meetings and gaming-tables, and almost infant daughters were carried off to an interminable round of Baby Balls, 'an innovation which Fashion herself forbade till now'.

Comparison of the two essays on the reform of the Great and Gay reveals Miss More's growing 'enthusiasm'. The second is more dogmatic, more vital, than its forebear. Hannah More became aware of this. She could, she stated drily, have made her protest 'more immediately evangelical', but had refrained, 'lest the condescending patience of her readers should come to an abrupt end when they detected the palpable enthusiast'.

The Religion of the Fashionable World was, like *The Manners of the Great*, published anonymously. It was rapidly sold out; within five years it had reached a fifth edition. Letters of appreciation, as before, poured in from her friends and admirers, who were not disconcerted by the anonymity of the author. Giants, Mrs Boscawen told her, could not be concealed. 'Aut Morus aut Angelus,' wrote the Bishop of London, before he had read six pages; 'there are but a few persons in Great Britain that could write such a book.'[20] To Newton it was 'a light shining in a dark place',[21] and gloomy Dr Watson of Llandaff conceded that it would do much good 'if any writing *can* do much good in a country debauched by its riches and prosperity'.[22] The fashionable and polite world read the book and reacted in different ways. Some admired the author's courage and deplored her enthusiasm. 'Good Hannah More', wrote Horace Walpole to Mary Berry, 'is labouring to amend our religion, and has just published a book called *An Estimate of the Religion of the Fashionable World*. It is prettily written, but her enthusiasm increases, and when she next comes to town I shall tell her that, if she preaches to people of fashion, she will be a Bishop *in partibus infidelium*.'[23]

Not all criticism was so good-natured. The tract was less easy to forgive or to ignore than its predecessor, and not a few of Miss More's contemporaries were unwilling to forgive it. One outraged lady of fashion staged a protest. At her Baby Ball she provided a guy dressed as Hannah More, rod in hand, and incited the children to show their resentment of one who interfered with their enjoyment.[24]

> Rouse the echoes of the hall
> With your sportive Baby Ball,
> Foot it nimbly on the floor
> Nor heed the carping Hannah More.[25]

And, according to Mrs Thrale, the boys at Westminster School burnt Miss More's effigy in the school-yard as an expression of their displeasure.[26] None the less the book, states a contemporary, became the fashion.

It paved the way for Hannah More's long and curious friendship with H.R.H. Maria, Duchess of Gloucester, the illegitimate daughter of Horace Walpole's elder brother, Sir Edward Walpole. Married first to the Earl Waldegrave, by whom she had three lovely daughters, the ladies Waldegrave and Euston and Lady Hugh Seymour, she took as her second husband William, Duke of Gloucester, brother of George III, a marriage unacceptable to the King. A highly decorous lady when Hannah More knew her, her interest in religion and morality and her friendship with Miss More were, it was said, encouraged by the Ministry and the sober members of the governing classes, to offset the scandalous behaviour of the Heir Apparent, who had brought Royalty into disrepute. In 1795 Hannah More paid her first visit to Gloucester House.

Lady Waldegrave [she told her sisters] presented me to the Duchess. We had two hours of solid, rational, religious conversation. It would be too little to say that the Duchess's behaviour is gracious in the extreme. She behaved to me with the affectionate familiarity of an equal, and though I took the opportunity of saying stronger things of a religious kind than perhaps she had ever heard, she bore it better than any great person I have ever conversed with and seemed not offended at the strictness of the gospel. I was resolved to preserve the simplicity of my own character and conversed with the greatest ease. . . The duchess presented me to the Princess Sophia and Prince William. The manners of these two young personages were very agreeable. They found many kind things to say to me and conversed with the greatest sweetness and familiarity.[27]

After this it was plain sailing. Evening readings at Gloucester House on the Epistle to the Ephesians and discussion on Mr Wilberforce's chapter on human corruption and other 'grand points' followed in regular succession.

The Duchess sang Miss More's praises; she read her works for the great and the humble, was her sturdy champion in the Blagdon Controversy, and pledged her children, Prince William and

Princess Sophia, to keep in touch with Miss More after their mother's death, a promise faithfully fulfilled by the young people.[28]

But the Duchess, like the other great ladies, accepted only what she pleased of her preceptor's instructions in living the Christian life. She refused to agree to Sunday observance, 'never having been brought up to regard the Sabbath as a day of humiliation and woe'.[29]

Ladies of quality, it would seem, though interested in religion and morals, were not prepared to change the even tenor of their way. What is most contrary to salvation, it has been said, is not sin but habit. Miss More would have agreed that *l'habitude* was an all-powerful handicap.[30] 'These people', she wrote despondently, 'come to me, but I cannot help them; they never see the slightest glimpses of the meaning of plucking out right eyes and cutting off right hands.' When duchesses came to her, and according to Zachary Macaulay's caustic remark they awaited her whenever she went to town, 'I can do no good.' It became clear to her that with few exceptions the quality 'read her but did not mind her'. 'I think I have done with the aristocracy. I am no longer a debtor to the Greeks but I am so to my poor barbarians.'[31] But even after tracts and schools for the lower orders almost wholly occupied her mind, she made a last appeal to the Great and the Gay to amend their lives.

(iii)

The third and most important of Hannah More's didactic works for the reform of the rich was her *Strictures on the Modern System of Female Education with a View to the Principles and Conduct of Women of Rank and Fortune*.[32] It was not published until 1799, after she had finished writing her tracts for the poor and while she was embroiled in difficulties with her schools in the Mendips. Like all Miss More's didactic writings, it is verbose and repetitive. Its thesis, that while men must be educated women should be trained, is too much out of tune with modern opinion to secure for it today a respectful hearing. It is, nevertheless, a vigorous and sensible condemnation of the education of girls of the upper classes at the end of the eighteenth century. Moreover, it is not impossible to find in it, as Mary Berry discovered to her amusement, an unexpected agreement between the views of Hannah More and her contemporary, Mary Wollstonecraft, 'on all the great points of the education of women'. 'Hannah More', wrote Miss Berry to her friend Mrs Cholmeley, 'will I daresay be very angry when she hears this, though I would lay a wager that she has never read the book.'[33] Miss Berry would, presumably, have won her wager. Hannah More detested Mary Wollstonecraft's views. As she had declared that she was invincibly resolved never to read *The Rights of Women*,[34] it is unlikely that she had looked inside *On the Education of Daughters*.

The main theme of the *Strictures*, as of her earlier essays, is the desperate need of a religious basis of society, which must be founded by the Great. She turned aside unwillingly from her work with the poor to make her last appeal to the rich.

Writing in 1799, when England was confronted by 'the most tremendous confederations against religion, order and government ever known', she found a marked increase of frivolity and irreligion among upper-class women, now accustomed to the alarms and excursions of the war. She appealed to them not, in Mary Wollstonecraft's harsh and prophetic tones, to vindicate their rights, but, in words unimpressive but none the less sincere, to fulfil their duties. Within the limits imposed by propriety, 'the first, second, and third requisite for women', she called on them 'as patriots at once firm and feminine' to raise the depressed tone of public morals and 'awaken the drowsy spirit of religious principles'. Once again, but with greater Evangelical fervour, she drove home the point that Christianity is a temper of mind and soul with which every wrong principle is incompatible. By religion alone could women, whose destiny it is to be daughters, wives, and mothers, influence society for good. The education of girls of rank fails lamentably in this object. It provides neither knowledge nor discipline. It aims merely at providing accomplishments for the transitory period of youth and lays up no resources for the future in this world or the next. Dancing, music, the fine arts, novel reading, and novel writing ('for every raw girl is tempted as she reads to fancy she can write'), a smattering of English literature, French philosophy, fantastic German imagery, or Italian love-songs form the curriculum. During recent years this 'frenzy of accomplishments' had taken an unexpected and dangerous turn. Hitherto restricted within the limits of rank and fortune, the contagion had spread to the middle classes, 'to the daughters of slenderly endowed curates, little tradesmen, and more opulent, but not more judicious, farmers'. A rapid revolution in the manners of the middle class, she asserted, had rendered obsolete the common saying that most worth and virtue are to be found in the middle station. This was an additional reason for reform from above.

The regeneration of society on a Christian basis could be achieved by the moral excellence of educated women. This is the gist of the book. Miss More made the surprising statement that only in religion were women the equal, and indeed the superior, of men. Paradoxically, she attributed this superiority to their faulty education, asserting, as her friend Soame Jenyns had done before her, that as girls were not taught the Greek and Latin Classics their education was free from pagan influences. The education of women could therefore the better establish Christian influence. To this end religious instruction from early years 'in a manner which would make religion a lively pleasure rather than a dry duty' was the first essential. Miss More had some good things to say on methods of instruction, closely associated with her own successful methods as a teacher. The dull learning by rote—the accepted method of her day—should be replaced, she urged, by 'animated conversation and lively discussion' between teacher and pupil, making the sensibilities of the pupil the first consideration. Teach them, as Christ taught his disciples, by 'interesting parables': seize upon 'surrounding objects, passing events, local circumstances' which will connect the pupil with the subject. 'Call,' she adds on a note of exaltation, 'on all creation to your aid and accustom the young to find:

> Tongues in trees, books in the running brooks,
> Sermons in stones and good in everything.'

By such methods children could be taught the Gospel of Jesus Christ in a lively and familiar manner which would make religion amiable, 'and her ways appear, what they really are, the ways of pleasantness'.

More difficult but even more imperative was it to make young people understand that the duties of Christianity grow out of its doctrines. Denial of 'the leading doctrines of Christianity', those of human corruption and the Atonement, was the source of false notions and wrong conduct.

Is it not a fundamental error to consider children as innocent beings, whose little weaknesses may, perhaps, want some correction, rather than as beings who bring into the world a corrupt nature, and evil disposition, which it should be the great end of education to rectify? This appears to be such a foundation truth that if I were asked what quality is most important in an instructor of youth I should not hesitate to reply such a strong impression of the corruption of our nature, as should ensure a disposition to counteract it.

Chapter XX of the *Strictures*, in which she set forth the 'peculiar doctrines of Christianity', aroused vehement opposition. In it, following closely Wilberforce's *Practical View*, she developed at length the doctrine of human corruption as the foundation of the Christian religion, but she refused to admit that it degraded and debased human nature or, as young persons disposed to turn away from the belief held, that 'it was a morose, unamiable and gloomy idea, for attached to it was the complementary doctrine of the Atonement which, if kindness and mercy have a tendency to warm and win the heart, provides every incentive to joy and cheerfulness. By it we know that Christ came into the world to save sinners, that he has died for all and that none are excluded from the Kingdom of God.' The chapter ends with 'the sublime doctrine of divine assistance' and the gradual transformation of man into the image of God under the influence of the Holy Spirit. This, she held, was a doctrine the more to be praised because of man's helplessness against the powers of the evil spirit, 'an article of our faith, by the way, which is growing into general disrepute among the politer classes of society as an ingenious allegory not as a literal truth',

The Great and the Gay

There is nothing in this expression of belief which is at variance with that of orthodox Anglicans in Hannah More's own day or since. Where she differed from the 'High Calvinists' on the one hand and with the 'indolent Christians' of her acquaintance on the other was in her contention that the doctrine of free grace was responsible for a material injury to the gospel of holiness. 'There is', she said, acutely, 'a worldly and fashionable as well as a low and sectarian antinomianism; an unwarrantable assurance that because Christ had died to save mankind there was nothing left for man to do.' This 'cheap and indolent Christianity' was nowhere taught in the Bible. On the contrary, 'grace must be used, or it will be withdrawn.' The Christian, she insisted, must fulfil the law of Christ, and the law of Christ demanded a complete change of heart and life in conformity with Christian holiness. 'Without this repentance there is no salvation, for though Christ has died for us and consequently to him alone we must look as a Saviour, yet he has himself declared that he will save none but true penitents.'

The greater part of the book deals trenchantly with the secular subjects of the curriculum, if secular they may be called, since *all* instruction was avowedly religious. Secular subjects had their use only in qualifying women for religious study. History was a subject of peculiar merit. To Miss More, as to Rollin, to whom she frequently refers, it was religion teaching by examples. No subject so clearly showed the controlling hand of Providence; none gave so true an insight into the corruption of human nature, 'for history is little else than the story of the crimes of the human race.' This invaluable subject was, however, taught to young women almost exclusively by the superficial method of question and answer, events were detached, and chronology, which passes for history, was simply a list of disconnected dates. Taught in such a manner, history was deprived of its moral purpose.

Literature, almost equally important, if carefully selected, was taught in a manner even less satisfactory. Girls of the fashionable world were not brought up on *books*. This is the gravamen of her charge. To make learning easier for pupil and teacher, swarms of

118

abridgments, compendiums and collections of extracts were in use. 'A few lines from the poets huddled together by some extract-maker to be learnt by heart is the prevailing method in the study of literature.' To the general inability of women to read books of solid worth Miss More ascribed their increasing dissipation and the decay of family life. Unable to find interest and occupation at home they frequented, night after night, 'the barbarous and gregarious assemblies', of upwards of 500 people, which in the 'nineties had replaced the 'animated and instructive conversation parties' of the 'eighties. To regenerate home life women must learn to read 'dry tough books'. Their minds needed ballast and concentration. She suggested as suitable works for the effete daughters of the aristo-cracy Locke's *Essay on the Human Understanding*, Butler's *Analogy of Religion*, and Watt's *Logic*, a reading list which provides a lively comment on the unfortunate habit of Blue Stockings of all ages to assess the intellectual taste and abilities of unformed minds by their own. The wind was not tempered to the shorn lamb.

The *Strictures* was received with extravagant approval by Miss More's friends and admirers and by the reading public. Five editions were published, the first three in 1799, and a total of over 19,000 copies was sold. The *British Critic* and the *Anti-Jacobin* reviews were warm in their praise;[35] Richard Cecil considered it 'one of the most perfect works in all its parts that any century or any country has produced';[36] Bishop Jebb of Limerick recommended the *Strictures* to Alexander Knox: 'Pray read the 18th and 19th Chapter of the *Strictures on Female Education* in which I think you will find more just reason and more good sense than is contained in many a volume of modern morality.'[37] 'You seem to me', wrote Knox to Hannah More after complying with Jebb's request, 'to have said what the world greatly needed but as far as I know had not been said before.'[38] The book placed her, in Pepys's opinion, among the foremost of English writers. Royalty in the persons of the Princess Royal, Princess Elizabeth, and Princess Mary, who read the book twice and decided to buy a copy for herself, added their eulogies in messages to Miss More, and the Bishop of London paid her the unusual compliment of recommending the *Strictures* in his Charge to the Clergy of his diocese, as

a work which presents to the reader such a fund of good sense, of wholesome counsel and sagacious observation, a knowledge of the world and of the female heart, and of high-tone morality and genuine Christian piety, and all this enlivened by such brilliancy of wit, such richness of imagery, such varied felicity of allusion, such neatness and elegance of diction, as are not, I conceive, easily to be found combined and blended together in any other work in the English language.[39]

Royal approval and episcopal eulogy did not prevent a storm of criticism and abuse. Hannah More's old friend, the Rev. Charles Daubeny, Vicar of Christ Church, Bath, tackled her in an open letter on a doctrinal point. He impugned as unscriptural her statement that the duties of Christians grow out of Christian doctrine 'as the natural and *necessary* production of such a living root', since the word 'necessary' led to the conclusion that, when once the doctrines of Christianity are assented to, everything necessary to salvation so inevitably follows as to render moral exertion superfluous, a conclusion he felt sure Miss More had not by her imprecise language[40] intended to suggest. Anyone reading the *Strictures* could discover without effort that she had not. But when a man of Daubeny's reputation unwillingly criticized a carelessly worded statement as expressing a doctrine both unscriptural and unrecognized by the Church of England, other critics, their wish being father to the thought, smelt the 'peculiar doctrines' of Calvinism.

The chapters on human corruption and Baby Balls gave great offence to the Great and the Gay. Friendships with the author snapped abruptly. Widespread and unpalatable publicity was attracted to the book by the ribald lampoon of 'Peter Pindar', who in *Nil Admirari*, a poem of 8 cantos, ridiculed the Bishop of London's extravagant praise of Hannah More's 'rushlight genius', and pilloried her for swallowing 'the praise her Stentor brays'.[41] He had attacked them both, wrote Porteus in distress to Hannah, not with neat ridicule and attic wit, but with 'gross and coarse ribaldry ... my

crime is too much complaisance: your's is too great asperity.'[42]
Other critics, among them the 'lazy clergy', detested the 'parade'
she made of the doctrine of natural corruption, and were shocked
by her application of it to 'innocent children'. 'No doctrine like this
was e're taught by our Lord.'[43] Mary Berry, comparing the *Strictures* with Maria Edgeworth's *Letters for Literary Ladies*, warmly ap-
praised the 'many excellent details' of Miss More's book, its 'much
good sense and infinity of wit', and roundly declared her opinion
that 'Hannah More's style is quite remarkable.' But she could not
accept the 'radically false' religious principles which, she held,
sapped 'the very foundation of morality—nay the very throne of
God'.[44] Anna Seward, 'the Swan of Lichfield', who in 1791 had
'liked infinitely, the charming writings of the celebrated Hannah
More', was more explicit than Mary Berry in her condemnation of
the *Strictures*. 'The absurd doctrine of original sin', she asserted, 'is
a dreadful and blasphemous supposition, formed only on a few dark
texts of St Paul, and nowhere authorized by Christ; on the contrary he repeatedly speaks of the primeval innocence of children,
and says "of such were the kingdom of heaven." '[45] To the principles
laid down in Chapter XX Hannah More referred her friends as her
deliberate confession of faith when, later, her religious opinions
were called in question.

Comparison of the three essays for the reform of the Great and
the Gay discovers her resolute courage and reveals the slow but un-
equivocal change in her religious determination. The Puritan of
Horace Walpole's ridicule in 1788 had become the Evangelical of
the early nineteenth century.

PART III

SOMERSET

'*The Old Bishop in Petticoats.*' William Cobbett

CHAPTER VI

THE TRACTS

'Antidotes to Tom Paine!'
Mrs Piozzi

(i)

HANNAH MORE'S connection with Somerset began with the building of a cottage at Cowslip Green early in the summer of 1784. Beginning to discover 'pleasure a laborious trade', 'tired of visiting', 'quite tired of assemblies', and perplexed and troubled by her indecision of mind and spirit, she looked around for a room of her own where she might find leisure and peace. After a ramble in Somerset, most lovely of English counties, she found an ideal spot in Wrington Vale. Not too far from London and conveniently near Bristol and her sisters, it would give her, she opined, 'the quiet and leisure I sigh for'. Here, after submitting plans and drawings to all her friends in turn, she built a cottage which acquired the name of Cowslip Green, 'first cousin at least', said Horace Walpole, who liked the drawing mightily, 'to Strawberry Hill'.[1] Here, when she was not in London for the season, or at Bristol helping the sisters, or could 'get off' visiting her aristocratic friends in the stately homes of England, she spent the summer months with one or more of her sisters, usually Patty, in 'the most perfect little hermitage that can be conceived', and here she developed, in common with middle-aged ladies at all times, a passion for gardening. 'I am growing a prodigious gardener,' she wrote to Mrs Boscawen, 'and make up by my industry for my want of science. I work at it for two or three hours every day, and by the time the hour of visiting arrives I am vastly glad of a pretence for sitting down.'[2] 'The world', she wrote half-humorously to Newton, 'is not half so formidable a rival to heaven in my heart as my garden.'[3] At Cowslip Green she planned

and in part wrote her early didactic essays, began to interest herself
in the religious instruction of the poor, and endeavoured to convert
'silence and solitude into seasons of prayer'.

The early 'nineties was a troubled period in Hannah More's
life. The Great and the Gay world appeared unaffected by her strictures; efforts to abolish the Slave Trade hung fire, and the setting up
of schools in the Mendips was depressing and exhausting work. The
diary for 1794 reveals that her attempts to live the Christian way of
life brought her no happiness, no assurance of God's love. She was
convinced of the supreme importance of vital religion and endeavoured to adapt herself to its demands, but her efforts to concentrate her mind on God and holy things were unavailing. 'My
mind rambles through a thousand vain and worldly thoughts but
seldom sticks close to God.' Only in works could this essentially
practical woman who confessed that she would 'rather work for
God than meditate upon him' find comfort, and good works, she
knew, did not carry with them the assurance she desired.[4]

Her efforts were complicated by the decision of the sisters, when
they retired in 1790 from the school at Bristol, to build for themselves a house in Great Pulteney Street, Bath. Few places in England
would appear to have been less well suited to pious, middle-aged,
unfashionable ladies, lacking in the social graces which their sister
had acquired, than 'voluptuous Bath', and it is clear, reading between the lines of Hannah More's correspondence, that the choice
of Bath as the future home of the five sisters occasioned a rare difference of opinion among them. For Hannah detested 'this foolish
frivolous place'. To her Bath was London, from which she was endeavouring to escape, in miniature. Wealth, ostentation, frivolity,
obtruded themselves in the contracted space of the lovely little city
as they could not in the metropolis. And the war, far from modifying the conduct of the city's habitués, provoked them to even
wilder extravagance. 'Gay, happy, inconsiderate Bath', wrote
Hannah to Mrs Boscawen in the fourth year of the Great War,
'bears no sign of the distress of the times . . . we go about all
the morning lamenting the impending calamities, deploring the

assessed taxes and pleading poverty and at night every place of diversion is over-flowing.'⁵ To get away from Bath and back to her cottage and her schools in the Mendips was her ardent desire, one impossible to fulfil in the winter months. For the 'thin-walled' summer cottage was too damp and wind-swept, 'when the waters were out', for a woman who suffered from a chronic form of asthma and bronchitis. Bath became for the next twelve years her permanent winter home. It is conceivable, had Hannah More been the woman of worldly ambition that William Shaw and Thomas de Quincey denounced her to be, that her distaste for Bath was associated with the embarrassments arising from a home shared with four unfashionable, unpolished, and somewhat eccentric sisters; for the difference between Hannah and her sisters in manners and appearance was great enough to cause contemporary comment. But there is no sign of this in her correspondence and no suggestion in the writings of her critics that the sisters were the social embarrassment to her that they may well have been.⁶

Her growing fame did not make things easier for her. Visitors to Pulteney Street were unceasing and her hiding place at Cowslip Green was no deterrent to resolute callers. 'So much company', laments the diary, 'unspiritualizes my mind and swallows up my time. Book goes on slowly.'⁷ Yet she was not prepared to deny herself to her Clapham friends, Wilberforce and Thornton, when they came to Bath to drink the waters, or to new friends they desired should meet her there. Samuel Hoare, a strong Abolitionist and the close associate of a notable group of men bent on mitigating the brutalities of the penal laws and of prison discipline, became an intimate friend and held her in high respect. Nor was she prepared to refuse a welcome to H.R.H. the Duchess of Gloucester and other of her aristocratic friends of the fashionable world who had retained their affection for her, when they in their turn visited Bath.⁸ To her local literary fame she was in no degree indifferent, in spite of her repeated complaints of the demands on her leisure and quietude. Bristol, so proud of its literary reputation, regarded Hannah More as the ornament and pride of the countryside. She herself had found a poet in a milk-woman, and the Yearsley Affair, in spite of the unhappy sequel, had testified to the patronage at her command in the Great and Gay world. She was proud of her position as a patron of literature, and welcomed young Mr Robert Southey to Cowslip Green, 'which more bishops and nobles and distinguished persons honoured with their presence than any private family in the Kingdom',[9] when Joseph Cottle, the Bristol book-seller and verse-maker and 'homely Maecenas' to penniless poets, brought the elegant young man 'brimful of conversation' to call on Miss More. Her report that he was one of the most intellectual young men the sisters had ever seen was highly gratifying to Cottle. It was presumably after this interview that Cottle's three young poets, Southey, Coleridge, and Robert Lovell, planned to express their admiration for Miss More by dedicating their 'fustian drama' *Robespierre* to her. If they did so, it may be safely assumed that Hannah More, who had no liking for revolutionaries of any kind, declined the honour.

Persons of lesser intellectual distinction or social importance who called 'in multitudes' at the Bath house were left to the care of the sisters. When Hannah was ill or depressed or at work, her bodyguard of four elderly ladies looked 'unutterable things' when the privilege of an interview was requested, and informed the *hoi polloi* with sturdy, unashamed snobbery that a duchess and a bishop had been denied entrance that day.[10] But in spite of the sisters' valiant efforts, 'company all day and every day' persisted.

Failing in her prolonged attempts to 'do the business of the world without catching the spirit of the world', she found at length no course open to her except to cut herself off completely from worldly interests. The annual visits to London for the season came to an abrupt end and visitors were resolutely restricted to those whose position would not permit refusal. Finding no Evangelical teaching in the churches of the Establishment in Bath, she and her sisters, who shared her Evangelical views, followed the lead of 'other strict Church people' in the city and frequented—'chiefly at six o'clock in the evening, an hour which did not interfere with the Church service'[11]—the Presbyterian Chapel in Argyle Street, where William Jay, famous among Dissenting ministers, officiated.

More drastic still was her rejection of all secular literature. 'It is now', she wrote in her diary for September 1794, 'five or six years since I have been enabled by the grace of God in a good degree to give up all human studies. I have not allowed myself to read any classic or pagan author for many years. I now read little of which religion is not the subject.'[12]

In the summer of 1795 a new guest, who could not be denied, made his way to Bath and Cowslip Green to visit Miss More. As her treatment of Zachary Macaulay was a subject of reproach in her lifetime, and has coloured judgements of her since, it demands consideration.

Appointed Governor of the Colony of Sierra Leone in 1793 when only twenty-six, Macaulay, home on leave in 1795, told Henry Thornton of his desire to meet Hannah More. His efforts to provide schooling for the native children of the Colony made the Mendip experiment of peculiar interest to him. Thornton sent him to call on the sisters at Cowslip Green. This was the beginning of a lasting friendship between the quiet, reserved young man, whose name throughout his troubled life was a synonym for integrity, and the More sisters. He was welcomed by them to the innermost circle of the family, was mobilized by the sisters to help with the Tracts they were writing for the poor, and straightway fell in love with Selina Mills, the sisters' successor at the Bristol school, who was living with them. It is not easy, in the face of conflicting statements, to unravel the story of Macaulay's courtship. Sir George Trevelyan in his *Life and Letters of Lord Macaulay* exempts Hannah More from blame. 'She advocated his cause with fairness and good feeling.' Lady Knutsford, on the contrary, in her *Life and Letters of Zachary Macaulay*, refuses to acquit Miss More of 'some duplicity' in her dealings with him. Mrs Babington, Macaulay's sister and confidante, roundly accuses the More sisters of 'a lack of perfect candour', and Macaulay himself expressed the opinion that 'our friends [the Mores] had not dealt kindly and candidly with me.'[13]

The Tracts

It seems probable that, with no prospects except those offered by the Gold Coast Colony, Macaulay would have left England at the end of his leave in February 1796 without proposing marriage to Selina Mills, but, 'deluged with letters of invitation from Patty and Hannah More', to whom he had 'rather unguardedly' betrayed himself, he paid a visit to Bath shortly before leaving England, determined to speak to Miss Mills. He informed Hannah on his arrival of his intention. She advised against it, giving him to understand, says Lady Knutsford, that 'the object of his regard was entirely indifferent to him.' Selina Mills, it may be assumed, when questioned by five affectionate elderly ladies on the state of her heart would have given them this impression. Macaulay, so informed, decided to leave Bath without approaching Miss Mills. On the evening of his departure he bade adieu to the five sisters in the upstairs drawing-room and made his way down to his carriage, when, unexpectedly seeing Miss Mills in a room alone weeping bitterly, prudence took wings. In a few moments a complete understanding was established between them. They arranged that Macaulay should return as soon as possible to break the news to the sisters. A day or two later the imperturbable young man presented himself at Pulteney Street, where he and Miss Mills met with 'stormy opposition', led by Patty More. Lady Knutsford admits that Hannah 'soon recovered some sense of what was due to Macaulay and endeavoured to mitigate the situation'. The sisters agreed to recognize the betrothal and Miss Mills, pleading duty, refused to return with Macaulay to Sierra Leone. She was persuaded by the sisters, says Lady Knutsford, to keep her engagement a secret from her family.

The explanation of Hannah More's strange conduct was attributed by Macaulay to the sisters' disapproval of marriage, and by Hannah More's critics to her sympathy with Patty's jealous affection for Selina Mills. Marriage, in Patty More's opinion, was 'hostile to friendship'. By this particular marriage, which involved Selina's residence abroad, she would lose her friend. The explanation is entirely out of keeping with Hannah More's life and character.

Nowhere is there evidence that she was antipathetic to the idea of marriage. On the contrary, it is easy to find illustrations of her sympathy in the matrimonial affairs of her contemporaries. More important is it that she was, to a marked degree, honest and fair-minded. Like other human beings she was capable of self-deception, but it is highly unlikely that she would have stirred a finger to secure Patty's happiness at the expense of that of Selina Mills. Other factors ignored by Miss More's critics require, but have never received, consideration. Selina Mills and her sister had taken over the Park Street school from the Mores in 1790. From 1791 to 1794 the school had provided a *cause célèbre* to press and public by the abduction of one of its pupils, Clementina Clerke, a West Indian heiress of fifteen years, by Perry, a Bristol apothecary, and the case against Perry, who was defended by the great Erskine, was in 1794 decided in his favour.[14] Miss Mills, as the Governess of the school, did not escape censure for her inadequate care of her pupil, or for her incompetence in handling the affair. On Hannah More's competent shoulders had fallen the burden of assisting Miss Mills to rescue the child from her 'atrocious companion'. With lawyers, officers, and Sir Sampson Wright's men she scoured London to find them. 'Every morning presents some fresh pursuit and every day closes in disappointment,' until Henry Thornton came to the rescue. 'His labours and influence have done more than all the lawyers: he got the King's Proclamation and did everything with the Secretary of State.'[15] Even then it was three years before Perry, who had carried off his wife to France, was brought to trial. It does not seem too much to assume that Miss Mills's duty, in the opinion of the sisters, who had made the school, and in her own opinion, since she pleaded duty as a reason for deferring her marriage with Macaulay, was to rebuild the school's reputation, badly shaken by the unpleasant publicity. Further, Hannah More was aware that the Mills family would oppose Selina's marriage with Macaulay. Not only were they 'set upon her making a better match',[16] but a marriage which involved residence on the distant and lethal Gold Coast was unlikely to please them. The sisters who had introduced

Macaulay to Miss Mills were not unreasonably apprehensive of family censure.

Considerations such as these, if they are accepted, do not excuse Hannah More's stupidity. She threw Macaulay and Selina Mills together and encouraged him to visit her, and then was surprised and perturbed when he proposed marriage; but they do something to exculpate her from the charge of exaggerated sympathy with Patty's emotional immaturity, and from the imputation of duplicity.

(ii)

In the 'nineties, when affairs began to wear a threatening and gloomy aspect in the country and French Revolutionary principles were spreading with dangerous rapidity among the lower orders, Miss More was inundated with 'letters by every post' calling on her to produce some little popular tracts which might serve as a counter-action to the poisonous writings of Tom Paine. His *Rights of Man*, the most vigorous and widely read of the replies to Burke's impassioned *Reflections on the Revolution in France*, published on 1 February 1791, sold over 50,000 copies in a few weeks, and 'what greatly surprised me', wrote Sir Samuel Romilly '[it] has made converts of many persons who before were enemies to the Revolution.'[17]

Paine's major contention, that of the majority of Burke's opponents, was that governmental institutions were neither sacred nor inviolable. Paine ridiculed Burke's defence of the Settlement of 1688 as a solemn agreement binding its creators and their descendants for ever. Government, he argued, must be based on the consent of the living. 'Mr Burke is contending for the authority of the dead.' He proceeded to argue that a comparison of French and English theories of government revealed the infinite superiority of the French. Methodically, he revealed the inferiority of the English constitution.

The response to *The Rights of Man* encouraged Paine to believe that the people of England were anxious for the triumph of liberty in England. Revolution, he asserted, was become 'the subject of universal conversation, and may be considered the order of the day'. Hence in Part II of *The Rights of Man*, which appeared in February 1792, he offered his readers stronger meat, developing his theme on the principles of democratic government with a vigorous attack on 'English monarchical usurpations and aristocratical institutions'. More than this, he introduced a new note into the controversy by a humane plea for the poorer classes of the community, and ended with a call for world revolution.

The Government had met Part I of *The Rights of Man* with silence. A pamphlet priced at 6s. would, it argued, be read only by 'judicious readers', and the 'unexpected gale' aroused by it would soon be over. Part II, with its note of concern for the poor and its call for world revolution, could not, however, be ignored. When it appeared in a cheap edition the Government began to move. It attempted first to hold up the publication of Part II by bribing the publishers; it paid for and sponsored the publication of a scurrilous *Life of Paine* by one Francis Oldys, a non-existent graduate of the University of Pennsylvania; it issued a Royal Proclamation against seditious writings; and finally it indicted the author of *The Rights of Man* for sedition. The sales of Part II far exceeded those of Part I. Remarkable skill and 'industry incredible' were shown in making it known. Copies were thrust into the hands of all sorts and conditions of persons in the public streets, they were quietly and unobtrusively introduced into cottage homes, were picked up on the public roads, and were found 'lurking at the bottom of mines and coal pits'. Even the children's sweetmeats were wrapt up in its pages. Savage sentences prevented the continuation of the initial success in circulating the pamphlet, but enough copies had been read by the lower orders, whose 'wild expressions of liberty and equality' alarmed the governing classes, to produce terror and despondency in England.[18]

It was at this stage that an antidote to Tom Paine was suggested in high places. Rumour had it that the Prime Minister himself had requested Hannah More to write some little popular tracts 'to dis-

pel the illusions so assiduously propagated among the vulgar', and
that she had consented to become an agent of the Government. Miss
More told a different story in a letter to Mrs Boscawen. 'Our dear
Bishop of London', she wrote from Bath in January 1793, 'came
to me with a dismal countenance and told me I should repent it on
my death-bed if I, who knew so much of the habits and sentiments
of the lower orders of people, did not write some little thing tend-
ing to open their eyes.' A strong Church and State woman, she was
in complete sympathy with Bishop Porteus's request, but, regarding it as a matter of politics, outside a woman's sphere, and as an
interference with the schools she was establishing in the Mendips,
she refused; but later

in an evil hour, against my will and my judgment, on one sick day, I scribbled
a little pamphlet called *Village Politics* by 'Will Chip'. . . It is as vulgar as heart
can wish; but it is only designed for the most vulgar class of readers. I heartily
hope I shall not be discovered; as it is the sort of writing repugnant to my
nature, though indeed it is a question of peace rather than of politics.[19]

Village Politics may be described as 'Burke for Beginners'. In it
Hannah More introduced her old friend, whose social and political
philosophy she shared, to the lower orders, as an antidote to the
poison of Paine's *Rights of Man*. She had parted company with
Burke on the great issue of the American Colonies, whose loss she
attributed to him, and on the trial of Warren Hastings, but, as her
letters and writings show, she retained her sympathy with and her
admiration for him. His cardinal principle of a divine purpose im-
manent in the existing order of things was her cardinal principle;
with him she held religion to be the basis of society, the source
of peace and trust and comfort. She was, too, dimly aware of the
significant role played by the historic purpose in moulding national
character, ideals and institutions. She had responded to the Revolution in 1789 with the characteristically complacent sympathy of
Englishmen for revolutions abroad. 'Poor France,' she wrote, 'I
cannot help hoping that some good will arise from the sum of
human misery.'[20] French excesses and fear of English contamination produced in her the horror which was responsible for trans-

forming English sympathy into fear and detestation. 'I have conceived', she wrote in 1790, 'an utter aversion to liberty according to
the present idea of it in France. What a cruel people they are!'[21]
Burke's *Reflections* she welcomed with ardour, though she was
level-headed enough to deplore his 'intemperate language'. The
book reinstated him in her opinion, as it did in that of tens of thousands of his countrymen. In the dreadful drama played out in
France she discovered evils which rendered his faults not only pardonable, but commendable. The *Reflections*, she held, combined
'the rhetoric of ancient Gaul', the 'patriot spirit of ancient Rome'
with 'the deepest political sagacity'. Above all she shared his resentment of the attacks of 'rash and presumptuous men', with their
abstract geometrical and arithmetical speculations, on English life
and institutions. They were out to alter for the sake of altering. This
she regarded as 'the infallible criterion' of unwise and evil men. Indeed only in their attitude towards the lower orders were they in
any marked disagreement. Good order, she agreed with him, was
the foundation of all good things: to achieve it the people must be
tractable and obedient, but her humanity made it impossible for her
to despise them or to refer to them in his unhappy phrase as the
'swinish multitude'. Her respect and affection for the poor was in
marked contrast to his contempt. The people were ignorant and
childish, easily excited by wicked men for their own ends; they
must be taught, she held, where truth lay in the great debate of the
day.[22]

Village Politics, which appeared in 1792, is a brisk dialogue, in
plain straightforward English, between two protagonists—Jack
Anvil, the village blacksmith, a sturdy champion of the existing
order of things, and Tom Hood, the village mason, who after reading *The Rights of Man* is of Paine's opinion that they order these
things better in France. The scales are heavily weighted against
him. He uses the language of revolution and reform without understanding it, and falls an easy victim to the blacksmith's heavy
blows of common sense. He wants a new constitution, embodying
liberty and equality and 'the Rights of Man'. His opponent insists

that we had already a fine Constitution, as much liberty as was good for us, and 'the best laws in the world'. He reduces to rubble the claims of his ill-equipped opponent by borrowing Solomon's question, 'How can he be wise whose talk is of oxen?' He defines French liberty as murder, French democracy as government by a thousand tyrants, French equality as the pulling down of everyone above him, French philosophy as disbelief in God, the devil, heaven and hell, 'the Rights of Man' as 'battle, murder, and sudden death', and the other 'hard words' which Paine's disciple finds a difficulty in understanding—'organization', 'function', 'incivism', 'inviolability', 'imprescription' and 'fraternization'—as 'downright hocus pocus'. The dialogue—it cannot be called the argument—ends with Tom's acceptance of Jack's conclusion: 'While old England is safe I'll glory in her, and pray for her; and when she is in danger I'll fight for her and die for her.'[23]

The Tract met with the usual extraordinary reception which all Hannah More's writings enjoyed. When internal evidence betrayed the author, thanks and congratulations poured in, not only from her friends among the great, but also, said Roberts with unconscious humour, 'from persons of the soundest judgements', who went so far as to say that the Tract had contributed under Providence to prevent revolution in England.[24] 'It is a masterpiece of its kind, supremely excellent, greatly admired at Windsor,' wrote the Bishop of London.[25] In Mrs Boscawen's opinion it was superior to Archdeacon Paley's recently published pamphlet *The British Public's Reasons for Contentment, addressed to the Labouring part of the British public*.[26] 'Swift', said Richard Owen Cambridge, who did not normally talk nonsense, 'could not have done it better.'[27] Miss More's friends, the Beauforts, Cremornes, Kennicotts, Montagus, Orfords, sent their thanks and congratulations. Roberts, carried away by enthusiasm when preparing Hannah More's correspondence for publication in 1834, attributed to 'the tact and intelligence of a single female a performance which wielded at will the fierce democratie of England'.[28]

Hannah More's first attempt to stem the torrent of French Jacobinism in England was followed by her open letter to the atheistical M. Dupont, a member of the French National Assembly. His call to the French people to overturn the altars of God moved her to make her second contribution to the pamphlet literature of the Revolution. 'Dupont's and Marvel's atheistical speeches have stuck in my throat all the winter, and I have been waiting for our bishops and our clergy to take some notice of them ... to counteract the poison.'[29] When no official effort was made to combat blasphemy and impiety so monstrous, the bishop in petticoats wrote her *Remarks on the Speech of M. Dupont*, calling the attention of religious people in the Church and the Sects to the horrors of French impiety.[30] The Tract was sold for the benefit of the exiled French priests in England. 'We plead not for their faith but their wants.' It received some charitable response, and aroused some violent abuse of Hannah More, who had opened her house in Bath to the unfortunate French priests, as a Papist wolf in Evangelical sheep's clothing and 'the notorious daughter of the Father of Lies'.[31]

After Tom Paine's *Age of Reason*, a vehement arraignment of Church and priesthood, had appeared in 1794, the success of Hannah More's Tracts moved the Bishop of London to appeal again for her help. The first impression of Paine's book, he told her, had been seized by the Government. Nevertheless copies had slipped through, and had done great mischief. 'Your help, therefore, is much needed, and it is as strongly called for as ever. I will venture to say that the eyes of many are fixed on *you* at this important crisis.' He suggested a 'very plain summary of the evidences of Christianity brought down to the level of Will Chip and Jack Anvil exactly as you have done in *Village Politics*'.[32] Miss More regretfully refused, entering in her diary, for 23 July 1794: 'Conjured by the Bishop of London to answer Paine's atheistical book, with a solemnity which made me grieve to refuse.'[33]

Hannah More's unwillingness to consider Bishop Porteus's urgent request was not due to a lack of sympathy, but to her preoccupation with her schools and the formulation of a large-scale plan to provide suitable literature for the children and adults attending them. She believed, as educational reformers had believed before her, that to teach the poor to read without providing them with 'safe' books was not conducive to religious or moral reform. Never did this appear more evident than in the last decades of the eighteenth century, when the Sunday schools were annually turning out tens of thousands of adolescents who, able to read, fell easy victims not only to the old vulgar chap-book and broad-sheet, but to the new publications of the 'school of Paine', which flooded the country. With the rapid decision and strong common sense which characterized her, she set out to supply a new type of literature for the inferior classes, which would be safe and cheap and unspeculative —the *Cheap Repository Tracts*. [34]

(iii)

Hannah More's drive and organizing power were seldom more conspicuous than in the exigent work of writing, editing, and vending for the Cheap Repository. That it was the concerted effort of herself, her sisters and an army of interested friends adds to rather than detracts from an estimate of her organizing talents. The help of her Clapham friends was at all times apparent. Henry Thornton undertook the work of treasurer; Babington was a tower of strength when publishers proved unkind; Grant went about explaining the Plan; Macaulay, to Hannah's satisfaction, agreed to act as an agent for the Repository; Wilberforce's purse was always open; and Dr Beilby Porteus, Bishop of London, threw the weight of his great influence into the scheme.

Tracts for the moral and religious instruction of the poor were not an innovation in the 'nineties, as the publications of the S.P.C.K. throughout the century attest. Wesley had used them, and more recently Hannah's friend Sarah Trimmer, author of 'that most delectable *Story of the Robins*', had published her *Instructive Tales*, and had produced two issues of *The Family Magazine, or Repository of religious instruction and rational amusement designed to counteract the pernicious tendency of immoral books which have circulated of late years among the poorer classes of people to the obstruction of their improvement in religion and morals.* Priced at 3s. a copy it was too expensive, and its format too superior, to attract the poorer classes, or to pay its way. Hannah More broke new ground when she decided to adopt not only the lively stories and ballads for community singing as supplied by chap-book and broad-sheet, but their format also, and by under-selling the hawkers and pedlars to beat them at their own game. 'It has occurred to me', she informed Mrs Bouverie, a generous contributor to the scheme, 'to write a variety of things, somewhere between vicious papers and hymns, for it is vain to write what people will not read. These verses are made to attack gross immorality or dishonest practice and by trying to make them a little amusing in the manner as well as ornamental in the appearance we may in time bring them to still higher things.' 'Dry morality or religion will not answer the end,' she told Sir Charles Middleton, 'for we must ever bear in mind that it is a pleasant poison to which we must find an antidote.'[35]

'The Plan', as she called it, was finished by the end of 1794. It was sent to the Bishop of London and to other friends for their comments. Subscriptions were invited, since it appeared unlikely that the Tracts would pay for themselves. Bishop Porteus warmly approved the scheme. He urged that it should be published immediately, with Miss More's name attached 'to give it éclat'.[36] Based on the monthly production of three Tracts—stories, ballads, and Sunday readings—the first essential for success was to secure an adequate supply of suitable contributions, and these, in the opinion of the editor, who contributed at least 50, probably more, of the 114 tracts published in the years 1795–8, were those which stressed morality, loyalty and religion. Neither the fears of her worldly friends, who warmly approved the scheme as an antidote to Tom Paine, that she would involve it in adverse criticism by being 'too Methodistical', nor the mild and deprecatory criticism of her Tracts by Henry Thornton on the same grounds moved her. Like the rest of the 'Sect', he deplored 'enthusiasm'.[37]

Of the remaining Tracts Sally appears to have contributed six, Patty one. The Clapham Sect responded nobly. 'Henry Thornton', wrote Hannah to Macaulay in 1796, 'is hard at work on some prayers.'[38] *Prayers to be used by a Child* was presumably one of his contributions. To Zachary Macaulay may be accredited the *Sacrament of the Lord's Supper*. John Venn was appealed to for a penny prayer; Mrs Chapone sent *Mary Wood the Housemaid*; John Newton and Selina Mills were called in to assist and made their assignments. *Babay* was borrowed from Mrs Trimmer's *Family Magazine*. Old favourites such as Dr Watts's *Divine Songs for Children*, and Henry Fielding's *True Example of the Interposition of Providence in the Discovery of Murder* found a place, and William Gilpin, the Vicar of Boldre, contributed the *Life and Funeral Sermon of William Baker*, a pious impostor who had completely deceived the simple-minded old man. Of six ballads offered by her old friend William Mason, three were firmly rejected by Miss More on the ground that there was too much love and too much politics in them. His *Ploughboy's Dream* she decided 'would do very well'. 'I know not', she remarked dubiously, 'what so great a man will say at having any of his offerings rejected.' It is satisfactory to know that Mason, with a firmness equal to her own, refused to make any alteration to his poems, which he asserted were 'of the true lyric dimensions and could not be mended'.[39]

Assured of a supply of Tracts, Hannah More dealt with the problems of their substance and format in a masterly fashion. She made a personal investigation into the stories and ballads sold by the hawkers and pedlars, and collected a remarkable library of *sans-culotte* literature sold by them for a penny. Not all, but more than enough, of the chap-books and ballads she waded through—as the remnant, still extant, testifies—were dirty and indecent stuff. Some glorified the 'smart-alec' character of the eighteenth-century 'spiv'; others were saturated with superstition. Even more disturbing to her were the new Jacobin imprints. Alluring novels, stories, and songs prepared by the 'School of Paine' were offered in the streets, and were hung up invitingly on walls and windows.

'Vulgar and indecent penny books', she wrote to Macaulay, 'were always common, but speculative infidelity brought down to the pockets and capacity of the poor forms a new era in our history. This requires strong counteraction.'⁴⁰ With the wisdom of the serpent, she produced her Tracts not only similar in size and general appearance to the chapmen's wares, but illustrated with the crude and lively woodcuts and written in the simple clear language to which the poor were accustomed. They were sold at a price within their means, at ½d., 1d., and 1½d. apiece. Finally she enhanced the interest of her readers and secured their co-operation in buying the Tracts by treating the longer stories as serials. 'Next month you may expect a full account of the many tricks and frolics of idle Jack Brown,' and again 'Do not forget to inquire for Jack Brown in prison.'

The Tracts were distributed through the normal book-selling channels. The names of Hazard of Bath, Marshall and White of London, Eldred of Edinburgh, and Wilson of Dublin appear on those sold respectively in England, Scotland, and Ireland. Other agents were named in a *Prospectus of the Plan* seen later by William de Morgan.⁴¹ Monthly issues of the tracts were delivered by the publishers to their agents and to private persons, Mrs Montagu, Mrs Boscawen, and Mrs Piozzi among them. Highly placed ecclesiastics helped in their dispersal. The Bishop of London turned his library at London House into a warehouse for the Tracts, some of which 'he gives to every hawker that passes.'⁴² Bishop Barrington of Durham 'hoped to spread the Plan much there'. The Archdeacon of Shrewsbury was 'a good Repository friend'. Not content with these methods of distribution, Miss More carried the war into the enemy's camp by persuading the pedlars and hawkers to sell her wares. They were invited to the opening ceremony of the Repository at Hazard's library in Bath, and arrived decently dressed with characteristic ribands in their hats. 'An assortment of the instructive and entertaining works in poetry and prose were presented to each man by means of a subscription raised by the ladies and gentlemen present.'⁴³

The demand of the public for the Tracts was astonishing. Enough subscriptions had been secured (over £1,000 in the first year) to allow the promoters to sell the Tracts at a price less than the expense incurred in printing and vending.[44] Three hundred thousand were sold between 3 March and 18 April 1795. 'I am afraid', wrote Hannah from London to Patty, 'that we shall be ruined by the very success of our Tracts. Cadell says he would not stand in my shoes ... for £500 over and above the subscription; nay, according to another calculation £1,000 would not do it.'[45] By July 1795, 700,000 copies had been sold; by March 1796, over two million. In 1797 Miss More reported that the *Cheap Repository Tracts* have 'gone on very well indeed', and that the bound volumes prepared for the more opulent classes 'have had an extensive sale'.[46] A response so great made further subscriptions unnecessary. The Tracts had paid for themselves.

Little information is available on the business side of this remarkable scheme. None of the business correspondence relating to it appears to be extant. Nor is it clear why the Plan petered out. The scraps of evidence available show that Hannah More's original scheme was to arrange for a local supply of Tracts from the press of Hazard, the Evangelical Bath printer. Before the Plan came into operation its area was extended to London. Henry Thornton, already engaged in writing Tracts for the Repository, promised his help in the extension of the Plan, and as Hazard, though a good printer, was a bad business man, 'mixing enthusiasm', said Thornton disparagingly, 'with worldly concerns, and hoping for a divine direction in a way which the Scriptures do not seem to promise it', Thornton selected John Marshall, 'a more worldly man', to run the London end of the scheme.[47] Marshall's wide experience as a printer of children's books, and his familiarity, through his firm, Cluer, Dicey, and Marshall, with the production of eighteenth-century chap-book literature, fitted him to manage Miss More's ever-expanding scheme. In February Hazard's name disappeared from the Tracts and Marshall remained alone as printer to the Repository until his dismissal in 1798.[48] That Hannah More agreed to Marshall's appointment demands, but does not receive, explanation. She had disliked and distrusted him ever since she had discovered his ungenerous financial treatment of Sarah Trimmer, who, popular as her writings were, had been treated by him as 'a mere bookseller's fag'.[49] 'Negligence and other faults' in his management of the Cheap Repository aroused her angry comments early in 1796. It would seem that Marshall was too worldly to adapt his standards to those of an imperious woman whose interests lay not in making money but in saving souls. 'Mr Babington', she wrote to Zachary Macaulay in January 1796, 'has promised to take M. in hand.' His 'judicious investigation' would, she hoped, produce 'some outward reformation, at least, in his management'. But the trouble persisted. 'Mr M.', she told Macaulay in September, 'has never belied my first impression of him, selfish, tricking and disobliging from first to last.'[50] In November 1797, as no reformation had taken place, she broke off her connection with Marshall and appointed Evans and Hatchard publishers to the Cheap Repository. Marshall at once claimed the copyright of the Tracts 'and threatened us', wrote Thornton, 'with a prosecution'.[51] His claim cannot have been sustained, for the right to publish reprints of the Tracts issued between 1795–7 was sold outright to Rivington.[52] 'I have settled all accounts with Marshall,' wrote Thornton on 20 September 1798.[53] Hannah's diary two days later records 'Cheap Repository closed. Bless the Lord, Oh my Soul! that I have been spared to accomplish that work.'[54]

But Marshall had a devastating shot left in his locker. The Tracts were a paying concern, too good to lose. Their fame was well established. When Hannah More severed her connection with him he produced a new series of tracts, with a similar format, to which he appropriated the name *Cheap Repository Tracts*. 'The Cheap Repository', wrote Henry Thornton mournfully, 'has received a great blow.'[55] Worse was to come. Marshall's standards of decorum were not those of Miss More. Most of his tracts were innocuous; others such as *The Baker's Dream, or Death no bad change to the poor and good*, would never have passed muster under Miss More's surveillance. Nor is it conceivable that the mild ribaldry of the ballad *The Contented Cobbler and his Wife* would have got past the censor.

The Tracts

The death of the triplets born to the Cobbler's distracted wife illustrated the sub-title of the ballad, 'All things turn out for the best.'

'Oh never you mind,'
Says I, 'Be resign'd,
There's no use to fret and to stew'.
Now sure I was right,
For before the next night
The two eldest took leave and withdrew.[56]

The collapse of the original Plan was not due solely to the machi-
nations of William Marshall. Other factors played their part. The
production of the Tracts, coincident with the organization of the
Mendip Schools, proved too heavy a physical strain for a woman of
Hannah More's age and indifferent health. It became less easy, as
the novelty of the Plan wore off, to secure sufficient contributions
for publication. 'I have often been driven to the necessity', she told
Macaulay, 'of furnishing the three monthly pieces myself.'[57] Hereafter she instructed the new publishers to concentrate on reprints;
only five new tracts found their way into the bound volumes for
1798.[58] No other contributions, if offered, appear to have been
accepted.

(iv)

It remains to assess the historical and literary value of the *Cheap
Repository Tracts*. The vast number published tends to exaggerate
their importance as factors in the reform of the poor, for the number of Tracts distributed to the lower orders was not identical with
the numbers published. It is significant of the growing solicitude of
Evangelicals for the middling classes that some of the Tracts were
addressed specifically to them as 'Stories for Persons of the Middle
Ranks'; others were published in a superior format. 'They were
bought by the gentry and middling classes full as much', wrote Miss
More, 'as by the common people,'[59] and shiploads, reported the
Bishop of London, were sent overseas. 'I hear of the immortal publication from every quarter of the globe.'[60] Large orders came from
America, accompanied by letters of congratulations on 'the un-
common success' of the Tracts. One correspondent—'a Mr

The Tracts

William Cobbett of Philadelphia', lately returned from America—informed Miss More that he would not lose a moment in paying his respects to her at Bath.[61] When, however, allowance is made for the demands of the superior classes and the immense overseas sales, it seems clear that no small number of the Tracts found their way into the homes of the poor, either indirectly, through schools, poor-houses, hospitals, prisons, and the army and navy, or directly—a more dubious point—through the pedlars and hawkers, who do not appear to have pushed their new wares. Thompson, writing five years after Hannah More's death, affirmed that the Tracts formed a principal part of the English cottagers' library. Some of the Tracts appeared in the lists returned in the *First Report of the Commissioners of Education in Ireland*, as forming the popular reading of the Irish peasantry, and so great was the demand for them in Scotland that in 1821 the New Edinburgh Tract Society begged Miss More's permission to reprint the Tracts on 'the most extensive scale'.[62] Nor did the importance of the Cheap Repository end when the monthly publication of the Tracts ceased. Miss More had blazed a trail which others followed in endless procession throughout the nineteenth century. In three years the Tracts had established themselves as the safe reading of the inferior classes. A year after the disbandment of Hannah More's organization the Religious Tract Society came into being.

The descriptive material of the Tracts, taken direct from the everyday circumstance and events in the life of the lower and middle classes at the end of the eighteenth century, is not without historical value. Farmers 'old and new style', labourers, craftsmen, shop-keepers, servants, beggars, poachers, thieves, prostitutes, informers, vagrants are depicted in the lively ballads and tales. Clerics, always treated with respect, for it was part of Miss More's deliberate intention to rehabilitate them in public estimation, squires, Justices of the Peace, Sir John Fielding's men, prison-warders, represent law and order. Hannah More, her sisters and friends, disguised as 'Mrs Jones' and 'Mrs White', appear as the social workers, organizing schools, women's clubs and district visiting. In some of the Tracts the harshness of the criminal law, the neglect of the poor law, the appalling state of the prisons and poor-houses provide a sombre background to the village dramas played in their pages. The most famous, *The Shepherd of Salisbury Plain*, 'a story from real life', portrays the honest, laborious poor, struggling to bring up a family of six on 8s. a week.[63] To Miss Charlotte Yonge, writing in 1888, and, presumably, to Hannah More and her contemporaries, *The Shepherd of Salisbury Plain* was an 'idyll of content and frugality'. It was also a revealing study of the material poverty and spiritual isolation of the poor in the west country villages, and an even more revealing study of the minds of the religious and philanthropic men and women who were constrained to convince the poor that poverty was a blessing in disguise. No word of criticism of the powers-that-be in Church or State escapes. The Tracts make clear that Hannah More shared Burke's views on the beneficent rôle of poverty. Annexed as a preface to the bound edition of *The Shepherd of Salisbury Plain* were his words:

... [Religion] is for the man in humble life, and to raise his nature and to put him in mind of a state in which the privileges of opulence will cease, when he will be equal by nature and maybe more than equal by virtue. . .[64]

But passive acceptance of ill conditions was no part of Hannah More's creed. The 'Old Bishop' harangued the upper and middling classes to remember their social responsibilities to the lower orders,[65] and, with equal vigour, she reminded the poor of their duty to relieve their poverty by amending their habits and manners. 'I have endeavoured', she wrote to Mrs Boscawen in 1795, when wheat was 75s. a quarter, 'to show them [the poor] that their distresses arise nearly as much from their own bad management as from the hardships of the times.' This tract, she added, with unconscious irony, 'is called *The Way to Plenty*.'[66]

The importance of the Tracts in stemming the tide of infidelity and disaffection it is not possible to determine. As one of the voluntary associations of the age, to whose influence Professor Halévy attributed the powerful moral authority which checked revolution in England, they merit consideration. It is not without significance

The Tracts

that the Age of Repression coincided with the Age of the Tracts. The Cheap Repository appeared when the appetite for literature among the lower orders, more voracious than it had yet been, was diverted by the efforts of Church and State from publications antipathetic to government and religion to literature which was safe. Canon Overton points out that, as the object of evidential writings is to convince persons of the truth of Christianity, 'Hannah More may in one sense claim a place in the very first rank of evidential writers.'[67] Some of the Tracts dealt directly with 'the new pestilential philosophy'. *Tis All for the Best* was an answer to Voltaire's *Candide*; *The History of Mr Fanton* to Paine's *Age of Reason*. Her ballad *Turn the Carpet* vindicated the justice of God in the apparently irregular distribution of good in the world by pointing to another world. 'Here you have Bishop Butler's *Analogy* all for a half-penny,'[68] wrote Porteus to her. It is probable that the Tracts did check disaffection and infidelity. The Prime Minister seemed to think so; Bishop Porteus had no doubt that 'they had enlightened the whole of England.' John Overton, author of the *True Church-man Ascertained*, said quaintly that it may be doubted whether even 'the exploits of Nelson have contributed more towards the preservation of national comforts than her excellent tracts', and J. C. Colquhoun, who approached the question as an authority on education, quoted with approval the widely held opinion that the great improvement in religion and morals of the past twenty years was due 'to Robert Raikes's Sunday Schools and to Hannah More's writings'.[70] Specific proof was offered by Miss More's friends and admirers. At Bath in 1796, 'the year of scarcity', the singing of her ballad *The Riot, or Half a Loaf is better than no Bread*, effectively checked 'a very formidable riot'. Equally successful was *Patient Joe, or the Newcastle Collier*, which, it was claimed, solved all the labour problems in the North of England. If these miracles be suspect, more reliable evidence is supplied by Cobbett's attack on Hannah More a quarter of a century later. She had taught piety and contentment to the poor; and had made one the cause of religion and the defence of the established order. Cobbett's *Monthly Religious Tracts*,

147

which set out to dissociate order and religion in 1821, provide a measure of Hannah More's success.[71]

One other point demands consideration. These vulgar tales were written for the vulgar. They were read not only by the vulgar but by those who, in Hannah More's words, 'could not be called vulgar'. They discovered to these superior classes a new nation. In the Tracts they met the patient and laborious poor, sometimes portrayed as irreligious and vicious, sometimes as the victims of Jacobin propaganda, but in general as God-fearing and loyal. Thirty years before Disraeli, forty years before Dickens, Hannah More did something to make the *Two Nations* known to one another. Unwittingly, for she had no sympathy with revolution of any kind, she had, in the words of a contemporary, made a revolution in thought when, in her Tracts, she 'let the poor know that the rich had faults'.[72]

The literary value of the fifty tales, ballads, and Sunday readings written by Miss More is easier to assess. Of their kind they rank high. Most of them are vivid, picturesque, and dramatic stories, written in simple, forceful, unpretentious English. They are characterized by Miss More's habitual and admirable good sense. There is, too, a pleasing vein of irony in the more ambitious of the tales. Character-drawing in them is at a minimum. The characters are merely pegs on which to hang principles. Mr Worthy, Mr Thrifty, Mr Truman, Mr Bragwell respond automatically to the names bestowed upon them in John Bunyan fashion. But lack of character-drawing is compensated by vigorous action. Death, suicide, repentance, punishment loom large. Differing in their medium—some are in prose, others in verse—the technique of these tales is the effective one of contrast. Often they take the form of a dialogue between two sharply contrasted types, the wise and the unwise, the religious and profane, and no one was left in doubt that it pays to be good, or that the hardship of this world would be compensated in the next.

The popularity of the Tracts did not exempt Hannah More from bitter and prolonged criticism. Their quasi-political character was

in part responsible for this. The rumour that she had been commissioned by the Prime Minister to write the Tracts persisted in
spite of her strong disclaimer. 'The very tracts', she wrote indignantly, 'have been specified for which the "venal hireling" was
paid by the Government.'[73] As the rumour spread, critics of the
Administration were at once up in arms. David Bogue, the Non-
comformist historian—an influential Dissenter—attributed the appearance of tracts for the poor at such a time to Hannah More's
friendship with the terrified aristocracy, and he reflected adversely
on the 'defective' religious principles exhibited in the Plan.
Zachary Macaulay, greatly perturbed, informed Henry Thornton
of Bogue's animadversions. 'You may assure Mr Bogue', wrote
Thornton, in hot indignation,

that it is not true that Mr Pitt desired Hannah More to write *Village Politics*: as
to her writing only for the poor, he ought to connote that no one before her
had ever written anything for them on the present plan, though many books
have been written for the Rich, some of them by Hannah More herself, and
that the same person cannot do everything, and even if defective in the Plan
this ought not to prevent her being zealous in doing even partial good. He little
knows her if he thinks she is afraid of the upper classes or is subject to them, for
she has, in fact, lost many of her great friends through the opposition she has
made to them, and the distance which her principles have thrown her; and
having tried them, almost in vain, she has turned to the poor, like the apostle
Paul when he said, 'so turn we to the Gentiles.'[74]

Rumour gave place in 1802 to an open attack upon the Tracts
and their promoter, compared with which Cobbett's later de-
nunciations were mild and restrained. William Shaw, Rector of
Chelvey, Somerset, in his *Life of Hannah More*, insisted that 'these
cheap little tracts intoxicated ignorant men with the hatred and
madness of war more effectively than the Gin-Shop,' and that
Hannah More's 'bloody piety' was paid for by the Government to
encourage the war spirit among the people. 'In spite of her profession of Christian principles, there cannot be found in all her
works one expression reprobating war and bloodshed.' To win the
approval of her great friends of the governing classes was, he
alleged, her dominating motive.[75]

The Tracts

An unexpected criticism of the *Cheap Repository Tracts* came from its reputed offspring, the Religious Tract Society of world fame. Founded in 1799 by Baptists, Presbyterians, Congregationalists, Quakers, Methodists, and Evangelical Churchmen, it was not, in its organization, methods, or personnel—with the single exception of Zachary Macaulay, who served on its early committees—connected with the Cheap Repository. The new society affirmed that it rejoiced in the 'wide diffusion' of Miss More's Tracts, but that it regarded them as 'doctrinally inadequate' because they 'did not contain a fuller statement of the great Evangelical principles of the Christian faith', nor were Miss More's lively tales approved by it until, in later years, the Society was driven by the necessity of selling its wares to adopt her methods of catering for the taste of the new reading public.[76]

CHAPTER VII

THE SCHOOLS

'Horace's Virginibus Puerisque may be her motto but in a sense much nobler than he has annexed to it.'
William Cowper on Hannah More

ROBERTS'S *Memoirs of the Life and Correspondence of Hannah More*, the main source of information for her religious and philanthropic work, was supplemented, during the years 1789–1800, by Patty More's *Journal.*[1] In it may be found a description of social work at the end of the eighteenth century which is unequalled for its authenticity and for its vivid and arresting detail.

For four years, 1785–9, Hannah More and her sisters had used Cowslip Green as a summer retreat for rest and quiet when in the August of 1789 William Wilberforce paid them a long-promised visit. 'Leisure and peace', noted Patty in her *Journal*, 'took wings' when Providence directed him to Cowslip Green. Incited by his hostess to visit the famous caves at Cheddar, he returned from his day's outing obsessed by the miseries of human nature rather than enraptured by the beauties of nature. He discovered to the horrified sisters Cheddar village as he had found it, a place, reports the *Journal*, 'where there was not any dawn of comfort, temporal or spiritual'. Like the rest of the world, the sisters knew of Robert Raikes's seminal work in educating the children of the poor in Gloucester and of the interest aroused by his scheme. Two Sunday schools, already set up, one in Wrington parish by the rector and another in the adjoining parish of Churchill, were, it may be assumed, supervised by the sisters, but Wilberforce's appeal to them 'to do something for Cheddar', eight miles distant, moved Hannah More to quick and immediate response. Before Wilberforce and the sisters parted company they had sketched out a plan for the moral reformation of the neighbourhood by the establishment of schools for the poor.

The Mendip scheme evoked wide contemporary interest. It operated in a peculiarly neglected and backward part of the country;[2] it was on a far larger scale than the similar efforts of Mrs Trimmer at Brentford, or of Countess Spencer at St Albans, or of the parish clergy who adopted Raikes's idea. It not only covered a large area of country including several parishes but provided infant and adult instruction. Before the end of the century a dozen schools, some day working schools, some Sunday schools, and several women's benefit clubs in association with them, had been set up.

It is this chapter of Hannah More's life which is responsible in great part for the unsympathetic portrait of her which has been handed down to posterity. In it she appears as a masterful, dogmatic woman, a high Tory in politics, a rigid Evangelical in religion, using her undeniable talents for organization to dragoon the wretched, ignorant, ill-nourished population into schools which did not attempt to offer an opportunity to children and adults to improve their material conditions.

My plan for instructing the poor is very limited and strict. They learn of weekdays such coarse works as may fit them for servants. I allow of no writing. My object has not been to teach dogmas and opinions, but to form the lower class to habits of industry and virtue. I know no way of teaching morals but by infusing principles of Christianity, nor of teaching Christianity without a thorough knowledge of Scripture. . . To make good members of society (and this can only be done by making good Christians) has been my aim. . . Principles not opinions are what I labour to give them.[3]

Both the spirit and the language, judged by later standards, are deplorable. That they were not so regarded by Miss More and the bulk of her contemporaries may be attributed in part to the failure of her age to recognize that the detestable conditions of poverty, ignorance, and vice which prevailed among the lowest orders were due not to the depravity of a class, but to the failure of the Great Society to realize its responsibilities to the ignorant and helpless members of the community. Hannah More reacted to the problem of poverty in a manner characteristic of reformers throughout the eighteenth century. To her the problem was a religious, not an economic, one. She was in no degree indifferent to the poverty and misery of the lower orders, but it was the spiritual and moral ills of the poor which aroused her to action, just as the spiritual and moral ills of the rich had moved her to courageous remonstrance. Because the poor were ignorant of religion they must be taught to read the Bible; because they were dirty, dishonest, and drunken they must be made fit to enter God's house to glorify him. But poverty and ignorance did not alone determine her attitude to the poor. The world of the eighteenth century was a static world; men and women were precluded by their ignorance of evolutionary ideas from imagining a world of social change and development. In this static world it was cruelty, not kindness, to educate a child beyond his station. Was it not the obligation of religion to train a child to do his duty in that state of life into which it shall please God to call him? The limitations of eighteenth-century thought explain, if they do not excuse, the attitude of mind to the problem of the poor. Worked out in practice, the hard lines of Miss More's dogmatic principles were blurred and softened by the personal relations which she established with cantankerous farmers, lazy clergy, inept teachers, with parents on whose goodwill she was dependent for her pupils, and with the pupils themselves. The warm heart and pleasing manners of London's popular Blue Stocking were not left behind in London.

The ten-mile circuit which the sisters marked out for their operations was both agricultural and industrial. In the fields and the mines and glass-houses the condition of the poor was everywhere much alike, one of desolating neglect by Government, Church, local authority, and fashionable philanthropy. It would be difficult to find elsewhere in England an area of similar dimensions better supplied by parish churches, many of them of great beauty, but in more than a dozen adjacent parishes there were no resident clergy of any kind. They were not long in discovering a sufficient number

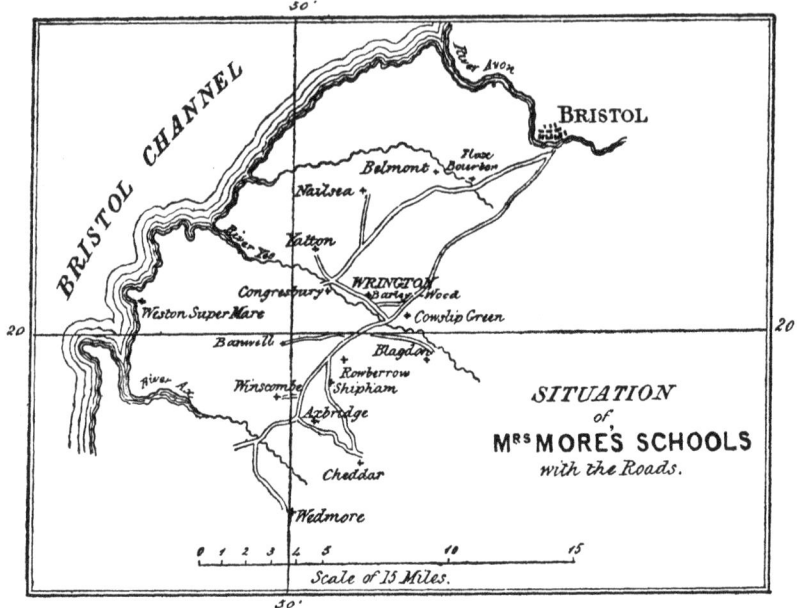

of wretched ignorant parishes in which there was 'as much knowledge of Christ as in the interior of Africa'. Cheddar, and Shipham
and Rowberrow, two mining villages at the top of the Mendips, in
which the people were 'savage and depraved, brutal in their natures
and ferocious in their manners', called for immediate attention.
Even when allowance is made for the sombre colours with which
social reformers paint the backgrounds to their work, the condition
of the poor in the Mendip villages revealed by the sisters' letters
and by the *Journal* was one of almost unrelieved gloom. How to
break down the opposition to the schools and to get at the children
was the problem to be solved. The sisters discovered that nothing
could be done at Cheddar, a village of 2,000 inhabitants, no gentry
and a dozen hard-hearted and ignorant farmers, without the concurrence of Farmer C., the big employer of labour in the district.
So they set off on a ten-mile trudge through ploughfields to call on
him. Like the farming class in general, he was opposed to the

religious education of the poor. Their reception, wrote Patty, was not favourable; indeed, Mr C. was very much shocked by the idea of Sunday schools for the children. Religion, he held, was a very dangerous thing; it would be the ruin of agriculture. So perturbed was he that the sisters prudently changed the subject and complimented him on the excellence of his wine, 'as though we had been soliciting a vote at an election'. This put him in a good temper. It was heightened, said Patty, with the lambent humour characteristic of her, 'by our declaring we should ask no subscription'. He then withdrew his objection.

Rather less unfavourable was their reception at eleven other farmhouses in the district, and, having leapt this hurdle, they approached, as was the custom, the incumbent of the parish to ask for his countenance and support. The Vicar of Cheddar was an absentee. He had 'something to do in the University of Oxford', said Hannah disrespectfully. The curate lived at Wells, twelve miles distant. He agreed to attend the opening of the school, and gave the infant congregation a twelve-minute address on the laws of the land and the divine right of kings. The Divine right of the King of Kings 'seemed to be a law above his comprehension'.

When the farmers were tamed and the clergy shamed, there remained the difficult problem of persuading the parents to send their children to the schools, and it is here that the Women's Friendly Societies, set up later by the sisters, may conveniently be considered. The co-operation of the parents would, they hoped, secure the children's attendance at school. This side of the sisters' work brought them into direct personal contact with the poor in their homes and in the poor-houses, and discovered to ignorant and horrified middle class ladies, unaware that they were living through an agrarian revolution, English rural society in the last stages of dissolution. A small clique of well-to-do farmers, 'as insolent aristocrats as any *ci-devant* nobles of France', exercised an uncontrolled tyranny over a mass of poverty-stricken and brutalized dependants and a tyranny, only less immediate because it was social rather than economic, over the miners of coal and calamine in the district.[4] The

The Schools

poverty, 'especially in those villages where there were no gentry', appalled the sisters.

I have been employing myself for many weeks every day that . . . I could spare from my schools [wrote Miss More to Mrs Bouverie, one of the most generous patrons of the schools] in visiting the cottages of the poor and I am persuaded that no labouring man, even if he be healthy and sober, can maintain a family of any size and . . . pay rent. Nothing is more common than for the father and mother and four children (of all ages and both sexes) to sleep in one bed. Hardly any poor man can now get a bit of ground for a cow, as all the land in a parish is swallowed up by a few great farms. Jobbers go round and buy up the butter, which they again sell to little shops, so that there are three profits before the poor get it. . . These husbandly labourers are quiet and patient, while the manufacturers, who get more than twice their wages, are rioting. I thank God that I am still able to prolong my campaign, though I fear I shall soon have my communication cut off from many of my villages, the waters being out and some of the roads nearly impassable.[5]

Writing again after a round of visiting the poor-houses in the neighbourhood, she tells her friends of the pitiful conditions of young and old in these 'mansions of misery':

I could now convict some overseers of murder if those who would redress these grievances would listen to me. I believe I see more misery in a week than some people believe exists in the whole world. . . I have written . . . to some of our young reformers [in Parliament] but those who do good have already so much to do, and the rest of the world cares so little whether it be done or not that I grow hopeless about all points of domestic reformation or redress.[6]

The devastating effects of disease on the ill-housed and under-fed poor was even more appalling to the sisters. Jones, the curate of Shipham, told them that in the winter before they began their work eighteen souls had died of putrid fever[7] in the parish and that 'he could not raise sixpence to save a life'.

Directly the early schools were under way the sisters called together the women in the villages of Cheddar and Shipham,[8] and proposed, with their co-operation, to found women's benefit societies ('Men already in this as in most other things', commented the *Journal* dourly, 'have the advantage of such comfort'). In return for subscriptions of 1½*d.* a week the sisters promised 3*s.* 6*d.* a week benefit for sickness and 7*s.* 6*d.*, 'a vast possession', for lying-in. Nor was this all. It was part of Hannah More's plan, which grew with feeding, to make the schools and clubs centres of social life in the neighbouring villages. The isolation of the poor distressed her no less than their poverty. Neither clergy nor gentry bothered about them. 'If I can do them little good I can at least sympathize with them,' she wrote in 1792. 'The simple idea of being cared for has always appeared to me to be a very cheering one.' To break down their isolation and at the same time to offer a bribe for cleanliness and decency and for the continuous and punctual attendance of the children at school, the sisters organized the annual club and school feasts, the one for club members, the other for the children attending the schools and their parents. To the feasts they invited those of the neighbouring clergy who approved of the schools, and some of the farmers and gentry, and when she had got them safely in her pocket, the 'old bishop', by some alchemy known to her alone, persuaded 'those who are presumptuously and impertinently called their betters' to help wait upon their guests.[9]

The annual feast days of clubs and schools, red-letter days in the Mendip villages, began in 1791, when 517 children and 300 elders picnicked in a 'fine high part of Mendip' and were made happy by as much beef, plum pudding, cakes and loaves and cider as their stomachs would hold. Preparations for the feasts, begun well ahead of the dates fixed for the meetings, provided opportunities for establishing social contacts. With the sisters' help the slatternly women made 'smart linen gowns with new finery', in which to appear. They were encouraged to assist in making garments for the children. 'Buying, contriving, cutting out and carrying through to every individual one or two articles of clothing, is no small job when your family consists of between one and two thousand,'[10] wrote Hannah to Mrs Bouverie. The girls of the schools were Miss More's especial care, 'as the morals of my own sex are the great object of my regard'. Those who after a year of married life could produce a certificate of good behaviour were presented with a Bible, a pair of stockings and five shillings 'as a trifling encouragement to sobriety and virtue'. This was 'the merry part of the feast', when Sally, 'the life and soul of the benefit societies',[11] and the elder women advised the brides how to dispose of their wedding portion, 'some dissuading them from eating it, others counselling expenditure on a teaspoon or a bit of plate'.

At the close of the club meetings Miss More or one of her sisters delivered a 'Charge' commending or condemning individual conduct and behaviour in the past year, urging again cleanliness and decency, and pleading for the application of religious principles to the affairs of everyday life. When occasion demanded, as in the desperate winter of 1801—a year of appalling poverty, when wheat was at famine price and labourers' wages in the neighbourhood of a shilling a day—Miss More did not forget to remind her hearers of the advantages—not easily discernible—which they derived from the generosity of man and the goodness of God:

It is with real concern that I am obliged to touch upon the subject which made part of my address to you last year. You will guess I allude to the continuation of the scarcity. Yet let me remind you that probably that very scarcity has been permitted by an all-wise and gracious Providence to *unite* all ranks of people *together* to show the *poor* how immediately they are dependent upon the *rich*, and show both *rich* and *poor* that they are all dependent on *Himself.* It has also enabled you to see more clearly the advantages you derive from the government and constitution of this country—to observe the benefits flowing from the distinction of rank and fortune, which has enabled the *high* so liberally to assist the *low*: for I leave you to judge what would have been the state of the poor of this country in this long, distressing scarcity had it not been for your superiors. I wish you to understand also that *you* are not the *only* sufferers. You have indeed borne your share, and a very heavy one it has been, in the late difficulties; but it has fallen in some degree on all ranks, nor would the gentry have been able to afford such large supplies to the distresses of the poor had they not denied themselves for your sakes many indulgences to which their fortune at other times entitles them. We trust the poor in general, especially those that are well instructed, have received what has been done for them as a matter of *favour*, not of *right*—if so, the same kindness will, I doubt not, always be extended to them, whenever it shall please God so to afflict the land.[12]

Nothing so poignantly reveals the limitations of Hannah More's mind as her 'Charges' to the women's clubs. The language, offensive as it is to modern ears, may be excused as common form; her paternalism, equally offensive today, was well suited to the needs of the semi-civilized poor in the Mendips, and in no way interfered with the warm and affectionate relations established by the sisters; but the identification of Christianity and social order, based on a fixed belief that the things that be are of God, and must not be questioned by man, involved her in the acceptance of social wrongs incompatible with the religion she professed and with her efforts for social betterment. Nowhere does she appear conscious that conditions such as these constituted a challenge to the followers of Christ.

The technical difficulties which emerged after employers, clergy, and parents had agreed to co-operate provided no easy problem. School housing was an acute embarrassment. No cottage was large enough for a school or weekly reading. None of the well-to-do classes offered a room, nor did they make the barns available as schoolrooms, hence no small part of the funds contributed by Wilberforce, Thornton, Mrs Bouverie, and the sisters was used perforce to build schoolhouses. Far more formidable was the difficulty of finding teachers for the schools. Men and women possessing enough education to teach children to read and instruct them in industrial and domestic work, were not easy to find in the Mendip villages. When to technical qualifications was added the requirement of character strong enough to keep order among hundreds of undisciplined children, and to make a stand against the incessant criticism of and interference by local opponents of the schools, the problem became wellnigh insoluble. Nor was this all. The sisters sought with untiring persistence to find teachers who were not 'merely moral', but were possessed of vital religion and were capable of conveying it to others.

'The grand object of instruction', Hannah told the young John Bowdler, 'is the Bible itself. . . The great thing is to get it faithfully explained, in such a way as shall be likely to touch the heart and influence the conduct.'[13] To help the teachers, Miss More drew up the *Mendip Schools Questions and Catechism*, and regularly on Sundays from May to December, except when the rising waters made travelling impossible, the sisters walked, or rode on horseback behind Charles, the groom, or, when they had guests, used a farm-wagon to convey them to the school whose turn it was for teaching and inspection.[14]

In the morning [wrote Hannah to Wilberforce] I open school with one of the Sunday School prayers from the Cheap Repository Tracts. I have a Bible Class —Testament Class—Psalter Class. Those who cannot read at all are questioned out of the first little *Question Book for the Mendip Schools*. Instructing the Bible or Testament class I always begin with the Parables, which we explain to them in the most familiar manner, one at a time, until they understand that one so perfectly that they are well able to give me back the full sense of it. We begin with the three parables in the fifteenth chapter of Luke, first fixing in their minds the literal sense, and then teaching them to make the practical application. When their understandings are a little exercised, we dwell for a long time on the three first chapters of Genesis, endeavouring from these to establish them in the doctrine of the fall of man. We keep them a good while close to the same subject, making them read the same part so often that the most important texts shall adhere to their memories; because on this knowledge only can I ground my general conversation with them, so as to be intelligible. I also encourage them by little bribes of a penny a chapter, to get by heart certain fundamental parts of Scripture, for instance the promises, prophecies and confessions of sin— such as the 9th of Isaiah, 50th of Isaiah, and 51st Psalm—the beatitudes, and indeed the whole Sermon on the Mount—together with the most striking parts of our Saviour's discourses in the Gospel of St John. It is my grand endeavour to make everything as entertaining as I can, and to try and engage their affections; to excite in them the love of God; and particularly to awaken their gratitude to their Redeemer.

When they seem to get a little tired we change the scene; and by standing up and singing a hymn their attention is relieved. . . Those who attend four Sundays without intermission, and come in time for morning prayer [at Church] receive a penny every fourth Sunday, but if they fail once, the other three Sundays go for nothing. They must begin again. Once in every six weeks I give a little gingerbread. Once a year I distribute little books according to merit— those who deserve most get a Bible; second rate merit gets a Prayer Book; the rest [she added with a pleasing touch of humour] Cheap Repository Tracts.[15]

Marianne Thornton, when staying with the sisters, accompanied them on their Sunday rounds. Morning school and service with the children in Church was followed by 'dinner at some farmer's who was proud to take us in'. When the distance was too great to allow of return in the same day, they were put up at a hospitable farm-house: then school again in the afternoon.

I chiefly recollect Mrs Hannah's or Mrs Patty's eloquent exhortation to the whole school in the most familiar, homely language, full of anecdotes of the people round them as well as of the good people that lived in old times, and full of practical piety brought down into such minute details... How she explained that the fifth commandment enjoined us to do errands for mother not saucily, or lazily, or stupidly...[16]

Cheddar, the first and throughout the sisters' lives the leading school of the circuit—'our University', the sisters called it—reacted in an astounding manner to the ministrations of Mrs Baber, a village schoolmistress, 'who with dauntless breast the little tyrants of her school withstood'. She controlled successfully a week-day school of industry in spite of the practice of avaricious employers to underpay the children for their work; she converted the 'great persecutor' of the school into a friend and supporter, and she frustrated the attempts of the great lady of the nearby hamlet to keep pupils away from school by bribing their parents with a glass of gin. The Sunday school which she opened in 1791 with 100 children had doubled four years later. An evening reading class for older lads and girls totalled 150 in the summer and 200 in the winter months. She kept excellent order, knew all her pupils and their parents, whose differences she settled. She nursed the sick and worked in great harmony with the new curate, Mr Boak, 'a very amiable and active young man'. She taught her children the plain Gospel truths and turned 'this seemingly forgotten people, buried as it were in their own cliffs', into 'an enlightened race'. 'They are now', reported the *Journal* in 1795, 'one large family.' Cheddar under Mrs Baber's control was the ideal school the sisters had envisaged. The *Journal* reports again and again the happiness of the managers in Mrs Baber's success. 'Everything flourishing'. 'Extraordinary progress in family and private prayer'. 'Cheerful, lively, affectionate, serious'. The respect and affection for this unknown village schoolmistress may in some degree be gauged by Patty's letter to Hannah telling her of Mrs Baber's funeral, 'one of the

The Schools

great masterpieces', says a modern critic, 'of macabre literature'.[17]

Monday August 18, 1795.

I took my letter to finish it at Cheddar; but, alas! hurry, grief, and agitation, render it almost impossible for me to write a word; however, I will endeavour to convey to you, that we have just deposited the remains of our excellent Mrs Baber, to mingle with her kindred dust. Who else has ever been so attended, so followed to the grave? Of the hundreds who attended, all had some token of mourning in their dress. All the black gowns in the village were exhibited, and those who had none had *some* broad, *some* little bits of narrow black ribbon, such as their few spare pence could provide. The house, the garden and place before the door was full. But how shall I describe it—not one single voice or step was heard—their very silence was dreadful—but it was not the least affecting part to see their poor little ragged pocket-handkerchiefs, not half sufficient to dry their tears—some had none, and those tears that did not fall to the ground, they wiped off with some part of their dress. When the procession moved off, Mr Boak, who was so good as to come to the very house, preceded the corpse, with his hat-band and gown on, which, as being unusual, added somewhat to the scene; then the *body*; then her sister and myself as chief mourners; a presumptuous title amidst such a weeping multitude—then the gentry two and two—*next*, her children, near two hundred—then all the parish in the same order—and though the stones were rugged, you did not hear one single footstep.

When we came to the outer gate of the churchyard, where all the people used to wait to pay their duty to her by bows and courtesies, we were obliged to halt for Mr Boak to go in and get his surplice on, to receive the corpse with the usual texts. This was too much for every creature, and Mr Boak's voice was nearly lost; when he came to 'I know that my Redeemer liveth', he could scarcely *utter* it; but to feel it, was a better thing. On our entrance into the church, the little remaining sight we had left discovered to us that it was almost full. How we were to be disposed of, I could not tell. I took my old seat with the children, and close by her place. Mr Boak gave us a discourse of thirty-five minutes *entirely* upon the subject. His text was from St John, 'Where I am, there shall also my servant be.' He said he chose it, because it was the last she had made use of to him (I was sitting on her bed at the time)—he added, she looked round her, and observed it was comfortable to have kind friends, but much better to have God with one. . .

When we drew near to the grave, and the last solemn rite was performed . . . everybody threw in their nosegays. I was almost choked. When Robert Reeves, John Marshall, and the six favourites let down the coffin, they stood over it in an attitude never to be described, and exhibited a grief never to be forgotten. They feared at one time Mr Crilling must have been taken out of Church . . .

the children sobbed a suitable hymn over the grave . . . I think almost enough tears were shed to lay the dust. We returned as we went, saving that we had left this 'mother in Israel' behind. When we got the children into the great room . . . I said a great deal as well as I could and I wrung their little hearts; for I knew but too well, that the world and young blood would make an excellent sponge to wipe out, full soon, the awful business of the day. . . Oh! that the rich and great would so live as to be so mourned! So passeth this world away, and so we go on sinning and take no warning.[18]

An experience quite new to the intrepid sisters met them in setting up the second of their 'Great Schools' at Shipham. Its inhabitants to a man were engaged in mining for calamine. More than a hundred mines were in the village itself, others in the yards and some in the very houses. Maton, writing in 1797, described the appearance of the miners popping in and out of their mines as being like that of rabbits from the burrows. In the squalid village there was no big employer of labour to confront and assuage. The miners were independent workers, according to the custom of Mendip. But their independence carried with it, in this decaying industry, precarious conditions. Their profits fluctuated from 5s. to £1 a week and the payment they owed to the lord of the soil varied from a tenth to a quarter of their profits. The life of the Shipham miners was arduous, poor, and squalid.[19] Their ignorance was abysmal. They were notorious among the Somerset peasantry for their grinding poverty and ferocious manners. 'No constable', reported the *Journal*, 'would venture to arrest a Shipham man' lest he should disappear in one of the pits in the hillside and never be heard of more.

The unsavoury reputation of its inhabitants did not deter the sisters, instead it acted as a spur to their courage. They were civilly received but could extract no promise of co-operation from the parents, who suspected that 'we should make our fortunes by selling their children as slaves'. The aged vicar, who lived a long way off and had not preached a sermon at Shipham for forty years and had never been known to catechise the children, agreed reluctantly to repair the old vicarage, derelict for three hundred years, as a schoolhouse. But if the vicar regarded the project of a school with indifference, the curate, later known through the Mendips as Jones of Shipham, greatly respected in his own person and to the joy of the sisters 'truly Evangelical' in his doctrine, was its ardent supporter. A year later, through Hannah's influence, the curate was presented to the living of Shipham. 'We had him secured to our schools,' exclaimed the sisters triumphantly.

Even more difficult at Shipham than at Cheddar was the tedious search for teachers. Mrs Babers did not grow on every blackberry bush. 'Normally', said Miss More in retrospect, 'we found one person in each place who would attempt the work.' At Shipham there was no one. Then, hearing casually that a young dairymaid, better educated than her fellows, 'had raised a little Sunday school' for her neighbours' children, 'we mounted our horses and went in pursuit of the girl,' who became, 'under instruction in our manner of teaching', one of the two mistresses of the school. A boys' school, less well-equipped, was not satisfactory. A succession of dull boys is 'very discouraging', noted Patty in the *Journal*, 'but still they have immortal souls.' By 1796, owing to the devoted work of all concerned, Shipham was a very fine school, a close rival to Cheddar, and, what was 'quite singular', every house in the parish sent children to the school. It was throughout the sisters' lives their very special care.[20]

Nailsea, nine miles south-west of Bristol, the third of the 'Great Schools', was not set up until 1792, when the curious propensity of the London lady for instructing the poor had become well known throughout the countryside. Like Cheddar and Shipham, Nailsea, the *Journal* states, abounded in sin and wickedness, 'the usual consequences of its main industries, glass-making and mining'. Situated in the midst of an almost inpenetrable clearing, its isolation was complete. Here, the farming Heads of the Parish, usually so antagonistic to the schools, welcomed the sisters and volunteered to put up a schoolhouse for them. A clergyman living in the parish blessed the scheme, and the usual fatiguing hunt for teachers began again. Finally, as no one could be found willing or able to act as teacher, the sisters broke with their normal custom and brought in a married couple from Bath, Younge by name, 'well-recommend-ed for religious zeal and industry'. On their visits of inspection the sisters found not only a flourishing school but a flourishing evening reading attended by the 'great boys' of the parish. Nowhere was the friendly relationship existing between the sisters and their pupils more pleasingly shown than at Nailsea. When the boys, for-getting the duty taught them at school of submission to the powers-that-be, marched to Bristol to join the strike of Somerset and Gloucestershire miners to raise their wages from 10s. to 12s. a week, the law-abiding, strike-detesting ladies awaited the return of the prodigals, not with reproach, but with joy at their return.[21] 'It would create a smile', wrote Patty, 'to behold our mutual pleasure on meeting.'

At Nailsea the indefatigable sisters visited the workers in the glass-houses. 'Whatever we had seen before was of a different nature,' says the *Journal*, in a vivid descriptive passage,

and though we had encountered savages, hard-hearted farmers, little cold country gentry, a supercilious Corporation, yet this was still new and unlike all we had imagined. Both sexes and all ages herded together, voluptuous beyond belief. The work of a glass-house is a very irregular thing, uncertain whether by night or day; not only infringing upon a man's rest, but constantly intruding upon the privileges of the Sabbath. The wages high, the eating, and drinking luxurious, the body scarcely covered, but fed with dainties of a shameful descrip-tion. The high building of the glass-house ranged before the door of the cot-tages, the great furnaces roaring—the swearing, eating and drinking of these half-dressed, black-looking beings, gave it a most infernal and horrid appear-ance. One if not two joints of the finest meat were roasting in each of these little hot kitchens, pots of ale standing about and plenty of early, delicate-looking vegetables.

The sisters' escort, 'a gentleman', said Patty politely, 'who being rather personally fearful of these wild savage beings, left us to pur-sue our own devices, which we did by entering and haranguing every separate family.' 'We were', ended this entry in the *Journal*, 'in our usual luck respecting the personal civility which we received even from the worst of these creatures, some welcoming us to "Botany Bay", others to ´Little Hell" as they themselves shockingly called it.' On this first visit the sisters did not talk religion. It would, they sagely remarked, have made 'an indiscreet and unsuccessful beginning'. And so they went back to the glass-houses again, and Patty entered in the *Journal* another vivid description of 'the Black Cyclopian figures and flaming horrible fires', and adds, 'Civilly and kindly received as usual . . . agreeably surprised as well as affected, for every one of these dismal looking beings laid down their tools and immediately surrounded us, speaking in the civillest terms.' Eighteen of the boys promised faithfully to attend the evening reading at the school to hear the Bible read and expounded.

This happy state of affairs was disturbed by a violent quarrel between Younge, the Nailsea schoolmaster, and the Heads of the Parish, whose children attended the school. The sisters, always steady champions of their underlings, inquired what complaint the farmers had against the schoolmaster. Nothing, they replied, against his industry or his character, nevertheless 'they begged us to be so good as to remove him.' The sisters flatly refused: they warned the farmers not to obstruct the new schoolmaster in his work, and retired. When the farmers persisted in their enmity, the Mores in 1795 reluctantly closed the day-school, 'the people being unworthy of it', removed Younge to the new school at Blagdon, and appointed a poor collier as a make-shift master of the Nailsea Sunday school. 'It is our business', remarked Patty lugubriously, 'to swallow great doses and go on.' A year later the success of the collier lad, a remarkable young man, moved the proud farmers to request the re-opening of the day-school under his care. They offered to subscribe to his wages. This in itself was unusual, for though in the Mendips the vocation of coal-mining does not appear to have carried with it the loss of caste which characterized the industry elsewhere, the farmers regarded themselves as a 'race' superior to the miners.[22] Yet the Nailsea farmers preferred an ignorant collier lad to the Mores' highly qualified teacher from Bath. Swallowing another bitter dose the sisters re-opened the school in 1796. 'It is astonishing', remarked Patty with undisguised annoyance, 'that these sages who persecuted a very able master should now consent to a poor collier as the instructor of their children.' Later, with her characteristic candour, she admitted that 'the stupid Heads of Nailsea' had in this case been wise, for no school of the circuit excelled as did Nailsea under the tutelage of the young collier and the two cronies who assisted him. 'Nailsea', the *Journal* reported in 1798, 'gives us the least trouble of all.' 'This extraordinary school flourishes remarkably.'

The 'lesser schools', so called because they were small in size and functioned only as Sunday schools and evening readings, offered less spectacular success than the three 'Great Schools'. They suffered in a marked degree from the usual embarrassments: opposition of gentry and farmers, indifference of the beneficed clergy and the perennial difficulty of finding competent teachers. 'The worst of our business', wrote Hannah in some dejection of spirit, 'is that having so many places, and all at a good distance from each other, to look after, when all goes smoothly in one place something breaks out in another, and hinders the instruction of the children and their parents.'[23] Sandford, a water-logged hamlet in Wrington parish, began well in 1791. Sixty children met on Sunday in the schoolmistress's cottage, and a reading class for older boys and girls was held once a week, but the shattered health of its mistress and the failure to find a successor brought the school to an end in 1791. Banwell's schoolmistress in the same parish struggled against the opposition of 'the rich, frigid farmers so hostile to us'. No one could be found to take any interest in Banwell at any time. In 1799, when the schoolmistress left the parish, the sisters put an end to the school and transferred the well-disposed pupils to Shipham. Congresbury and Yatton differed from the majority of the schools in the mixture of classes in attendance. At Congresbury 'what is called gentlemen-farmers', reports the *Journal* contemptuously, sent their children to be instructed with the very poor. Here the teaching problem was met by taking over a pay-school in the neighbourhood—'we had no alternative'—run by a schoolmaster and his wife whose knowledge the sisters suspected was 'very moderate', and whose spiritual gifts were even less. 'Two stones, who increased in hardness', the mordant Patty called them. Under them the children made no progress. After three years' continuous work they were still in the fifth chapter of Genesis. 'This', she adds, with dry humour, 'is proof of perseverance not despair.' 'Poor Congresbury', the sisters lament in 1797. The pupils steadily dwindled in number and when the schoolmaster, 'an old rogue', was guilty of some unnamed 'atrocious action', the sisters put an end to the school.

An unusual welcome met them from the curate, gentry, farmers, and village people at Yatton. The bells were set ringing when the sisters appeared, the gentry and clergy agreed to do their duty by the school, attending it on alternate Sundays and collecting money to clothe the children. But the 'respected village woman' and the 'two decent men' appointed as teachers failed to play their part. The school steadily decreased in numbers, and 'aversion to religion' increased. In 1800 the sisters reluctantly decided to transfer the money and time spent on the Yatton school to a new school at Chew Magna, 'populous, ignorant, and wicked, three pretty substantial reasons for fixing there'.

Axbridge, a few miles from Cheddar, was the only urban school of the circuit: 'an old beggarly town', was the Mores' succinct description. An ancient, 'unfeeling hard-hearted Corporation' spent the town's money in riotous living, surrounded by half-starved adults and by children, 'poor, little, dirty, wretched'. How to begin in such a place to canvass for a school puzzled the sisters. The incumbent, 'intoxicated about six times a week', was civil but uninterested, the Corporation good-natured but indifferent, the townsfolk solidly unfavourable. Only the presence of the good Mr Boak, curate of Cheddar, in the town emboldened them to open a school in 1791. Two 'moral teachers' were appointed. Under their care the children at first came on capitally. The school, notes the *Journal* in 1792, is 'a good school'. They pray for 'a couple of spiritual teachers'. But in 1793 the boys were reported as 'dumb in spiritual things'. By 1794 the teachers were no longer careful of the children's morals, and in 1796 Boak dismissed the 'deplorable teachers'. Even the good work of the new schoolmistress, Mrs Carrol, later denounced as a woman of 'rank Methodist principles', who worked a reformation in cleanliness and decency and collected a large evening reading, could not save Axbridge school. Violent opposition of the great folk to the evening reading forced the sisters in 1799 to suspend the school and to transfer the schoolmistress to the new school at Wedmore.

The controversy which blasted the plans of the sisters, and made them the objects of calumny throughout the Kingdom, began in Wedmore, the last of the schools to be set up. Situated fifteen miles from Barley Wood, it was the largest and most populous parish in the diocese. The village people clamoured for a school, the curate and other religious friends supported them; but the sisters were reluctant to commit themselves to a project larger and more remote than anything they had previously undertaken. 'Time, distance, money, health rushed in upon our minds and served to render it impracticable.' When, however, the shocking accounts of the wickedness of Wedmore incited them to take action, they met with violent opposition from the farmers. 'The poor', declared the forbidding wife of the big man of the village, 'were intended to be servants and slaves'; it was 'preordained that they should be ignorant.' 'We cannot alter what is decreed,' she stormed; 'the lordly savage', her husband, added with a fine disregard for logic, 'If a school were set up it would be all over with property, and if property is not to rule what is to become of us?' 'The day a school was opened there would be the beginning of such rebellion in England as had taken place in Ireland and France.' 'It was very affecting', wrote Hannah, 'to see the poor standing trembling behind [when he vented his rage], lest the project should fail.' Fearing lest the villagers might be imprudently inflamed against the farmer and his property, and determined that they should have their school, the sisters, with their usual courage, took prompt action. They set up a school, appointed a schoolmaster, and gave instructions for the building of a large schoolhouse. But they were uneasy in their minds. During the summer months their anxiety increased. The schoolmaster, Harvard by name, though a worthy man was not discreet; when provoked he said strong things in return, 'so that there was a prodigious soreness against him'. The Heads of the Parish began to set him at defiance. At the end of the summer they presented a petition 'of the most impudent description' against the sisters to the Dean of Wells, in whose jurisdiction Wedmore, a peculiar, lay. They charged the schoolmaster with calling the bishops 'dumb dogs', with threatening all who did not come to school with hell fire, and with distributing books called *A Guide to Methodism.* Hannah was, at last, obliged to write letters to Dr Moss and other high powers for permission to go 'twenty-eight miles of a Sunday to instruct their poor and spend £70 a year on them'. As a compromise solution of the quarrel the schoolmaster was withdrawn, and when Axbridge school was suspended the schoolmistress was appointed to Wedmore in the hope that female influence 'might soften these barbarians'. 'Poor dwindling Wedmore,' runs a last entry in the *Journal* for 1800, 'the parish is as depraved and shocking as ever.'

Blagdon School, on the northern slopes of the Mendips, may best be considered out of the chronological order of its foundation. It was financed by Henry Thornton and was set up by the sisters in 1795 in response to a deputation of the curate, Mr Bere, and churchwardens, who waited on Miss More at Cowslip Green. They wanted, they said, to be reformed, like Cheddar. Notorious as Blagdon was throughout the countryside for crime and litigation, the recent sentence of death by hanging passed on a woman for attempting to riot and purloining butter, offered for sale at a price she thought unreasonable, had caused a wave of hysteria throughout the parish. The deputation begged the sisters to come and do them a little good. Had the deputation been less solemn 'it would have been almost ridiculous,' wrote Patty. 'A six-foot giant implored us, with particular eagerness, to come. There were, he said, places in the parish where he was personally afraid to go. It was here', she remarked with acid humour, that 'he wished to send two nervous women.' The school was opened in the autumn of 1795, when a ragged banditti of 170 young persons from eleven to twenty-one years gathered at the church to meet the sisters. 'As I was coming out of the church', wrote Hannah to Wilberforce, 'some musical gentleman, drawn from a distance by curiosity . . . struck up quite unexpectedly that beautiful anthem "Inasmuch as ye have done it to one of the least of these ye have done it unto Me." '[25]

Never had a school a more promising beginning. Clergy, churchwardens, and villagers were of one mind in desiring a school. The sisters had heroically responded and the work was crowned by the appointment of their cherished schoolmaster Younge, late of Nailsea. Unlike other smaller schools of the circuit, Blagdon offered to lads of the superior poor who attended the school instruction in the three Rs, to fit them to become overseers, constables, jurymen, farmers, and tradesmen. 'Everything augurs well,' reported the *Journal* after the three visits of the sisters in 1795. 'Blagdon full and flourishing', was the entry for the summer of 1796. The school and Sunday reading introduced by the curate in 1797 'prospered beyond our hopes'. Not a single man or woman from Blagdon, formerly notorious for crime, appeared at the last assizes and quarter sessions. 'Even pilfering was quite out of fashion.'

But in 1798 a curious incident happened. Bere, the curate of Blagdon and a Justice of the Peace, preached a sermon at Axbridge against the school and, it was alleged, against the Trinity, which flung Blagdon parish into confusion. The number of pupils dropped from two hundred to thirty-five. The sisters, greatly perturbed, hurried to Blagdon and threatened to remove the school if parents and children did not pull themselves together and support it. Peace was restored, but 'Satan was busy.' Malicious tales grew and spread rapidly against the schoolmaster. In 1800 came a violent explosion, long pent up. The curate 'no longer concealed the cloven foot'. In 'an impudent letter' to Miss More he demanded the instant dismissal of the schoolmaster. The sisters, away in London, referred the matter to Sir Abraham Elton, a neighbouring J.P., and asked him to investigate the charges against the schoolmaster. The *Journal* ends abruptly a few pages after this entry.

CHAPTER VIII

THE BLAGDON CONTROVERSY

'This She-Bishop and her dangerous institutions.'
E. Spencer

(i)

THE Blagdon Controversy was a *cause célèbre* in the early years of the nineteenth century. From 1800 to 1803 twenty-three pamphlets were published on one side or the other;[1] the local papers gave tongue, the London monthlies and quarterlies took up the cry, and for three successive years the *Anti-Jacobin Review* seldom missed an issue in its attack on Hannah More. As the Controversy developed, criticism of her work and of herself became more scurrilous and outrageous. It would be difficult to find a dispute, even in an age which indulged in disputes, comparable in virulence and lack of common decency to the Blagdon controversy.

The ostensible cause of the controversy was the quarrel between the curate and the schoolmaster of Blagdon. The real issue behind this unimportant quarrel was whether the lower orders should be educated at all, and, if so, by whom. Neither of these was a new problem. They had marked the establishment of charity schools in the early half of the eighteenth century, and had held their place in religious controversy since. The Sunday school movement, which, as an organized movement, dated from Robert Raikes's seminal work in Gloucester in 1780, brought the question again to the fore. After a remarkable beginning as an undenominational effort it came under suspicion, during the years of repression, as a radical, subversive, and Jacobinical movement. Opposition to schools for the poor was still based on social and economic grounds. They would unfit the poor for their functions as hewers of wood and drawers of water. At the end of the century the charge of disseminating heterodox religious and political opinions provided a new ground of opposition, which threatened to call a halt to the Sunday school movement. 'Schools of Jacobinical politics abound in this country,' said Dr Samuel Horsley, Bishop of Rochester, in his 'Charge' to the clergy of his diocese in 1800. 'In them the minds of many of the lowest orders are taught to despise religion and the laws of subordination.' The antidote to the poison of Jacobinical schools, he declared, was the establishment of schools for the same class of children under the management of the parochial clergy. 'Sunday schools must be under clerical inspection and control.'³ The Blagdon Controversy affords a rare opportunity for examining a cross-section of public opinion on the education of the poor during the years of the Great War.

In 1800 Bere, the curate of Blagdon, a Justice of the Peace and an effective penman, published in support of his demand for the schoolmaster's dismissal the voluminous correspondence of the protagonists in this village drama: a schoolmaster of alleged Methodistical enthusiasm, a curate smeared with Socinianism, an absentee rector, an enfeebled diocesan, a hot-headed and far from impartial Justice of the Peace, and an imperious old bishop in petticoats, accustomed to command, convinced, not without justice, of the excellence of her schools, and strongly objecting to criticism of her underlings. The curate alleged that the schoolmaster had turned the evening reading into a 'private' unlicensed conventicle—a chargeable offence—in which he disseminated fiery Calvinistic doctrines at variance with those of the Church of England. He had adopted the class discipline of the Methodists, encouraged his pupils to indulge in extempore prayer, questioned them on their spiritual experiences, and, in addition, had traduced the curate's character. Nor did his charge end here. Miss More, he held, had acted with a lack of candour in sending Younge to Blagdon when he had previously behaved himself in a reprehensible manner at Nailsea. She had refused to discuss the curate's objections and, using her great influence, had taken the matter over his head to Dr Moss, the Bishop of Bath and Wells. 'To protect her teacher Miss More had attached her establishment to the man. I want to detach the man from her establishment.'[4]

Here was a strong case, well put, and the aged diocesan, after laboriously studying the evidence against the schoolmaster, requested Miss More to remove him. Her compliance did not end the quarrel. The curate's conduct in handling the affair confused the issues. He had, said the schoolmaster's party, called witnesses to testify against Younge, whose credibility could not be accepted. Furthermore, he had, as Justice of the Peace, taken the *affidavits* in his own cause and, ignoring the first principle of justice, he had not called the accused to answer his accusers. Pressed by the Chancellor of the diocese to meet the clamours aroused by his conduct, he agreed to re-swear the witnesses in the presence of the most respectable gentlemen in the neighbourhood; and proceeded to pack a meeting with his friends among the local gentry and clergy, who without any vestige of authority pronounced judgement in his favour, and denounced the schoolmaster and the school. Miss More immediately closed the school. Flushed with victory, the curate illuminated the rectory, rang the church bells, and remarked jubilantly, 'The Church has carried it.' Shocked by this unseemly behaviour, the Bishop of Bath and Wells requested the rector to dismiss the curate and asked Miss More to re-open the school. It reassembled in January 1801.

The curate now replaced the schoolmaster as the victim of ecclesiastical tyranny. Denying as stoutly as did the schoolmaster the charges made against him, he defied the rector and the Chancellor to show that he had been guilty of any offence against morality or ecclesiastical law. After long and embittered correspondence he won his points. There was no case against him. He retained his curacy, and as he maintained his hostility to the school, Miss More again dissolved it.

The curate's victory added fuel to the fire. Rumour insisted that Miss More's hidden hand was behind the attempt to get rid of him, and with redoubled fury the curate's party led an attack on her schools, her religious principles, and her personal character. Miss

The Blagdon Controversy

More's supporters replied in language not less unmeasured. So bitter was the partisanship that 'the charities and courtesies of social life were suspended.' Opponents in the controversy could not safely be invited to meet at the same table. In Blagdon village there was no more peace. Bills posted at the turnpike directed visitors to 'the menagerie of five female savages of the most desperate kind' who had 'wounded a black bear with a poisoned dart while he was guarding his young ones'.[5] Bere's pamphlet was answered by one, equally acrimonious, by Elton,[6] and it, in its turn, by an anonymous layman.[7] Nine resident clergy of five parishes in which Miss More had set up schools, rushed into the fray and testified in their 'Statement of Facts Relative to Miss More's Schools'—a contribution based on ascertainable facts—that the schools were conducted with meticulous care, were subject to the inspection and control of the clergy of the parish, who selected the teachers, and that 'universally beneficial effects flow from them.'[8] The 'Ninepins', as he contemptuously called them, were knocked down by one Edward Spencer of Wells in one of the most scurrilous of the pamphlets. He insisted, in his *Truth respecting Miss More's Meeting Houses*, that only in those parishes whose clergy were in 'the vortex of the She-Bishop's petticoats' did their statements hold true. Events had shown beyond dispute that the schools were not properly conducted. Why else, he pertinently asked, were they withdrawn from Banwell, Yatton, Congresbury, Axbridge, and Blagdon? Teachers such as Younge, Mrs Carrol, and Harvard, appointed by Miss More, were well known as rank enthusiasts. They worshipped with Methodists and encouraged Methodism, which had now assumed formidable proportions in the district. In Wedmore alone the number of Methodists had increased from 30 in 1799, when the school was set up, to 300 in 1801.

An attack on the 'She-Bishop' followed. She had changed, he alleged, Robert Raikes's admirable idea for the instruction of children into the most powerful engine of sectarianism. Her conduct had shown that she was a woman without principles. She professed to be a pillar of the Church yet she not only supported

Methodism but had several times attended and communicated at Jay's Dissenting chapel at Bath. She was out for power; 'the ramifications of her scheme were yet to be developed,' and he solemnly warned his readers that 'the anniversary meetings of fanatic sectaries on the peak of a mountain' would terminate in Jacobin assemblies. Finally descending from the hill-tops to the gutter, he alleged immoral conduct on the part of Miss More's Sunday school teachers and of the lads and girls attending the evening seminaries. He recalled to his readers that several dames of Miss More's large and fashionable school at Bristol had earned unenviable notoriety in public life, and that Hannah More herself in her youth 'had not kept her mind in temperance, sobriety, and chastity'.[9]

On these, and other pamphlets, the London reviews and their correspondents played their heavy guns for three years. Rumour supplemented their laboured articles. It charged Hannah More with spreading Jacobinical principles, with praying in the schools for the success of the French, and with fanatical attempts to overthrow the Church. Ridiculous as were these and kindred allegations, they aroused the anxiety of her friends, the Bishop of London among them, for charges of disaffection based on evidence less flimsy were not unknown in the age of repression. They urged her to reply to her traducers, and Lord Chancellor Loughborough advised her to take legal action.[10] She flatly refused to make public reply, or to budge from Cowslip Green. Even when Bishop Porteus, in a note as ambiguous as it was alarming, informed the sisters by special messenger that Hannah was 'in grave danger',[11] she kept a stiff upper lip and offered neither explanation nor excuse. But her letters make clear that she was badly shaken by the malignity of a seemingly endless spate of abuse. 'I have prayed earnestly', she wrote to Wilberforce, 'but I cannot command my nerves, and though pretty well during the bustle of the day I get such disturbed and agitated nights that I cannot answer for my lasting if the thing were to go on much longer.'[12]

It became apparent in 1802 that the storm was wearing itself out. Hannah More's detractors had overshot the mark when they dragged her personal character into the controversy. One of the last of the pamphlets written against her, the *Life of Mrs Hannah More* by the Reverend William Shaw, Rector of Chelvey, tried and failed to revive the controversy. Public interest was abating. The Bishop of Rochester, watch-dog of the schools, expressed his surprise at a London dinner-party that anyone could have given credence to Bere's allegations against Miss More;[14] the *Anti-Jacobin Review* piped down, and in 1802 the appointment of Dr Richard Beadon to the see of Bath and Wells drew the remaining teeth of the opposition. To him in a full, clear, and balanced statement she presented her case. The charge of intrusion she denied. 'Not one school have I ever attempted to establish without the hearty concurrence of the clergyman.' That she had introduced Methodism into the schools she rebutted with vigour. She admitted that she had mistaken the instruments she employed, but asserted that her greatest mistake, obvious only *after* the event, was that 'I did not instantly dismiss Younge. I grant that it would have saved me infinite distress but I not only thought myself bound to protect an innocent man, whom I still consider to have been falsely accused, but I was convinced that, as the event proved, the object in view was not merely to ruin *him*, but to strike at the principle of all my schools and to stigmatize them as the seminaries of fanaticism, vice, and sedition.' She pleaded that the enthusiasm of teachers and pupils charged with Methodism was but 'the coarse way' in which illiterates, when they have become religious, express themselves. That which appears to be enthusiasm is 'only vulgarity or quaintness', and she made a bold bid for Bishop Beadon's sympathy when she added 'I am persuaded your Lordship will allow that this does not furnish a reason why the poor should be left destitute of religious instruction. . . If the possibility that a *few might* become enthusiasts should be proved, could that be justly pleaded as an argument for giving them all up to actual vice and barbarism?'

With becoming restraint she dealt briefly with the charges directed against herself. She denied ever having attended a Methodist conventicle, expressed her detestation of Calvinism and challenged his lordship to find a single Calvinistic passage in any of her writings. She admitted attendance at William Jay's chapel in Bath, and acknowledged that on one occasion, nine or ten years earlier, she had remained to receive the Holy Communion at his hands, a 'single irregularity which I regretted, and never repeated'. She ended by asking her diocesan if he would inform her whether he wished her to continue or dismiss the remaining schools.[15] 'I wanted no declaration or evidence of either your faith or your patriotism,' he replied, promising her every protection and encouragement for her schools; 'I can only say that if you are not a sincere and zealous friend to the constitutional establishment both in Church and State you are one of the greatest hypocrites as well as one of the best writers in His Majesty's dominions.'[16]

(ii)

Bishop Beadon's acceptance of Hannah More's vindication does not offer an explanation of the virulent animosity shown to Miss More in the Blagdon Controversy. Some of it was the honest expression of those who believed that she was a Methodist or Dissenter and as such should not be entrusted with the care of parish schools. To them Methodism was an enemy to the state-ecclesiastical; it was a third column operating within the country when an apparently invincible military power prepared an invasion at its leisure. They did not realize that Methodism was an antidote to Jacobinism. Some of the animosity may be ascribed to the reprehensible tendency of eighteenth-century publicists to pull down rather than to build up the reputation of contemporary public figures;[17] some of it to the growing imperiousness from which the high-minded and competent not seldom suffer when confronted by ignorant and pig-headed opponents. Hannah More's tact, one of her leading characteristics, failed her more than once in the Controversy, and the failure left a legacy of unconcealed bitterness.[18]

But the 'persecution', as her friends called it, though distorted by the intrusion of personal antipathies, cannot be explained in terms of personalities. Hannah More was attacked because she represented, during the years of the prolonged war of nerves, two unpopular concepts, 'a calumniated religion' and a radical innovation, each of which was a challenge to her age. The one was an implied criticism of the lives and religion of orthodox clergy and laymen, deeply resented by them, the other was an open challenge to the monopoly exercised by the big farmers and little gentry over the bodies and souls of the children of the rural poor. This was the background, often forgotten, sometimes obscure, to the bitter Blagdon Controversy.

Two main issues emerge from the spate of indictment and counter-indictment, those of 'Methody' and 'intrusion'. Was Miss More a Methodist? Were her schools Methodist schools? Had she established them with or without the consent of the clergy in whose parishes the schools were set up? Miss More insisted that she was not a Methodist,[19] and that her schools were not Methodist institutions. The *British Critic*, most influential of reviews, supported her. The *Anti-Jacobin Review* opposed her. Tolerant of Roman Catholics and Dissenters, she was not tolerant of Methodists and Methodism. 'I dread it,' 'Call me not a Methodist,' were recurring themes in her letters. In the Mendips, remote and neglected by the Church, Methodism was strong. It put up steady opposition to Miss More's schools as rivals to the Methodist meeting. 'They are more enflamed against me than the High Church bigots.' She complained not once but several times of Methodist interference and stated bluntly in a letter to John Bowdler: 'It has been my avowed object to counteract the Methodists, they are the enemies of my schools.'[20]

The seemingly illogical charge of Methodism made against a convinced opponent of Methodism rests in part on the difficulty of defining terms in the years under discussion. 'Methodism' at the time was a measure of enthusiasm, not a doctrinal term capable of definition. The clear-cut distinction between Methodist and Evangelical accepted in later times was not then in common use, as contemporary writing testifies. To some publicists, Sydney Smith among them, there was no difference: a Methodist was an enthusiast outside the Church, an Evangelical an enthusiast within the Church. Anyone, said an ingenious correspondent of the *Christian Observer* who had collected over one hundred meanings given to the term Methodism, thirty-three of which were in daily use, was dubbed a Methodist who carried his religion into practice.[21] Hannah More's untiring advocacy of piety and holiness appeared not seldom, even in the eyes of the most staunch of her friends, 'Methodistical'. Her devoted allegiance to the Anglican Church they sometimes forgot. Conscious of the dangers to which Evangelicals were exposed, she endeavoured to conduct herself as Orthodoxy demanded, but it was not easy to confine vital religion within prescribed limits or to maintain the fiction of an exemplary clergy, which she had assiduously cultivated in her Tracts, when they exasperated her in the flesh.

As the schools increased in number, the perennial difficulty of staffing added to her embarrassments. The qualifications she demanded, good conduct, ability to teach, and vital religion, were so difficult to find in combination that she was driven across the border line separating Methodist from Evangelical to secure the teachers she required. Wilberforce's advice was sought early on this acute problem. Steadfastly regarding the Methodists as Churchmen, he replied, 'Send for a comet. Whiston had them at his command and John Wesley is not unprovided'.[22] Miss More's biographer insists that this advice was not followed. But the *Journal* reports as early as 1791 that Miss More appointed a new assistant teacher at Cheddar and remarked, with apparent misgiving, 'I am afraid she must be called a Methodist.'[23] Her letters disclose that she knew Harvard was a Methodist and it seems improbable that she was unaware that Younge and Mrs Carrol were at least predisposed to Methodism.

Again, finding that communal singing was a counter-attraction offered by the Methodist meeting, she deliberately taught her pupils to sing psalms, so as to combat the Methodists with their own weapons, and, on occasion, instead of the church singers chanting Sternhold and Hopkins, 'Heaven was won by violence of song' when the children were allowed to sing in church, an innovation as much enjoyed by them as it was displeasing to the orthodox clergy, gentry, and farmers. As for the church singers, they were 'sorely affronted' and reinforced the growing army of Miss More's critics.

Further, and it is the main consideration, Miss More, early in the history of the schools, was faced by the crying need for adult education. 'We were struck', says the *Journal* in 1791, 'with an idea of at least attempting to teach the parents of these children, by reading a chapter and a sermon to them on Sunday evenings, to sing a psalm and read a prayer.'[24] The suggestion was warmly welcomed, and was not confined to parents and Sunday evenings. Week-night readings for adults rapidly appeared. But the plan for adult education was neither as safe nor as simple as it seemed. 'Surely', wrote Hannah to Patty from London after giving the matter 'sober and careful consideration', 'no harm can arise from giving leave to parents as desire to come in the evenings to be instructed themselves.'[25] But surely, in the opinion of orthodox clerics and laymen, much harm could come from a device so closely akin to the Methodist class. The sisters took the risk and suffered the consequences, for the *gravamen* of the charge of Methodism made against Hannah More rests on this point. Not the schools, whose curriculum and methods were carefully prescribed in her *Hints for the Schools*, and whose inspection was carried out with meticulous care, but the evening readings, seldom inspected by the sisters because of the difficulty of night travel, were suspect of Methody. Wedmore and Blagdon supplied her critics with indictments based on chapter and verse. The clergy and churchwardens at Wedmore, the curate and his supporters at Blagdon, asserted that the adult evening 'private' schools had assumed the character and privileges of licensed conventicles without the licence. In them Methody was rife. Extempore prayer, interrogation into spiritual concerns, singing hymns and reading sermons '*not* wrote by the clergy of the Church of England', and the teaching of 'fiery Calvinistic doctrines' by men who boldly proclaimed themselves to be Calvinists were alleged against them. These 'Methodists within the Church in conjunction with Methodists outside the Church, led by the She-Bishop and her institutions, were consolidating their power to destroy the Church.'[26] The only way to convince her opponents of her loyalty to the Church would have been to dismiss her suspected teachers. This she did not do.

The question of 'intrusion'[27] raised a point no less open to censure. Hannah More's desire was to make the schools auxiliaries to the Church. The schoolhouses, whenever possible, were built near the Church, and church-attendance was part of the appropriate discipline. As an Anglican she was aware that the permission and co-operation of the parish clergy was a first essential. There is ample evidence to attest her efforts to secure their help, and of her success, especially with the subalterns. Her conduct, however, at Wedmore and possibly elsewhere played into the hands of her critics. When Eyre, the curate, had given permission to establish the school, Miss More appeared in the parish with two 'extra-parochial' clergy as her assistants.[27] The curate was ignored. His suggestion for a schoolmaster was set aside as unsuitable and Harvard, Miss More's nominee, later admitted by Miss More to have been one of Wesley's preachers, was appointed schoolmaster in a parish which, said Miss More in exasperation 'would prefer a Mahometan to a Methodist'. Eyre refused to testify with the 'Ninepins' that Wedmore school was under the control of the parish clergy; instead he joined his vicar and churchwardens in a request to the Dean of Wells that Miss More's school, a 'meeting place for people who were not respectful to the regular ministry of the Church', should be closed. There were strong reasons why at Wedmore, a large parish with a bad character, neglected by its absentee rector and ineffective curate, extra-parochial assistance was needed. Technically it was not intrusion, but the action aroused vehement opposition.

Seen in retrospect the punishment meted out to Hannah More and her sisters, for they shared the contumely showered upon her, was cruel and undeserved. It may be explained, though not excused, by the vehemence of public feeling during the long-drawn-out war of nerves. 'Parties' or individuals whose conduct was open to suspicion of disloyalty to Church and State received no mercy. Hannah More, a Tory who championed the radical causes of anti-slavery and the education of the poor, a Churchwoman who attended a Dissenting Meeting House and employed Methodist teachers, was an easy target for vituperation and abuse.

CHAPTER IX

THE MAKING OF MANY BOOKS

'*I, of all people, ought not to find fault with authors for writing too much.*'

Hannah More: Letter to Daniel Wilson

(i)

ALTHOUGH the storm did not at once die down, the championship of the new Bishop of Bath and Wells, the moderated tone of the *Anti-Jacobin Review*, and the vulgar but effective pamphlet written against Bere by Miss More's neighbour, the Reverend Septimus Whalley,[1] ended the controversy in Hannah More's favour. But at the cost of intense humiliation, broken nerves, and, more distressing to her than either, the conviction of God's displeasure. To a woman of her religious views the humiliation she had suffered could be explained only as an expression of his anger. Puzzled, as the pages of her Diary for 1803 reveal, to find a reason why she, who had in great measure left the world to serve God, and had 'laboured to assist others to the knowledge of his truth', had been so severely punished, she, in George Herbert's words, 'dressed and undressed her soul' night and day to discover her wrong-doing. She found it in her old weakness, 'though I did not then know it'—too great an appreciation of human esteem, too little humility of heart, too little resignation to God's will. 'I hoped I had learnt to value praise and reputation only as an instrument of usefulness.' It was characteristic of her courage and honesty that, when she believed she had discovered the reason for her suffering, she rededicated herself to God's service. 'Grant that I may not be content in *saying* this,' she prayed; 'do thou enable me to *do* it.' Acceptance of 'God's trials of my health and fame' gave her eventually the serenity of mind, and the spiritual assurance of his love which crowned the Evangelical profession of faith. 'I have had a life of so much prosperity that I needed powerful correction.'[2]

Ill health had dogged her from childhood. Chronic asthma had not been improved by twelve years' supervision of schools many miles distant from one another, in all sorts and conditions of weather, nor by the nervous strain of the years of controversy. In 1801 the sisters, closing their ranks, decided to leave Bath and join Hannah in building a commodious and charming house at Barley Wood in Wrington Parish, with views of vale and hills, to accommodate the five sisters. They were of one mind in their desire to retire from the world and to devote the remaining years of their lives to the care of the poor and to reading and reflection. They envisaged a life of retirement undisturbed by contacts with the world. 'We could not more be royal,' said Hannah drily; 'we give no invitations and we pay no calls.'

'Battered, hacked, scalped, tomahawked', discouraged by the failure of her schools and prevented by ill health from leaving the house in the cold and wet, she was averse from effort of any kind. 'I used to watch for all occasions for introducing useful subjects,' records the Diary for 1803. 'I am now backward to do it from the idea that all I say may be called enthusiasm—alas, I know not how to act. Lord, direct me by thy spirit'; and again, 'I fear that I am become more intent on reading Scripture and cultivating retirement than willing to advance others. I have hitherto erred on the other side. The danger now is lest the slanders I have met with should drive me into too much caution and silence.'[3]

But a nature both resilient and courageous does not easily succumb. Doubts of her future usefulness were quashed not only by the insistent and flattering requests from her army of admirers for her writings, but by a slowly growing assurance of God's love and approbation. 'I have a comfortable evidence', she wrote in 1804, 'of growth in grace.'[4]

During the twenty-five years of her life at Barley Wood Hannah More produced a series of books, essays, ballads, and tracts which made her name even more widely known among all classes of society and in far distant lands. She had found a public which would greedily devour anything she wrote. Friends and strangers united in demanding books from her pen and publishers clamoured for the privilege of producing them. Her only claim to fame, she remarked cheerfully in her old age, was that she had written eleven books after she was sixty. As a voracious reader of English classics in her younger days she did not lack literary standards. She was well aware of her shortcomings as a scholar and a writer. 'To what is called learning I have never had any pretence,' she said, and the remarkable public response embarrassed her. 'I am almost ashamed to tell you that I have made over £30,000 by my books.'[5]

The Blagdon Controversy, these publications bear witness, did nothing to reduce her activity, nor did it modify her religious convictions. None the less it disciplined her conduct and tempered the austerity of her methods. After Bishop Porteus's gentle reprimand that it would have been better if she had not received Holy Communion in a Dissenting Chapel, she restrained her unorthodox freedom of action and broke off her 'worshipping intercourse' with Nonconformists, endeavouring by spiritual self-denial, 'which I find the most trying of all self-denial',[6] to remove a cause of offence to friends dear to her and generous to her charities.

In 1805 an urgent appeal from Dr Robert Gray,[7] Prebendary of Durham, who had known her in her Bristol days, acted as a trumpet call to a weary war-horse. He convinced her that she alone could prepare a guide for the education of the heir-presumptive to the throne, whose disastrous upbringing was becoming a matter of profound concern to the nation. She would repent it on her deathbed, he assured her, if she did not do so. The loyal elderly lady, sharing the extravagant public admiration for the King which made George III, after his illness, the most popular man in England, and abounding in sympathetic admiration for his efforts to provide a fitting education for his grand-daughter, responded immediately and produced in 1805, in her usual unscholarly haste, her *Hints towards forming the Character of a Young Princess*.[8]

It was a book in the grand tradition of royal pedagogics, follow-

ing in the footsteps of Archbishop Fénelon's *Telemachus*, which had
been devoted to the education of Louis XIV's grandson and heir,
the Duke of Burgundy. Published anonymously, it was soon
known that 'the celebrated Miss Hannah More' was responsible for
one of the last of such tracts written for the instruction of royalty.
   The young princess, the preface made clear, was Charlotte
Augusta, daughter of George Prince of Wales and his wife Caroline
of Brunswick. All the world knew that the natural guardians of this
important and neglected child were a dissolute father, an indecor-
ous if not wanton mother, and a mentally unstable grandfather at
loggerheads with his son. From babyhood to her ninth year in 1805
the child had lived apart from her parents under the care of her
governess, the easy-going Lady Elgin, and a succession of sub-
governesses and attendants. Early in 1804, when the princess was
approaching her ninth birthday, her father and grandfather, who
had been on acrimonious terms for years, agreed upon a plan of
education. Lady Elgin resigned and Dr John Fisher, Bishop of
Exeter, an ecclesiastic of High Tory principles, considerable learning, and uncertain temper, was appointed preceptor-in-chief with
two sub-preceptors to assist him. The feminine subjects of the curriculum and the care of the princess's conduct were entrusted to the
kind but fussy Lady de Clifford, assisted by two sub-governesses
and a host of art, music, and dancing masters. While the *entourage*
was assembling, Hannah More finished the *Hints* and dedicated it
with respectful compliments to the Bishop of Exeter. He accepted
it with gratitude, informing Bishop Jebb of Limerick that he had
gained from it more information on the subject of his duties than
he had received in all his other reading.[9] Copies of the book were
presented to the King and Queen and to the Prince and Princess of
Wales. Queen Charlotte, who read her copy, invited Miss More to
meet her and Lady Elgin at Weymouth, that they might seek her
advice on the education of the princess, and the Duchess of Gloucester, her warm admirer, gave a great breakfast party at Gloucester
Lodge in her honour. From this time, says Hannah's clerical biographer with some complacency, 'Miss More was honoured with

the intimacy of some members of the Royal Family, having long enjoyed the esteem of all.'[10]

Like most English pedagogics since the publication of John Locke's essay *Some Thoughts Concerning Education*, the *Hints* proclaimed the grand object of all education to be the formation of character. A carefully selected curriculum, formed of subjects of moral and utilitarian worth, provided means to this end. The natural sciences were ruled out as lacking in vocational value for kings, and the fine arts were likewise excluded, for excellence in artistic performance, to Miss More as to Plato, smelt of the professional, while mediocre performance diminished the dignity of a sovereign. Languages were admitted on the ground of utility. The masters of English literature found a place in the curriculum if 'vulgarity, indecent levity, and gross descriptions' were carefully expurgated.

History, in the *Hints* as in the *Strictures*, held pride of place among the lay subjects of instruction. For royalty this 'School of Princes' was the ideal instrument of education. The greater part of the book was devoted to its study. Never profound, Hannah More had nevertheless worked out for herself a philosophy of history which she illustrated with immense erudition and 'some deplorable errata'.[11] In history she sapiently discovered not isolated events, but, in modern phraseology, a repeating pattern of logic and social conduct, and since every theory of social action is ultimately a philosophy of history, she found hers, as Bossuet, Vico, and Rollin had found theirs, in the domain of Providence in the affairs of man. A good cosmopolitan, she selected her illustrations from universal, i.e., European history. This depicted 'the dependence of man on the guidance of God on an immense canvas' and introduced to the pupil the splendid characters and the laws and customs of other nations. But since lack of time made selection from so vast a scheme imperative, she advocated, in contrast to the contemporary curricula for boys, the study of *modern* history. It best provided the royal pupil with the examples and warnings her vocation required. Interpreted by Hannah More, history assumed an amazing simplicity.

Events and persons classified themselves as good or bad, and received appropriate rewards and punishments. And if, as not infrequently happened, the wicked appeared to flourish as the bay-tree, Miss More was content to leave the final verdict to history, sure, as Lord Acton was sure, of 'the undying penalty which history has the power to inflict on wrong'.[12]

Revealed religion, as would be expected from a woman of Hannah More's characteristic religious sincerity, informed the *Hints* from start to finish. The *Monthly Review* complained that Miss More had refrained from avowing her rigid religious tenets when writing on religion for royalty—in other words, she had tempered the wind to the royal lamb.[13] This was unfair. The book was an attempt to construct a curriculum for the future sovereign, not to define doctrine, nor did Miss More forget to point out that the royal child did not escape from 'the grand peculiarity of Christianity, the knowledge of ourselves as fallen creatures'. 'No instruction', she roundly asserted, 'can be more indispensable to her than the knowledge that in this respect she stands on a level with the meanest of her fellow creatures.' None the less there was ground for asserting that religion was not treated in the *Hints* as in her earlier didactic writings. Two chapters, suggesting by their place near the end of the book that they were an afterthought, were devoted to the history of the Anglican Church as the visible Church of Christ. Perhaps these disparate chapters owed their place to a sudden realization that some knowledge of the Established Church, its liturgy, articles, and creeds, was of supreme importance to the Defender of the Faith. What was astonishing, though her critics passed it by, was the faint adumbration in these chapters of the *via media* as a function of the Anglican Church. It is not without significance that Alexander Knox, the precursor of the High Churchmanship of the later nineteenth century, was a guest at Barley Wood when Hannah More was writing the *Hints*.[14]

The reception of the book was remarkable. It rehabilitated Miss More in public esteem, which had been shaken by the Blagdon affair. It had the good fortune to please the Court and serious persons of high rank, who deplored the scandalous behaviour of the Prince and Princess of Wales. To Miss More's surprise, persons of the 'Second Class', among whom her animadversions on the Great and the Gay had been immensely popular, read the *Hints* with avidity and quickly swallowed up six editions. Written in haste 'to meet a national emergency', it is the most ill-arranged of all Miss More's literary efforts. 'Transition is made abruptly from one subject to another,' complained the *Edinburgh Review* in a highly critical article, 'in a manner embarrassing to the reader',[15] yet the book is marked by Hannah More's excellent good sense, and by her characteristic religious candour. The chapters on 'The Arts of Popularity' and on 'The Abuse of Terms of Religion' are still worth reading.

What effect, if any, the *Hints* had upon the education of Princess Charlotte it is impossible to estimate. 'The Bishop of Salisbury is here,' records the princess in her Diary, 'and reads with me an hour or two every day from Mrs Hannah More's *Hints for forming the character of a Pss*. This, I believe', she adds mournfully, 'is what makes me find the hours so long. *I am not quite good* enough for that yet.'[16] To it Miss More's admirers ascribed the change from the noisy garrulous hoyden of Princess Charlotte's childhood to the gentle girl of irreproachable conduct and piety whom Parliament, pulpit, and press discovered to a lamenting British public when she died in childbirth before her twentieth birthday. Miss More's admiring references to *Telemachus* suggest that she hoped her modest *Hints* might, if intelligently applied, have produced the civilizing effects on Princess Charlotte which Archbishop Fénelon's ideals had produced on the Duke of Burgundy, whose savage temper, bitter wit, and ungovernable rage were transmuted into saintly self-discipline and piety. Princess Charlotte provided no such dramatic opportunity to Hannah More, but the fact that the princess had read the *Hints* on her eighteenth birthday, and was reading it before her sudden and unexpected death, encouraged Miss More's admirers to attribute Princess Charlotte's reputed change of mind and character to the *Hints*. With more good sense any such change

might be attributed to the happy marriage of a girl starved in childhood and youth of affection and sympathy.

(ii)

Convalescing after persistent bouts of illness in 1808, Hannah More
conceived an idea startling in its audacity. She would write a
novel. Always apprehensive of adverse criticism, she made known
her bold intention only to the sisters; hence when *Coelebs*, published anonymously, appeared in 1808 its authorship provided
lively speculation. 'Junius's Letters and Chatterton's poem hardly
occasioned more curious research or eager controversy in public
than *Coelebs* did in private,' wrote James Stephen to Miss More,
when, the success of the novel established, she acknowledged it as
her own.[17] No moralist of her age had written with more vehement
disapproval of novel reading and novel writing than she. Her
Strictures of 1799 had condemned root and branch the novels of the
'nineties as 'the most pernicious source of moral corruption'. Comparing them with the novels of Richardson and Fielding, she found
the old masters relatively innocuous, for they were dangerous to
morality 'only in one respect'. The modern novel, on the contrary,
characterized by 'a pernicious subtlety', was a thousand times more
dangerous. It diffused destructive politics, deplorable profligacy,
and impudent infidelity. As a good patriot Hannah More had no
doubt that French influence in general, and that of Rousseau in
particular, was responsible for the deplorable change. 'Eloisa' and
'Emilius' illustrated his immoral influence, for Rousseau did not
attempt, as the English novelists of the old school had done, 'to present an innocent woman ruined, repentant and restored', but with
a far more mischievous refinement had annihilated the value of
chastity and attempted to make his heroine appear more amiable
without it. He struck at 'the very root of honour by elevating a
crime into a principle'.[18]

Writing her *Strictures* when French influence was waning, she
made an important contribution to current controversy when she

reserved her strongest condemnation for the publications of the German *Illuminati* then appearing in England.[19] Drama, poetry, romance, history had become 'the vehicles of unparalleled vice and infidelity'. Incredible pains were taken to make English translations of every book likely to be of use in 'corrupting the heart and misleading the understanding'. Kotzebue's play *The Stranger* called for particular notice. It was 'the first attempt at representing an adulteress in an exemplary light', and, as such, had created 'an era in literature'. And the evil did not end with the translations of immoral novels and plays. English writers had followed suit. 'They taught that chastity is only individual attachment, that no duty exists which is not prompted by feeling, that impulse is the mainspring of virtuous action, while laws and religion are only unjust restraints.' The new teaching, she insisted, was deliberately designed to break down the standards of feminine morals by encouraging women to indulge in the freedom 'which custom, not religion, had tolerated in the male sex'.

Nor had her trenchant criticism ceased with her castigation of French and German writers and their schools. The 'nineties had witnessed an abnormal increase in the output of light fiction. John Lane's Minerva Press and the large and well-equipped circulating library attached to it in Leadenhall Street was but one of the several channels of modern fiction which 'glutted the imagination with cheap sentiment and plentiful incident', creating in their turn a universal source of moral corruption. And the circulation of these books was not confined to the superior orders. Miss Flinders's library in Walpole Street and Miss Minigen's library in Newcastle Street catered for domestic servants and supplied the apprentices of milliners and mantua-makers with novels. It had become a custom in the workrooms for one girl to read aloud to the others, 'thus increasing the scope of this pernicious influence'. In the decade 1799–1809 the output from the Minerva Press alone was immense and gave point to Miss More's caustic remark that, like the prolific progeny of Banquo, each new and trivial romance was followed by 'Another and another and another'.[20]

The Making of Many Books

'I wrote *Coelebs*', said Hannah More rather apologetically to William Weller Pepys in 1809, '[because] I thought there were already good books enough in the world for good people, but that there was a larger class of readers whose wants had not been attended to—the subscribers to the circulating library. A little to raise the tone of that mart of mischief and to counteract its corruption I thought was an object worth attempting.'[21] If the sale of a book were the test of its worth, Miss More was more than justified in her attempt. Within three days she prepared, at her publisher's request, a second edition; in less than a fortnight the book was out of print and the booksellers all over the country were clamouring for copies. Within nine months the eleventh edition appeared, and a twelfth was in preparation. 'Though the expenses were heavy', wrote Hannah to Mrs Kennicott, 'since the expense of printing, paper, etc., are extraordinarily increased, and I had near £5,000 to pay for expenses, *I have cleared within the year* £2,000.'[22] Once again Hannah More had shown her remarkable *flair* for discovering, in spite of ample evidence pointing to a dissolute and irreligious age, a reading public steadily growing in size, which would absorb all she wrote and ask for more. The immense vogue of *Coelebs* in England and America, where thirty editions of a thousand copies each were sold before Hannah More's death in 1834, and the importance which contemporaries attached to it may be attributed to two main factors. It presented a 'calumniated religion' as the religion of the home in an easy and attractive guise and thus contributed to the growing popularity of Evangelicalism. At the same time it offered to its readers among the middle classes, anxious for instruction in 'decorous conduct', a valued guide to feminine propriety written by a woman of recognized religious and social position.

Coelebs, who tells the story, was a young man of the upper middle class endowed with wealth, gentle birth, attractive appearance, and careful upbringing. He set off on a round of visits to find a wife whose character, intelligence, and piety would meet with his requirements. 'In such a companion', he mused as he drove along in his post-chaise

The Making of Many Books

I do not want a Helen, a Saint Cecilia, or a Madame Dacier; yet she must be elegant, or I should not love her; sensible, or I should not respect her; well-informed, or she could not educate my children; well-bred, or she could not entertain my friends [and] I should offend the shade of my mother; pious, or I should not be happy with her, because the prime comfort in a companion for life is the delightful hope that she will be a companion for eternity.

As an ironical study of an insufferable egoist much could have been done with Coelebs, but Hannah More, whose model of male excellence he was, made of him a totally uninteresting prig. After months of wandering among fine folk in London he arrived at the country house of his father's old friend, Mr Stanley. Here he met his future wife Lucilla, the epitome of all the virtues, and the novel straightway becomes an Evangelical and feminist tract.

It is at once apparent that Hannah More's purpose in writing *Coelebs* was to present a plea for the Christian life in its Evangelical dress. Underlying her verbiage and digressions is her conviction that the household of faith is a happy and contented household. In the ordered lives of parents and children the 'drudgery of the world', cards, play-going, dancing, polite conversation, censorious judgements, the care of over-loaded establishments, were replaced by the habitual services of God, in which there was not only perfect freedom but abiding happiness. Coelebs, the newcomer, found children who spent their time in steady work, affectionate intercourse, unremitting charities and gay and animated conversation, and parents who discharged their duties, the chief of which was charity, ôn the estate and in the home. Morning and evening they called the household to family prayer. Daily they instructed the children in secular studies and in religious duties as prescribed by the Catechism. Together parents and children read works in which *belles lettres* shared an honourable place with books of devotion. On Sundays parents, children and dependants attended the parish church, where the rector—a replica, said Miss More, 'of the country parson of the ingenious Mr George Herbert'—conducted the service. Grave and solidly pious, he was a clergyman all the week as well as on Sunday. He epitomized as pastor and preacher the

194

Evangelical ideal of *Zeal without Innovation*.[23] 'Content to dwell in decencies' he did not scamper through the liturgy, or treat it as a background for an elaborate discourse of his own making. 'His charity was large, his spirit truly catholic.'

In this household of piety and cheerfulness, as in other Evangelical homes, one recreation was permitted and encouraged. 'Rational, animated conversation' on matters of doctrine and conduct, and on the providential guidance of God in things both great and small, occupied, it would appear, all leisure time. 'Religion', said Miss More, 'requires discussion'. At Stanley Grove no one could complain of its lack.

As an exposition of womanly duties and conduct, 'always the great object of my regard', *Coelebs* was no less successful. Hannah More's pastoral drama of the 'sixties had acclaimed the feminine virtues of modesty, humility, and propriety. Her *Essays* of 1777, following suit, were criticized by Mrs Walsingham and others of her Bas Bleu friends. They deplored that she was not a better feminist. In the *Strictures* she had condemned forthright the follies and weakness of her sex, and with equal vehemence had condemned 'the infamous doctrine of the Rights of Women'. Propriety, 'the first, second, and third requisite for woman', she had offered instead.[24] *Coelebs* presented a portrait of the ideal English lady which, it must be presumed, met with the approval of no small section of the upper and middle classes, since it became the standardized picture of the Victorian gentlewoman. Pleasing in appearance, modestly dressed, pious and charitable, and in matters of conduct the essence of propriety, Hannah More's heroine left her mark on English life and literature throughout the nineteenth century. One social activity was, by her example, permanently attached to English womanhood, that of benevolence. Charity, said Miss More, unwittingly inserting the thin edge of the wedge into masculine preserves, was the calling of a lady. 'The care of the poor is her profession.'[25]

Hannah More's obvious sincerity, the satirical quality of her wit and her power of turning neat and epigrammatic remarks suggest that she possessed some at least of the requisites for good novel writing. But, as it stands, *Coelebs* is completely lacking in artistic quality. Miss More fights shy of incident, forgetting Dr Johnson's sharp reproof, 'Incident, child, incident is what a biographer [and by inference a novelist] wants—did he break his leg?'[26] Nor did she 'discover' her characters. She built them brick by brick. Nevertheless, by her friends and admirers *Coelebs* was greeted as a delightful achievement. Even those who had doubted the propriety of combining fiction and religion were reconciled to the new technique. Evangelicals welcomed this new and powerful instrument to correct the irreligious tastes and manners of the age. 'I look upon *Coelebs*', wrote John Venn, 'as one of the most useful works which has ever been written for the purpose which it was intended to answer.'[27] 'I have not met with such writing since the days of Burke,' wrote the literary young man of her London days, Sir William Weller Pepys, now an old man of seventy.[28] Madame de Staël later contributed a glowing appraisement to the *Constitutionnel*,[29] and Jane Austen, who did not like Evangelicals, said grudgingly, 'Of course I shall be delighted when I read it, like other people.'[30]

But in spite of these and other encomia from men and women not lacking in standards of religion and literary taste, the book profoundly troubled some, at least, of her friends. 'Hannah More's new book *Coelebs*, an odd kind of redivived religious courtship, is not exactly what it should be,' wrote Alexander Knox of Dublin to Bishop Jebb of Limerick, in some perturbation of mind, 'I am puzzled to know how to speak of it.'[31] Her old friends, the Henry Thorntons, were more than puzzled, they were dismayed. 'They affirm', wrote Wilberforce, 'that it cannot be H. More's and are strong against it, surely without reason. It is Hannah More all over.'[32] A letter from Charmile Grant to Mrs Thornton discovers their objection. 'All of us are guessing who the author is,' she wrote, 'We think him, as you do, vain, coarse and somewhat presumptuous. A report has reached us that it was written by Mrs H. More, which till we have it from herself, or from you, I will not believe.

I earnestly hope', she added with charming naïveté, 'that it may be written by someone I have already thought disagreeable.'[33]

It was unfortunate for *Coelebs* that its publication coincided with the ebullient youth of the *Edinburgh Review*, which introduced a new note into English literary criticism. Hannah More's plays and verses, her essays on religion and educational subjects, though she had not escaped criticism from the Kendricks and Wolcots, had been treated in general with deference by the literary world of the eighteenth century. The *Edinburgh*, brilliant, brutally outspoken, imperiously demanding a high standard of literary excellence, and the *London Review*, taking its tone from the *Edinburgh*, fell upon *Coelebs* and enjoyed a Roman holiday. The religious motive of the book did not save it from the unsparing criticism of Sydney Smith, into whose hands it was given for review. His strong and consistent dislike of 'the trash and folly of Methodism', a term used by him to cover 'all fanaticism within or without the Church', barbed his literary criticism of

this good lady, who wants to see men chatting together on the Pelagian heresy, to hear in the afternoon the theological rumours of the day, and to glean polemical tittle-tattle at a tea-table rout. All the disciples of this school fall into the same mistake. They are perpetually calling upon their votaries for religious thoughts and religious conversation in everything, inviting them to ride, row, wrestle and drive out religiously. . . No Christian is safe who is not dull.

Equally mordant was his criticism of Hannah More's plea for feminine modesty in dress:

Oh! if women in general knew what was their real interest! if they could guess with what a charm even the *appearance* of modesty invests its possessor, they would dress decorously from mere self-love, if not from principles. The designing would assume modesty as an artifice, the coquet would adopt it as an allurement, the pure as her appropriate attraction, the voluptuous as the most infallible art of seduction.

'If there is any truth in this passage', remarked Mr Smith, with justifiable acerbity, 'nudity becomes a virtue, and no decent women in the future can be seen in garments.' He bore witness to Hannah More's good sense, her real piety and her occasional very original and very profound observations, but he laughed at her representation of life and manners as false, trite, and artificial, and, in spite of her not infrequent brilliant style, he refused to allow the book a vestige of claim to be considered as a work of literature. Most unkindest cut of all, he compared it, to its detriment, with 'the brick and mortar novels' of the Minerva Press.[34]

Richard Cumberland's hysterical outburst in the *London Review* was urbane in comparison. In her 'sucking babes of grace', 'wallowing in Hell's broth', he professed to see an insidious attempt to undermine and sap the Church, and ended with a vehement *caveat emptor*. But it was left to the *Christian Observer*, whose unfortunate editor had not recognized Hannah More in the anonymous author, to deliver the *coup de grâce*. The *bruta fulmina* of the *Edinburgh* caused no surprise or resentment. When one entered the lists of secular literature, criticism of the literary merit of a work was to be expected and Hannah More, always humble where her literary merits were concerned, does not appear to have been disconcerted by Sydney Smith's critique. Evangelicals knew what they had to expect from Chesterton's 'admirable old heathen'. Cumberland's obloquy in the *London Review* could be explained as 'the stored up malice of a splenetic old man'. But the disparaging comments of the organ of Evangelicalism could not be dismissed. In an otherwise laudatory review it complained that *Coelebs* was 'apt to be vulgar', and, discovering in the novel 'some want of taste and strict moral delicacy',[36] neither of which is discernible to the modern eye, brought the career of Hannah More, a precursor of Jane Austen as a novelist of manners, to an abrupt end. Angry and indignant, she informed Macaulay in no measured words of her opinion, and then followed up her letter by a second, apologizing for the first.[37] *Coelebs* was her first and last novel, neither friends nor publishers nor public response[38] would induce her to provide a successor. 'A new and profitable vein of religious instruction', deplored James Stephen, 'ought not to be abandoned as not worth further working'.[39]

The Making of Many Books

(iii)

Undeterred by her success as a novelist, Hannah More returned to the essay as the literary form best suited to her genius. Three didactic works followed *Coelebs*. They were old friends in a new guise. Aware of this, she called them 'reproductions' of herself and apologized for repeating what she had said before. The new essays were a significant demonstration of the growing popularization of Evangelicalism. They were written for a new class of readers—the young generation of the war years. Women engaged in setting up schools for girls of the middle classes, acquaintances concerned with the education of their daughters, old friends who wanted spiritual pabulum for their children, such as she had provided for their elders in the 'nineties, assured her that there was an unsatisfied demand for works from her pen. Her personal contacts with young men from Oxford who had taken or were about to take Holy Orders, and with the 'engaging young' who lived in the neighbourhood or came with their parents on visits to Barley Wood, and 'in whose affection she was singularly happy', convinced her that she 'carried some weight with them'. For these 'amiable young readers' she produced her essays.

Like her didactic works of the 'nineties, the new works were concerned directly with religion and morals, but the harsh and at times censorious note of the *Strictures* was absent. 'I have deliberately avoided, so far as Christian sincerity will permit, whatever may tend to disputation.'[40] Her ability 'to come with power into the conscience, and to reiterate truths long since familiar but with unceasing variety', impressed even the critical among her army of readers.[41]

Devoted to the love and service of God, *Practical Piety: or the Influence of the Religion of the Heart on the Conduct of Life*, written in 1811, was a simple and straightforward persuasive to the Christian life.[42] It developed Hannah More's dominant conviction that Christianity brought happiness to all who accepted it. So valuable did her readers find her book that its lack of method, its diffuse and heavily antithetical style, and the absence in it of any 'intellectual exercise' did not discourage them. That it met the needs of young and old was affirmed by the amazing response of the public. Its sales exceeded those of *Coelebs*, hitherto Hannah More's best seller, by one edition and three thousand copies. It brought superlative praise from friends new and old,[43] but its non-controversial character did not exempt it from criticism. 'The very high Calvinists' declared war against it.[44]

Christian Morals (1812),[45] a sister volume to *Practical Piety*, offered, like *Manners of the Great*, direct moral instruction in Christian conduct. Addressed primarily to the young of rank and education, it reminded them of their responsibilities as represented in the parable of the talents; recalled to them their duty of charity in time and money to the poor, and stressed the vital importance of building up right conduct by habitual right action. She presented, with a vigour which aroused the opposition of her critics, her conviction of the control of Providence in the affairs of man. This was not, as her opponents averred, an assertion that God worked by miracles. It was a claim that the world was a moral world in which all things worked together for good to them that love God.

No sooner was *Christian Morals* announced than the whole edition was bespoken. Eleven editions were published and nearly ten thousand copies were sold.

The *Character and Practical Writings of St Paul* (1815)[46] was the last of Miss More's major writings.[47] It was a venture in Christian biography, for which she was ill-equipped. Conscious of her lack of ancient learning and of her deficiencies as a theologian, she disarmed criticism by treating St Paul and his works as a model for Christian imitation. Her talents did not lie in depicting character, nor were her critical and constructive powers competent to deal adequately with the materials for so complex a study. It was the least successful of her efforts, yet the first edition was sold out on the day of publication and over 7,000 copies of the book were sold.

While none of Hannah More's writings under review may claim consideration as contributions to literature or learning, they serve to illustrate a modification in her methods of religious and moral

PLATE II

HANNAH MORE
'From a drawing by Mr Slater, taken at Barley Wood in November 1813'

instruction. Her *Strictures* of the 'nineties had given place to *Persuasives*. The severe criticism she had suffered from High, or 'Daubenian' clergy on her doctrinal views, the charges of Calvinism, Methodism, and Dissent preferred against her, had convinced her that she was 'unfitted to be one of the prize-fighters in theology'.[48] Possibly too she was influenced by the works of her friend Thomas Gisborne, when he urged that concentration on the practice of piety would meet the common reproach that Evangelicals were more absorbed in the doctrinal plan of conversion than in the education and development of Christian character. Be that as it may, Miss More's later writings, novels and essays, spoke 'the language of sympathy rather than that of dictation, of feeling rather than of document'. 'By her strictly commonplace writing', said a not unsympathetic observer, 'she calmed the religious apprehensions of a huge public, whose hearts were stronger than their heads'.[49] By so doing she popularized Evangelicalism among the upper and middle classes, and thereby strengthened its influence.

(iv)

The series of moral and religious publications was broken abruptly in 1817, when 'urgent representations from the highest quarters' diverted Miss More from her didactic writings, and 'led me to undertake as a duty a task I should gladly have avoided'.[50]

Over twenty years of exhausting war with France, coinciding with slow but revolutionary changes in agriculture, industry, population, and economic opinion, and aggravated by unemployment and rising prices when the war was over, imposed conditions of intolerable hardship on the labouring classes, and presented the Government of Liverpool, Eldon, Castlereagh, and Sidmouth with a series of problems unequalled in their complexity. With honourable exceptions, Whigs and Tories alike failed to understand that hard economic facts were, in the main, responsible for the futile and pitiful expressions of despair, the bread-riots, machine-breaking, rick-burning, and hunger-marching. The growing conviction that in neither official party were there men of principle, prepared to make a stand to relieve misery and insist on prior and immediate consideration of political and economic reform, explains the embittered determination of all sorts and conditions of radicals to arouse public opinion to *demand* reform.

It is still debatable whether the state of the country justified the repressive measures taken by the Government in 1817, but the solid support given to it by the upper and middle classes, and the ineffectiveness of radical leadership, make the suspension of the Habeas Corpus Act in 1817 and the new penal legislation appear as the excessive precautions of an apprehensive government, ignorant of the state of public opinion.[51] The Circular Letter of Lord Sidmouth, most repressive of Home Secretaries, restricted the freedom of the press by calling the attention of the Lords-Lieutenant to the dissemination of blasphemous and seditious literature. His injunction to the magistrates to apprehend the writers, publishers, and vendors of such literature, while equally oppressive, may be credited with the psychological insight and political acumen with which Professor Halévy endowed the Secret Committees of both Houses appointed in 1816 to examine the evidence of disaffection in the country. The Circular Letter, like the Reports of the Committees, stressed the irreligious character of revolutionary propaganda, and thereby enlisted the support of innumerable men and women of all classes and conditions to whom, in an age of growing piety, blasphemy was the sin of sins.[52]

The appearance of William Cobbett's *Twopenny Trash*, a cheap copy of his *Weekly Political Register*, in 1816 and its immense circulation moved the governing classes to find an antidote 'to a kind of fourth estate in the politics of the Country'. The services of '20,000 parsons, 4,000 to 5,000 lawyers, the two Universities, the two Houses of Parliament, many thousands of magistrates and many hundreds of writers for pay' were, according to Cobbett, mobilized without success to this end. In January 1817 'the highest quarters', still seeking for antidotes to disaffection, remembered the effects ascribed to Hannah More's *Village Politics* and *Repository Tracts* in the 'nineties, and, informing her that 'Revolution showed itself in all the great towns,' appealed for her 'powerful assistance in supplying antidotes to the spreading poison'.[53]

Her response was immediate. The Government which needed her help she regarded as 'a virtuous government'. It was manned by her friends, Sidmouth, Home Secretary, and Vansittart, Chancellor of the Exchequer, and it was supported by Wilberforce, whose opinion she revered above that of all living men. She had read with horror and distress the parodies of the Creed, the Catechism, and the Litany written by Hone in 1817, over 100,000 of which, it was said, had been sold, and she agreed with Wilberforce that Cobbett's papers were blasphemous. A Government which needed the help of an old woman, in her seventy-second year, to counteract these evils, could not be refused. 'I did not think to turn ballad-maker in my old age,' she wrote to J. S. Harford, her neighbour at Blaise Castle, 'but the blasphemous and seditious tracts which have deluged the whole country called on every lover of religion and social order to provide some counter-action. I, for one, have set to work, and I think in 6–8 weeks I produced over a dozen of these *d*. and 1*d*. productions.'[54]

Little is known of the tracts and songs contributed by Hannah More to the anti-Cobbett drive in 1817. Some of them were old friends—*Village Politics* in a new guise as *Village Disputants*; others, such as *The Loyal Subjects' Political Creed, The Delegate, The Market House Orator*, were written to cope with the new conditions in the country. Tens of thousands were distributed by a central London Committee, others by her own efforts and those of her friends. From February to April 1817 she contributed to the *Anti-Cobbett or Weekly Patriotic Register*, published at the price of 1½*d*. 'I am pushing the *Anti-Cobbett*,' she wrote to Pepys, 'a useful tract which I hope you will recommend as an antidote to the *Twopenny Register*. The songs in the first two numbers are written by your old friend.'[55] The *Anti-Cobbett* ceased publication abruptly in April 1817, when Cobbett fled the country after the suspension of the Habeas Corpus Act; 'all further exposure of his conduct', announced the last number triumphantly, and with peculiar ineptitude, 'becomes unnecessary.'

Compared with Hannah More's lively tracts of the 'nineties, with their vigorous moral teaching, the politico-religious tracts of the post-war years are poor stuff, repetitive, garrulous, and unconvincing. Content to express *ad nauseam* the view that government and law were not responsible for the country's distress, they read today as ineffective replies to the shattering blows of Cobbett's 'mutton fist'; yet if, as it is difficult to deny, the strong and consolidated opposition to revolution was in part due to the abhorrence of anti-Christian propaganda, Hannah More's tracts and ballads addressed to the labouring classes merit consideration. Her skill in teaching 'plain and plebeian understandings' could not be gainsaid. Cobbett made no mistake when he dubbed her 'The old bishop in petticoats'.[56] It is a tribute to the power of her pen and his sagacity that alone among the Evangelicals he detested she was given episcopal rank. He could not deny that she fed her hungry sheep even while he abhorred the pabulum she gave them.

Hannah More's 'antidotes' reveal what had long been implicit in her writings, the identification in her mind of religion and social order, characteristic of most contemporary religious thought. Providence, she insisted, as she had insisted in her didactic writings, controlled events and conditions. Applied to present conditions, the reason for distress was not to be found, as irreligious men asserted, in 'our government and laws', but in God's will. Distress was the expression of his displeasure with the atheism and sedition of the times. Religion demanded acquiescence in his will and reverence to authority. The sanction of habitual usage was the sanction of religion.

> I do believe these times were sent
> For warning and for punishment,
> Of God's displeasure they're the token
> Because his holy laws were broken.

Her tracts reveal, too, an inability to discriminate between agitation for reform and agitation for revolution, and between the revolutionary and constitutional methods employed, an inability which she shared with her Evangelical and Tory friends. Spence, whose 'foul doctrines' she abhorred, Major Cartwright and his Hampden men, Orator Hunt, and William Cobbett were tarred with the same brush. They were 'all, all irreligious men', out to overturn established usage for their own ends. And Cobbett, with whom she had so many points in common, his love of the English countryside, his deep affection for the poor, his courage, his passion for instructing others, she regarded, as did Wilberforce, as 'the most pernicious'[57] of all the leaders of reform.

> I think those men that magnify
> Our wants and raise a hue and cry,
> Intend to make those wants a cause,
> To shake our government and laws.

Finally the tracts and ballads loudly proclaim that in common with her age she had no social philosophy wherewith to meet the urgent social problems of the post-war world. She could not believe, and history confirms her judgement, that the poor would benefit from parliamentary reform. Their distress, which she strenuously and unceasingly endeavoured to ameliorate, could not be alleviated, she held, by annual parliaments, borough reform, and the abolition of sinecures. But she had no alternative to offer. The duty of charity *to* the poor, the duty of acquiescence *by* the poor, defined her social philosophy. The generosity of squire and parson, gentlefolk's soup and flannel subscriptions were practical blessings which the reform of the parliamentary franchise and public finance could never secure.

> If Birmingham *ten* members had
> Think you the times would be less bad?
> That annual parliaments would tend
> The price of bread or malt to mend?
>
> . . . .
>
> I do believe what hurts the grain
> Is not the pensions but the rain.
> I do not think that rotten boroughs
> Can mar the wheat or drench the furrows.[58]

CHAPTER X

LADIES IN RETIREMENT

'Her diocese embraced almost every city of her native land and extended to many of the remote dependencies.'

James Stephen on Hannah More

(i)

THE writing of many books did not absorb the energies of the untiring elderly lady, nor did it preclude the active interest of herself and her sisters in contemporary affairs. When they settled at Barley Wood in 1802 the war was about to enter its most bitter phase. The sisters, unlike Miss Austen's ladies of the same period, were not unaware of its existence. Somerset, as its inhabitants, old and young, believed, was a first line of defence. 'Able to do little or nothing to serve our country', the patriotic ladies offered Barley Wood, 'conveniently situated should the French land at Uphill, eight miles distant' to the Officers-Commanding at Bristol.[1] They were prepared to move to Bath if their offer, which was declined, had been accepted. War tidings and invasion scares penetrated even to their rural retreat, for Hiley Addington, their near neighbour and brother to the Prime Minister, kept them well abreast of the war news, and in the last years of the war Vansittart, Chancellor of the Exchequer, sent them, as a special privilege, copies of the *Gazette Extraordinary*.[2] Hannah's diary for 1804 records their apprehension and their confidence. 'The foe hourly expected... Mr Addington declares the country to be in a complete state of defence.'[3]

Nothing, not even the prospect of immediate invasion, was allowed to interfere with the sisters' charities in the pitiable years of the war. When the hounds of peace following on war's traces brought increased suffering to their poverty-stricken neighbours, the sisters redoubled their efforts to meet distress unparalleled in their experience. At Barley Wood they relieved the day-to-day necessities of the villagers, visited the poor-houses, assisted the women's clubs to keep afloat, maintained the three Great Schools 'on a peace footing', rivalled Dorcas in the garments they made for the children, and sent their doctor to attend to the sick when the common scourge, typhus fever, made 'great ravages in the neighbourhood'.[4] In the appalling winter of 1817 they carried through an extraordinary piece of organized charity. Three hundred calamine miners at Shipham were thrown out of work when the brass foundries closed down and the demand for calamine ceased. The sisters came to the rescue of '1,200 starving creatures'. Not content with providing food and clothing, Hannah, with the help of Hiley Addington and others of her friends, 'turned merchant', bought up all the ore the miners produced, and 'stored it against better times'.[5]

To the pious and philanthropic sisterhood the early years of the century brought new and abiding interests which the war and its attendant tragedies could not eclipse. On a scale hitherto unparalleled, the first group of religious societies, which stamped the nineteenth century with its distinctive character of social and religious responsibility, came into being. The support they received affords overwhelming proof of the change in the public attitude of mind. One after another, societies which twenty-five years earlier would have perished for lack of personal and financial support were established on foundations strong enough to withstand opposition and indifference. The ladies of Barley Wood waxed enthusiastic when, with the weighty support of their Clapham friends, two of the great nineteenth-century societies were established. The British and Foreign Bible Society began its remarkable career in 1804. It was the answer to the despairing cry of the Welsh people for Bibles in the Principality. Later in its history it supplied Bibles to all peoples throughout the world. An unsectarian society, open to all Christians, it began to publish the Authorized Version without note or comment, a singular act of faith in an age of religious controversy. No less remarkable was the episcopal sanction it received 'after a reasonable delay' from Bishop Porteus and three other bishops. Later, royal dukes, Heads of Houses, and professors at Cambridge and Oxford supported it as patrons, and the Clapham friends provided the President, Secretary, and members of Committee in the persons respectively of Lord Teignmouth, Henry Thornton, Wilberforce, Grant, and Granville Sharp.[6]

By no one was this ecumenical event greeted with greater enthusiasm than by Hannah More. 'Bible Christianity is what I love,' had been her reiterated cry.[7] Hence when, after a happy beginning, characterized by admirable tolerance of mind and spirit, opposition declared itself, her indignation was vociferous. It appeared to her incredible that there could be objections to a society which had as its object 'the wider dispersion of the Scriptures'. No one, she asserted roundly, could object to the Bible Society except through 'ignorance, infidelity or popery',[8] opprobrious terms which could not be applied to Dr Christopher Wordsworth, future Master of Trinity College, or Dr Herbert Marsh, Lady Margaret's Professor of Divinity at Cambridge. They, and those who thought like them, considered the new society as antipathetic to Church order and discipline, since it encouraged men to believe that they might draw their religion from the Bible without reference 'to the authoritatively commissioned priests of the only apostolic church'. They vindicated the sole right of the old Society for the Promotion of Christian Knowledge, which for over a hundred years had supplied Churchmen with Bibles and devotional literature, to receive Anglican support. This 'effusion of high church bigotry'[9] produced a counter-charge of 'heresy and schism'.[10] The bitter controversy did not destroy the young society. It was too well entrenched in public estimation, but it deepened the antagonism between Anglicans ready to work with Dissent and those who would not pretend to a unity which did not exist. Dreading controversy and deploring the creation of parties, Hannah More shut her eyes to incompatible differences. She urged the approximation of the old and new societies; she commended her own example—membership of both societies;[11] and indignantly expostulated with her friends Alexander Knox and Sir Thomas Acland, when, after supporting the Bible Society, Knox withdrew, convinced of the 'utter hopelessness of bringing home religious principles to the mass of the people by distributing Bibles', and incited Acland to do likewise.[12]

Neither High Church opposition nor the defection of her friends made a whit of difference to Miss More's approval of the new society. It was recognized by Bishop Porteus and eleven other Bishops. That was sufficient for her. Thus when Bible Societies became 'a sort of rage'[13] and local branches were set up throughout England, she established in Wrington Parish one of the 2,439 branches returned in the Society's Report for 1814. Stupendous efforts were made by the sisters to arouse the interest and support of their lay and clerical neighbours, whose 'spiritual climate' was they found 'rather cold'. 'We had', wrote Miss More triumphantly to Wilberforce after the first of the annual meetings in 1816, 'near forty clergymen of the Establishment' who could not be placed in a 'hot-bed of heresy and schism'. By invitation of the sisters 'the superior part of the company' resorted to Barley Wood, a hundred and one to dinner and a hundred and sixty to tea in the grounds, which had 'all the gaiety of a public garden'. 'Some may think', she added, meeting criticism before it was offered, 'it would be better to add to one's subscription and save ourselves so much trouble, but we take this trouble, from a conviction to the contrary. The many young persons of fortune present by assisting at the little festivity, will learn to connect the idea of innocent cheerfulness with that of religious societies and may go and do likewise. For no other cause on earth would we encounter the fatigue.'[14]

The creation of the Church Missionary Society, founded on Church principles in 1801, aroused Hannah More's enthusiasm. It was in general free from the antagonisms which disturbed the Bible Society. The sole qualification for membership of the C.M.S. was membership of the Church of England. Evangelical principles, doctrines, and methods, says its historian, are not mentioned in the laws of the society; non-Evangelical Christians were always in a majority on the Committee of twenty-four laymen who guarded its destinies. None the less it may rank as one of the greatest, if not the greatest, of Evangelical enterprises in the nineteenth century, for 'a society has traditions as well as laws' and the traditions of the C.M.S. were those of Evangelicalism.[15] With Teignmouth, Babington, and Vansittart among its Vice-Presidents and a whole posse of lay and clerical friends actively engaged in its work, Hannah More, prevented by failing health from attending its meetings, was kept well informed of the sustained efforts of the society to carry the Gospel to distant lands, a logical development of Evangelicalism at home. From her friends, in person and by letter, she learned of its highly efficient organization, of its methods of collecting funds by penny subscriptions, and of the success of its deputations. The enthusiasm aroused at the May meetings, which became an easy target for satire, delighted her.[16] 'If the reading of the prosperous state of these blessed institutions is so exhilarating,' she wrote to Daniel Wilson after the 'Sainte Semaine' in London in 1818, 'what must it be to witness them? These have been pleasures out of my reach, but my interest in them is not lessened by want of personal participation. I shall pity you when you come, you will be so teased and tired by questions.'[17] When anniversary meetings were held in Bristol, which by 1815 was a leading provincial association, it became a matter of course for clerics and laymen to pay their respects to the 'old bishop' at Barley Wood. 'All the orators came to see me,' she wrote after the meeting of 1821. 'All were old friends except Mr Jowett with whom I was singularly pleased. I thought him almost too good for a missionary, by which I mean', she added hurriedly, 'that a coarser tool might be fitter for the wear and tear of holy itinerary.' 'Last Thursday', she wrote again to Wilson in the April of her eighty-second year, 'was the missionary meeting [at Bristol]. The next day brought me three carriages full of holy missionaries and missionesses.' She received them in her room. 'They made me a long and pleasant visit; it was not the worst part of it that Mr Bickersteth closed it with a fine prayer.'[18]

Hannah More's lively interest in missionary work was not confined to activities overseas. From three notable men of her acquaintance she learned of the 'Home Heathen Problem' which accompanied the Industrial Revolution. The rural parishes of Somerset had presented conditions of apathy and neglect which dismayed and angered her. The urban parishes of the Tron, Glasgow, St James's, Bristol, and Islington, served, respectively, by her friends Thomas Chalmers,[19] the leading Scotsman of his day, Thomas Biddulph, 'virtually Bishop of Bristol',[20] and the impetuous and imperious Daniel Wilson, a 'king of Evangelicals,'[21] posed novel and complex problems, the outcome in the main of new and impersonal social and economic forces. The amazing changes in the size of the population, one of the concomitants of the revolution, made overcrowding, insanitation, and disease problems of the first magnitude. No less deplorable were the moral and spiritual ills which accompanied them. Piety, courage, and decency could not flourish in conditions such as these. A passion for ignorant and neglected humanity moved these men and others like them, irrespective of Church or party, to provide spiritual and moral help for their growing flocks. Services on Sunday and week-day evenings, weekly meetings for communicants, house-to-house visiting, 'powerful preaching' to crowded congregations and parish schools for the children set standards for the transformation of the urban parish, 'one of the revolutionary achievements of the Church in the nineteenth century'.[22] 'Islington', said the biographer of Thomas Wilson, telling of Wilson's untiring work in his large and neglected parish, 'slept under its old vicar. It has never slept since.'[23] Hannah More, following the reforms with lively interest, informed her friends of the good work. Other hard-working Christians, she reported, were endeavouring in Smithfield to try out Chalmers's scheme for general instruction in religion in great cities.[24]

In curious contrast to Hannah More's enthusiasm for Bible and Missionary Societies was her attitude to the National Society for Promoting the Education of the Poor in the principles of the Established Church. It may be assumed that the rival British and Foreign School Society, an undenominational society associated with the 'Prince of Schismatics', Joseph Lancaster, was as unpalatable to her as it was to Mrs Trimmer and Zachary Macaulay, since to Orthodox and Evangelical Churchmen alike undenominational religion was a 'Moral Monster', but it is surprising that nowhere in her published correspondence is there direct reference to the founding of the National Society in 1812. That it was associated with the 'Hackney Phalanx' of the High Church party rather than with the 'Clapham Sect' does not explain Miss More's lack of co-operation. She was not a party man. The few references in her letters reveal that her vehement disapproval was aroused not by the Society as such, but by its educational programme. It offered what was euphemistically called a 'literary education' to the children of the poor. This she denounced as 'ridiculous'. 'My views of popular education are narrow,' she admitted, but thirty-six years of experience had shown her that the only safe method of instructing the poor was by confining instruction to reading 'the Scriptures and such books as were preparatory to and connected with them.'[25] The new education of the three R's she held was dangerous. Its tendencies were revolutionary. 'I am not the champion of ignorance but I am alarmed by the violence of the contrast.'[26] She begged her Parliamentary friends to steer a middle course 'between the Scylla of brutal ignorance and the Charybdis of a literary education. The one is cruel, the other preposterous.'[27] The sober mean of Christian instruction lay between the two extremes.

(ii)

More exigent than the daily charities and religious interests were Miss More's gargantuan correspondence and the incessant demands on the sisters' leisure by guests who made their way to Barley Wood. As Hannah's reputation grew with the publication of each new book, a seemingly endless procession of friends and acquaintances, old and new, native and foreign, came to pay their respects or wrote letters which called for reply. The sisters' asseverated desire to retire from the world was not proof against the determination of the world to visit them, and indeed, in spite of recur-

ring complaints in the letters of 'tormenting company', it is clear
that nothing gave the lively and intelligent sisters more pleasure
than the plethora of guests with whom they could discuss the war,
religion, philanthropy, even politics, and, with due caution and
circumspection, the literary innovations of Walter Scott and
Madame de Staël. A variety of guests, amongst them men of distinction in scholarship and affairs, allowed the sisters to indulge in
the one recreation which Evangelicalism permitted and of which
they were fine exponents, sober conversation.

Among the new friends, almost all of whom reflect her absorbing religious interests, appear high ecclesiastics as of yore. Bishop
Beadon, though he had no Evangelical sympathies, was a warm admirer. He came with his wife from Wells to stay with Miss More.
Two successive Bishops of Bristol, Dr Mansel and Dr Gray, visited
her. Henry Ryder, Bishop of Gloucester in 1815 and of Lichfield
in 1824, the first Evangelical Churchman to be made a Bishop, was
a frequent guest. The 'excellent Thomas Burgess', Bishop of Salisbury, one of the first scholars of the Bench, was an intimate friend.
As Bishop of St David's he had consulted Miss More in his 'Her-
culean labour of raising the tone of morals, learning and piety of a
large Welsh diocese'. The collegiate education which he secured
for his clergy, 'marked', she held, 'an era in the History of Wales'.[28]
From Ireland came two distinguished men: Bishop Jebb of Limerick and his *alter ego*, Alexander Knox, a Dublin layman who dubbed
himself a 'Methodist High Churchman'. Their friendship with
'this most extraordinary woman' provides one of the most interesting chapters of Hannah More's life. It is impossible to read Knox's
letters to Miss More (*theses* would be the more appropriate term for
his dissertations, one of them covering thirty-five pages, which
are as fresh and interesting today as when they were written), or the
relevant letters in the *Thirty Years' Correspondence* of Knox and
Bishop Jebb, without recognizing the affection and respect of these
highly critical men for her. 'There is', wrote Jebb, 'no modern
author, whom I hold in such estimation, indeed veneration . . .
would more adequately express my feelings.'[29] Nor is it possible to

read her *Hints on the Education of a Young Princess* without becoming conscious of the response of her pious and eager mind to the adumbration of the *via media* which they propounded in their writings. Knox's neo-Anglican theory envisaged a Church in which profound piety, akin to and embodying the perfectionist ethics of Wesley, would be united with an equally profound understanding of the traditional piety embodied in the liturgy of the Anglican Church. The Protestant Churches of the Reformation, he held, in protesting against the errors of the Catholic Church had cut themselves off from the spiritual blessings which 'the Church of all the ages' had to bestow.[30] 'What perverse influence the nickname of Protestant has had on our Church,' he wrote. 'Dread of transubstantiation, has made the sacrament into a ceremony, and to ward off infallibility every man has been encouraged to shape a creed for himself . . . if Popery can be a Charybdis, there is a Scylla on the other side not less dangerous. . . [In] the mixed mass of the Roman Catholic religion, there is gold and silver, and precious stones, as well as wood, and hay and stubble.'[31]

Few of Hannah More's letters to Alexander Knox are extant, but it is not difficult to guess their content from the answers the leisured scholar made to questions raised by her. He reassured her that reunion with Rome was no part of his theology; indeed it was his essential point that the Church of England, which alone among the Protestant Churches had retained in its liturgy the sublime piety of the primitive Church, was to follow a *middle* course and to act as an intermediate link. 'By a most singular arrangement of Providence' the Anglican Church united a Catholic soul with a Lutheran body.[32]

To meet the woman he so greatly admired, Knox, on his infrequent visits to England, made Barley Wood a port of call, and from there wrote to Bishop Jebb his impressions of this 'very great character', whose 'power of mind united with such simplicity of purpose and humility of heart' profoundly impressed him.[33] 'It looks like vanity thus to adjoin my mind to that of Hannah More; but truly I felt her superiority of native powers and acquired knowledge.' 'Hannah More and I are substantially of the same school, that is, we both make it our object to pass through the form of Godliness to the power thereof.'[34]

It is apparent from the Knox-Jebb correspondence that the two men hoped to win Hannah More's support in the propagation of their views. 'Were Hannah More decidedly of your way of thinking,' wrote Jebb, 'with the high character she has acquired and the weight which attaches to her sentiments among Evangelical people she might be an instrument of great good.'[35] In this hope they were disappointed. The 'amazing harmony' of their minds, on which Knox insisted, did not extend to her acceptance of the doctrines he propounded. And he, for his part, could not accept her views on Bible Christianity.[36] She was at bottom a Puritan, albeit of the eighteenth-century variety, and Puritanism is a 'book religion'. He was 'not one whit puritanic'.[37] Knox's defection from the Bible Society defined their positions. 'We both value and wish for the same religious affections', he wrote regretfully to Jebb, 'but we have quite different ideas of the best ways of exciting them.'[38]

Among her guests and correspondents, making Barley Wood a 'minor Evangelical centre',[39] were clerics whose lives and works do not suggest that 'the austere spirit of Newton and Thomas Scott had between 1820 and 1830 given way a good deal to the influence of increasing popularity.'[40] Daniel Wilson, Claudius Buchanan, Legh Richmond, Josiah Pratt, Edward Bickersteth, Thomas Biddulph, Fountain Elwin, Francis Randolph, Rowland Hill, John Hensman, J. W. Cunningham and others whose names are forgotten were not 'degenerate sons' of their saintly Evangelical Fathers.

To the tolerant ladies of Barley Wood came letters and visits from distinguished members of the denominations. The Quaker, Elizabeth Fry, 'that wise and active disciple of her master' revered by Hannah More as 'the most heroic of women', came with her distinguished brother, J. J. Gurney, in the summer of 1823. 'We were delighted with our interview with the extraordinary and excellent person,' wrote Mr Gurney in his diary. 'She is now seventy-eight years old but most vivacious and productive. *Very* like Wilberforce.'[41] Mrs Barbauld, in spite of Hannah More's disapproval of

Unitarianism, still visited her. The Baptist friends of the Anglican lady, men of intellectual and spiritual power, paid her a high compliment. They combined stiff criticism of her religious views with a very real appreciation of herself. John Foster, author of the astringent *Essays*, which in his day required no further definition, subjected her writings to trenchant criticism in the *Eclectic Review*, but his diary reports, after a visit to Hannah More, 'If ever I saw the spirit of the Redeemer and his religion realized, it is in her conversation and character.'[42] Joseph Hughes, Secretary of the Religious Tract Society, who did not approve of her theology, remained the old and tried friend of her Bristol and Battersea days. Robert Hall of Cambridge, who by general consent stood as a preacher of the Gospel 'in solitary grandeur', criticized her literary style as 'exceedingly faulty' but the substance of her writing as 'truly admirable.' Always generous in her estimates, she held unequivocally that there was 'no man in or out of the Church comparable with Robert Hall'.[43] With William Jay, minister of the Presbyterian Chapel, Bath, her friendship was long and intimate. As an old friend who knew her well he was invited by Cadell, the publisher, to write Miss More's biography. He refused on the ground that as 'she was an Episcopalian and I a Dissenter a tincture of my own principle would hardly be avoidable', but he left on record the discerning appreciation of a man of unusual qualities of mind for her conversation 'seasoned with salt', for 'the moderation of her doctrinal sentiments', for her power, during heated polemics, of harmonizing different parts of her company 'so that those who met as foes separated as friends', and for the absence of censoriousness in her character. 'Upon her tongue', he quoted, endowing her with the most lovely of epithets, 'was the law of kindness.'[44]

Laymen were not behind her clerical friends in their warm affection. The neighbouring gentry, the Whalleys, the Addingtons, the Harfords, the Hart-Davises, the de Quinceys called with the regularity of friendship. From Stowey Mead came Lord Mount-Sandford and his intelligent young god-daughter Clarissa Trant. 'I am happy', wrote Miss More to Pepys, 'in the esteem of my neighbours.'⁴⁵ Two young men among them, the generous and buoyant Sir Thomas Dyke-Acland, her 'recreant Knight of Devon', and grave John Harford of Blaise Castle, the prototype, it was said, of Miss More's ideal of manly perfection, *Coelebs*, constituted themselves the 'old bishop's' lay helpers. Harford's thumbnail sketch in 1809 of the sisters, five in number, who 'in their style of dress and manners belonged to a society far away', makes clear that the individuality of each had not diminished with the years. Mary, grave and dignified, was still the acknowledged head of the family; the household management remained in Betty's care, and 'plenty and good cheer followed in her train.' Sally had not lost her ebullient sense of humour, which still delighted and still alarmed the sisters. 'The gay and fragrant flowers bore witness to her ruling passion.' Patty's untiring philanthropy was evident in her benevolent expression; and Hannah, 'whose brilliant eyes lit up a pale but sensible countenance, was most frank and cordial. There was no effort to shine, but again and again pointed and bright things fell from her lips in the most easy and natural manner.'⁴⁶

Nor did men from across the seas fail to pay their respects. They came to tell her of the avidity with which the Cingalese read the translations of her tracts; or of the efforts of the Muscovite Princess Metschersky to translate *Charles the Footman* and the *Two Wealthy Farmers* into Russian. Two Persian noblemen presented themselves at Barley Wood. They were received with befitting dignity and were presented with two copies of *Practical Piety*. Lion-hunters from America, where her fame was well established, came in a steady stream to pay their respects to the author of *Coelebs*. 'There is hardly a City in North America', remarked Miss More with conscious pride, 'in which I have not a correspondent... You would be surprised to see the number of superior Americans who visit me.' The growth of the American Episcopalian Church she regarded with joy. One of its nine bishops, Bishop Chase of Ohio, escorted by Sir Thomas Acland to Barley Wood, made an excellent impression upon its mistress.⁴⁷

The 'multitude' of distinguished guests at Barley Wood in the first three decades of the nineteenth century is not only a testimony to the affection of Hannah More's friends, and to her remarkable reputation: it has a wider significance, for it serves to affirm the growth of Evangelicalism among the middling and upper classes of society in the Age of Elegance. The number of men and women of the 'superior classes' whose lives were profoundly affected by acceptance of the Evangelical teaching of 'Christ Crucified as the only foundation of a sinner's hope'[48] was a phenomenon of supreme importance in the religious and social history of the nineteenth century. 'It is', wrote Miss More, eight years before her death, 'a singular satisfaction to me that I have lived to see such an increase of genuine religion among the higher classes of society. Mr Wilberforce and I agree that whereas we knew one instance thirty years ago there are now a dozen or more.'[49]

Far more pleasing, however, to the old lady than her new acquaintances were the friends of earlier times. Those of her London days did not neglect her, as her voluminous correspondence and the visits of the few of her London contemporaries still living testified. The Dowager Duchess of Beaufort, Countess Spencer, the Duke of Gloucester, son to Duchess Maria, Countess Waldegrave, Lady Olivia Sparrow were received with the consideration their rank demanded when they called at Barley Wood. But the welcome of welcomes was reserved for her Clapham friends, Wilberforce, Thornton, Newton, Macaulay, Venn, Babington, Stephen, Teignmouth, Gisborne, and their contemporaries Bishop Porteus, Lord Barham, and Mrs Siddons, and—earliest of all her friends—Richard Lovell Gwatkin. And they did not come alone. Those who had families brought their wives and children for her inspection. Wilberforce came with his two boys; Teignmouth with his four girls; James Stephen and Charles Grant with their daughters. The beloved Thorntons with members of their large family were especially welcome. 'I have this year visited the paradise of my childhood,' wrote Marianne Thornton in 1856,

and fancied I could once more see the venerable forms and hear the kind greetings of the five hospitable sisters. Surely there never was a house so full of intellect and piety and active benevolence. They lived in such uninterrupted harmony with each other; were so full of their separate pursuits, enjoyed with such intense vivacity all the pleasures of their beautiful home, so wholly laid aside the forms of society that were irksome, that young and old felt in a brighter and happier world. . . I can imagine our arrival and 'the ladies', as they were always called, rushing out to cover us with kisses, and then take us out to the kitchen to exhibit us to Mary and Charles, the housemaid and coachman, then running to fetch the tea-things, Mrs Betty letting no one but herself fry the bacon and eggs for the darlings. . .

She tells of the loaves of mahogany colour and enormous size, baked only once a week, of the two cats called 'Passive Obedience' and 'Non-resistance' who 'were fed by all of us all day long'; of the crowns of flowers the children made for themselves and the garlands for the sheep, and, when they laid themselves down on the hay to rest, 'Charles the coachman, gardener, bailiff and carpenter made us a syllabub under the cow.'[50]

Even more welcome than the Thornton family were the Macaulay's, with Tom and Hannah,[51] Miss More's god-daughter, as especial favourites. The letters of Hannah More to Zachary Macaulay abound in references to Tom, regarded by parents and friends as a remarkable child.

Mrs Macaulay [says Sir George Trevelyan] gladly sent her boy to a house where he was encouraged without being spoiled, and where he never failed to be a welcome guest. . . Hannah More . . . was the most affectionate and the wisest of friends, and readily undertook the superintendence of his studies, his pleasures, and his health. She would keep him with her for weeks, listening to him as he read prose by the ell, declaimed poetry by the hour and discussed and compared his favourite heroes, ancient, modern and fictitious under all points of view and in every possible combination; coaxing him into the garden under pretence of a lecture on botany, sending him from his books to run round the grounds or play at cooking in the kitchen; giving him Bible-lessons which invariably ended in a theological argument, and following him with her advice and sympathy through his multifarious literary enterprises.

It was to the broad and more genial aspect of life at Barley Wood that Sir George attributed Lord Macaulay's childish squibs and parodies; it was to Hannah More that the small boy owed the foundation of 'the most readable of libraries'. 'Though you are a little boy now', she wrote when he was six years old in one of the most charming of her letters, 'you will one day if it please God, be a man: but long before you are a man I hope you will be a scholar. I therefore wish you to purchase such books as will be useful and agreeable to you *then* . . . employ this very small sum in laying a little tiny corner-stone for your future library.' A year or two later she thanks him for his two recent letters, 'so neat and free from blots'. 'By this obvious improvement you have entitled yourself to another book. You must go to Hatchard's and choose. I think we have nearly exhausted the Epics. What say you to a little good prose? Johnson's *Hebrides* or Walton's *Lives*, unless you would like a neat edition of Cowper's poems, or *Paradise Lost* for your own eating? In any case choose something which you do not possess.' And she added surprisingly, 'I want you to become the complete Frenchman that I may give you *Racine*, the only dramatic poet I know in any modern language that is perfectly pure and good.'[52] Aware that no details were too trivial for the insatiable appetite of parents she gathered up the small *memorabilia* of Tom's visits to Barley Wood in her letters to Zachary and Selina Macaulay. 'We have poetry for breakfast, dinner and supper,' she wrote, regaling them with references to Tom's passion for writing verse. 'Sometimes we converse in ballad-rhymes, sometimes in Johnsonian sesquipedalians; at tea we condescend to riddles and charades.'[53]

In due course the parents consulted her on the all-important question of Tom's education. She shared the strong Evangelical disapproval of the Public Schools, 'these nurseries of vice', in which there was an almost complete absence of religious education. 'I think sufficiently ill of them,' but she discriminated, as did few of her Evangelical contemporaries, between the intellectual and religious training which they offered. 'Next to religion there is no such drill to the mind, no such tamer, as the hard study and discipline of these schools.' She advised that as Tom, 'no vulgar boy', needed competitors he should be sent as a day-boy to Westminster School. In the vehement controversy on the Public Schools at the turn of the century Westminster was almost exempt from Evangelical attack.[54] Home life, Miss More held, would protect the boy against evil influence, and the school would provide him with rivals 'worthy to break a lance with him'. But the Evangelical prejudice against the schools was too strong. Tom was sent to the Reverend Mr Preston's private school at Little Shelford until he went to Cambridge. She rejoiced with the parents on the success of their 'wonderful son' at Trinity College. 'The verses', she wrote when he won the Chancellor's Medal for his poem *Pompeii* in 1819, 'are really worthy of any poet of any age,' and, bursting with vicarious pride in this 'jewel of a boy', she set the Bishop of Gloucester to read *Pompeii* aloud to a distinguished house-party at Barley Wood, Professor Farish, a name to conjure with in Evangelical Cambridge, one of the guests, 'gave us a pleasing account of the Commencement and Tom's share in it'. 'I should not tell *him* all these flattering things,' she added, 'but I could not keep them from his mother.'[55]

The warm friendship between the young man and the old lady splintered in her extreme old age on the question of Reform. Soon after his election to Parliament in 1830 he called on her at Clifton. In an unguarded moment, forgetting or ignoring his elderly friend's political prejudices, he argued with his characteristic vivacity for Reform. Conscious that he had offended, he persuaded his mother not to send a copy of his highly praised speech of 3 March 1831, to Hannah More: 'if you do she'll cut me off with a prayer-book.'[56] By a codicil to her will added in the following year, Miss More revoked the bequest of books from her valuable library to Thomas Babington Macaulay. Not even a prayer-book escaped the ban.

(iii)

Madame de Bunsen, writing in 1812, deplored the effect on Hannah More's writings of her retirement from the world and from the civilized society of her Garrick and Walpole days to the narrow family circle of the four sisters and 'religious sectaries' in a Somerset village.[57] She was unaware of the 'polished society' which, says de Quincey,[58] was to be found at Barley Wood, or of the

literary interests which the sisters shared in common. Hannah
More's voluminous correspondence in the last three decades of her
life reveals her old enthusiasm for literature. She deplored that she
had none of the leisure which she had hoped old age would allow
for reading, but her letters provide a reading list of massive proportions and of a catholic taste seldom accredited to Evangelicals of her
day. As always, religious works predominated. The old Anglican
and Nonconformist classics still held pride of place. 'I like nothing so
much as the lean of their fat.' 'I have fagged hard at old Bishop
Reynold's folio of near 1,200 pages which I have almost got
through,' 'such solid Christianity'. Archbishop Leighton's *Com-
mentary on St Peter* was a never failing 'mine of intellectual and
spiritual wealth'. 'My dear friend Mrs Boscawen', she told Wilberforce, 'has left me a legacy of about 400 volumes, chiefly Port Royal
authors; I am so fascinated by them that I can scarcely even look into
another book.' 'Almost every day', she wrote to Knox, 'I read a
portion of Nicole or some other good Jansenist. I cannot but believe
Heaven open to a conscientious papist.' Among the moderns,
Archdeacon Paley's *Natural Theology* interested but perturbed her.
She was not insensitive to the remarkable clarity of his style, 'as
pellucid as crystal', but she deplored his prudential morality—'a
very able book . . . but deficient in some essential points'. Trenchant criticism was meted out to the biographers of her friends,
William Cowper and Elizabeth Carter, because 'they fought shy of
religion.' Hayley, she averred, 'had forgotten, or did not know, that
religion was the grand feature of Cowper's life'. Montague
Pennington's life of his aunt provoked her to spirited criticism:

In order to do away with the terrors of her piety and learning [he] has laboured
to make her a woman of the world, and produced no less than five letters to
prove that she subscribed to a ball. He respects her fondness for cards as much
as if it were a passport to immortality. Every novel reading miss will now visit
the circulating library with a warrant from Mrs Carter. . . Her *mind* is not at all
turned inside out.[59]

All books, sacred and profane, were subject to the same religious
test. Jowett's *Christian Researches in the Mediterranean,* 'the work of

an accomplished scholar', was preferred to Dodwell's *Tour in Greece*, 'purely classical'. When Pepys introduced her to *Corinne* she could not restrain her disapproval. 'Never was such a book. Such a compound of genius and bad taste. She [Madame de Staël] never stumbles so much as when she attempts to introduce Christianity, as there is no subject on which she is so completely ignorant . . . yet let me acknowledge that though, like Pistol, I swallowed and execrated I went on swallowing.' 'I admire her genius so much', she told Wilberforce after reading *L'Allemagne* in 1814, 'that I hate to say anything disparaging, but to speak the truth her religion appears to me to be of a very questionable sort. . . She seems to admire its mysteries in common with those of free-masonry.' Undeterred by her ignorance of German literature, Miss More heroically tackled Elizabeth Smith's *Klopstock*, 'though to own an unfashionable truth I am not at all fond of German poetry'.[60]

The English literary renaissance in the last three decades of Hannah More's life provided a severe test of an elderly lady's adaptability to new forms and new ideas. Evangelicals who were courageous enough to read Coleridge, Wordsworth, de Quincey, or Byron, Shelley, and Keats found themselves reading literature which profoundly shocked them, for the Romantic poets, though they did not speak with one voice, were to a man antagonistic to Evangelicalism and the Evangelical Plan. Miss More, who combined her Evangelicalism with a literary reputation based, in their opinion, on the flimsiest of foundations, was treated by them with amused contempt and disrespectful comment. Coleridge, brought to Barley Wood by the ubiquitous Cottle, still engaged in seeking support for penniless poets, confused the minds of five elderly ladies, unversed in metaphysics, by 'the bright colours without form sublimely void' of his brilliant conversation. Coleridge, for his part, found 'the flattery of religious persons the worst kind of flattery'. 'Never shall I forget the amoeban eclogue between Miss Hannah More and an Evangelical Countess which I heard at the breakfast table at Miss More's.'[61] Byron introduced 'Coelebs' wife in search of lovers' into *Don Juan* and listened with unmitigated enjoyment to de Quincey's scurrilous account of Hannah More's broken engagement to William Turner fifty years earlier. De Quincey, Hannah More's neighbour at West Hay, and during his Oxford vacations a frequent guest at Barley Wood, attributed his mother's tiresome anxiety for her 'wayward boy's' irreligious views and intellectual precocity to Miss More's Evangelical influence and did not attempt to hide his dislike or control his tongue. In an essay, published anonymously within three months of Hannah More's death, he tore her literary reputation to tatters, and, granting her 'sincere piety', denounced her as a woman of worldly mind and social ambitions.[62]

There is little reference in Hannah More's published correspondence of the 'nineties to poetry, which in her younger days had been her chief literary pleasure. The republicanism and 'semi-atheism' of the early Romantics put their work in these years automatically outside her sphere of interest or approval. When her self-imposed discipline was relaxed in the early decades of the nineteenth century she found herself in a new and strange literary world which delighted while it alarmed her. Scott was her harbinger of change. She greeted his poems with enthusiasm. The *Lay of the Last Minstrel*, the *Lady of the Lake*, and *Marmion* enchanted her. 'I had thought poetry was dead until I read Walter Scott,' she wrote to Pepys, and with characteristic enthusiasm she ordered her bookseller to send her 'everything of Walter Scott's (I mean his poetry) as soon as it shall descend to the attainable price of 12s.' When *Rokeby* arrived, she and the sisters 'fell to' and sat up half the night reading it aloud in turns. 'It had not', she remarked, 'the same attraction as the *Lady of the Lake*, but I am not disposed to be critical where pleasure is the prevailing feeling.'[63] Unhappily, pleasure did not remain the prevailing feeling. Scott, she discovered, had few maxims for the improvement of life and manners. 'I would not have it supposed I had not read with delight and admiration all his poetry. This is a repast which may be taken with safety, though certainly not with profit,' for the poems though 'not anti-moral' were 'non-moral'. But the novels were taboo. She had read one and a half volumes when she discovered from the reviews that 'the absence of evil rather than the presence of good' characterized them. And the seemingly endless spate of Waverley romances perturbed her. To attempt to read thirty novels would be 'a misapplication of time' involving a waste of thousands of hours, 'too much for our poor scanty three score years and ten'.[64]

Of the younger group of Romantic poets Byron alone is mentioned, only to be condemned. 'No one', said Miss More flatly, 'should read Byron and his compeers in sin and infamy.' Unlike Scott, he was 'an anti-moralist'. She did not see, as a later critic has suggested, that Byron was 'the only one of the greater romantics whom Biblical Evangelical Christianity had got *inside*', and that it was 'the Orthodox Evangelical doctrine of sin and guilt and retribution with which Byron is always inwardly at war'.[65]

In 1814 she made a discovery redounding to her credit. Since she depended on the reviews for an estimate of new writers, Wordsworth was but a name to her. He too had been a republican and semi-atheist; he too was not averse from philosophical speculations, but the *Excursion*, introduced to her by Jeffrey's savage review in the *Edinburgh*, wiped away all Wordsworth's earlier errors. Perhaps the 'natural Methodism' which Charles Lamb discovered in Wordsworth revealed itself to her. 'She could not believe', reported James Hogg, that 'these noble Miltonic lines had been written by a man whom the reviewers had been assailing for years,'[66] and whom Evangelicals of her day denounced as anti-Christian. 'William', wrote de Quincey satirically from West Hay to Dorothy Wordsworth, telling her of Wordsworth's visit to Barley Wood, 'has made a conquest of Holy Hannah.'[67]

(iv)

During the lifetime of the sisters it was possible by a division of duties to cope with the innumerable charities, the care of the house and estate, and the 'tormenting guests', but when 'the bright sisterhood' which for over sixty years had enjoyed each other's company, 'just as if they were acquaintances of last winter',[68] was broken by the death of Mary in 1813, followed by that of Elizabeth in 1816, Sally in 1817, and the dearly loved Patty in 1819, Hannah was left to maintain family standards of hospitality at an age when the grasshopper is a burden. At no period of her life had she enjoyed, in Dr Johnson's phrase, 'a plentiful lack of time'.

As to myself [she wrote to Wilberforce] I think I have never been more hurried and more engaged, more loaded with cares than at present. I do not mean afflictions, but a total want of that article for which I built my house and planted my grove. I mean retirement. It is a thing I only know by name. . . I saw fifty persons last week and it is commonly the same every week. I know not how to help it. If my guests are old I see them out of respect. If young I hope I may do some little good. If they come from a distance I feel I ought to see them on that account. . . Oh, what a comfort to think that there really remaineth a rest for the people of God.[69]

A plethora of guests was not the only burden of her old age. For nearly half a century the loving and admiring sisters had relieved her of school and household duties and had shared the burden of her philanthropy. In her seventy-fifth year, except for the help of a series of young and not always competent companions, she was left alone to administer the innumerable charities and to control a large and overstaffed house. Chronic ill health kept her for seven years, 1818–25, a prisoner in two upstairs rooms 'opening out of one another so that I may have room for exercise'. 'It is no want of strength,' she averred cheerfully to her friends, 'but my kindly physician will not allow me to walk out, as a cold has so often threatened to be fatal to me.'[70] It was during these years in the upstairs rooms that the domestic tragedy which ended Hannah More's days at Barley Wood was prepared.

Without experience of household management and unable for long stretches of time to move about the house and grounds, she became dependent on the senior servants, some of whom had been with the family for years, to run the house as her sisters had done. Consistently considerate to servants, constitutionally afraid of giving trouble, she added to their number lest her illness and frequent guests should make their work burdensome to them. The extra-

PLATE III

HANNAH MORE IN OLD AGE AT BARLEY WOOD

ordinary increase in her expenses in the years following Patty's death, so that expenditure greatly exceeded income, she attributed to her own incompetence. But rumours that all was not well below stairs at Barley Wood spread among her neighbours and were reported to Zachary Macaulay. In a letter to the old lady he informed her of her servants' habits of intemperance, profusion, and neglect,[71] and followed up his letter by a visit, when he produced in person witnesses to the shameful peculation in the house and home-farm by 'eight pampered minions', who, when they had put Miss More to bed after family prayers in her rooms, entertained their guests to evening parties in the kitchen quarters, or slunk out of the house after dark to dance in Wrington village, leaving their mistress unattended. To Macaulay's urgent plea that she should leave Barley Wood and move to Clifton, where her friends could the more easily care for her, Hannah More, overwhelmed by the defection of her servants and distressed by the anxiety of her friends, gave a reluctant assent. Escorted by a dozen gentlemen of the neighbourhood, she left Barley Wood in April 1828. 'I am driven like Eve out of Paradise, but not like Eve by angels.'[72] Five years later, still interested and cheerful till her mind failed in the last months of her life, she died at Clifton Wood.

CONCLUSION

'Her writings may continue to sell during her lifetime, but they will not be heard of later.'
Eclectic Review, quoted by Hannah More, 1827

(i)

THE prophesy by the *Eclectic Review* of the swift decline of Hannah More's contemporary reputation, requires modification. The several editions of her writings published in the nineteenth century show that she was not without readers after her death; none the less the nineteenth century so effectively destroyed her reputation that today those who remember her name vaguely associate it with schools set up in the Mendip villages and with a series of unread and unreadable books.

The reaction of a new age to its predecessor explains in the main the indifference of many and the distaste of others for Hannah More and her writings. The length of her life made its contribution to the decline of her reputation. She belonged to a past era and because of her great age she formed part of the 'overlapping generation' whose presence in politics or literature or religion is unwelcome to a new generation bursting with fresh ideas and opinions and impatient of the old ways and old people.

Hannah More's character and personality did not escape criticism in her day. It persisted after her death and made its contribution to the decline of her reputation. For this the extravagant over-praise of her innumerable admirers was in great part responsible. Nothing is more unconvincing than indiscriminate praise. From her early days in Bristol to her death in 1833 Hannah More had been exposed by her friends and followers to a conspiracy of adulation. She made indifferent plays and they hailed her as a dramatist;

she wrote fugitive verse and they called her a poet; she was a Puritan and they dubbed her a saint. Later generations, who did not know her personally and were dependent on her writings for their estimates of her, found it difficult to accept the encomium of her contemporaries. The last of the eulogies, the *Memoirs of the Life and Correspondence* published in 1834, did little to convince posterity that Hannah More had earned their respect, or that scores of men, women, and children of her own day had regarded her with well deserved admiration and warm affection. 'Hannah More', said W. H. Prescott, after reading the *Memoirs*, 'has been done to death by her friend Roberts.'[1]

A life of eighty-nine years, stretching across one of the most complex and changing periods of English history, offers ample room and verge enough for the discovery of inconsistencies of conduct and faults of character. They may be found without difficulty in Hannah More's life. An old-fashioned Tory who wore the radical insignia of the abolition of the slave trade and the provision of instruction for the poor, an anti-feminist who enjoyed a freedom condemned by her as unsuitable for other women, a denouncer of plays who permitted the re-publication of her own dramatic writings does not appear as a model of consistency. Nor does her life disguise her faults of character. 'She was', said wise old Marianne Thornton, who knew her well, 'a little hardened by contumely and criticism, a little spoilt by her success.'[2] She was too great a respecter of persons, a fault she recognized and deplored, and she did not lack the spiritual vanity which has been called 'the besetting sin of Evangelicals'.[3] All this must be admitted, but the allegations of religious hypocrisy and worldly-mindedness made by William Shaw and Thomas de Quincey and other minor detractors cannot stand against the evidence of her life or the bulk of contemporary opinion. Her singleness of aim and generosity of temper are everywhere apparent. She emerges as a woman of integrity, piety, and moral courage, on whose tongue was the law of kindness. 'Don't believe anything you hear that she said or did,' wrote Miss Thornton, the last of Lord Macaulay's generation, to one of the

younger generation thirty years after Hannah More's death, 'she
was a fine creature overflowing with affection and feeling and
generosity.'[4]

(ii)

When the nineteenth century got into its stride, Hannah More's
close association with Evangelicism brought her under criticism of
the same nature as that to which it was exposed. That Evangelicism
was, in Mr Gladstone's words, 'a strong, systematic, outspoken
and determined reaction against the prevailing standards both of
life and preaching'[5] which exercised a profound influence on
spiritual understanding and moral conduct, conferred on it no immunity from harsh and prolonged criticism. The doctrines which
Miss More expounded were regarded as rigid and narrow. She
had followed Wilberforce in the emphasis which he laid upon the
need for precise and definite doctrine. The 'peculiar doctrines of
Christianity', defined by him in the *Practical View* as the corruption
of man, the efficiency of the Atonement, the sanctifying influence
of the Holy Spirit, and the unqualified prediction of eternal punishment for those who refused Christ's offer of Redemption, were her
peculiar doctrines. She said nothing on the doctrine of the Trinity
or of the Incarnation, and barely mentioned the life of Christ leading up to the Atonement. *Christus Redemptor*, not *Christus Con-
summator*, defined her doctrinal position. The doctrine of eternal
punishment cannot have failed to trouble her profoundly, as it
could not fail to trouble all religious minds, but she accepted it
without submitting it to the grave inquiry of nineteenth-century
thought. In the eyes of later generations of religious men she represented a restricted and above all a disproportionate view of
Christian doctrine.

Moreover the Evangelical Plan was open to adverse criticism on
counts other than that of doctrine. Neo-Anglicanism asserted that
Evangelicalism had neglected the Catholic aspects of the Christian
system. It is true that Evangelicals laid little emphasis on the
Church as a divine institution; the organization of episcopacy was

230

apparently a matter of secondary importance to them, and, with notable exceptions, sacramental observances were not stressed in their teaching. They conceived of religion primarily as a subjective relationship between the individual soul and God. Hannah More's teaching, no less than that of her fellow Evangelicals, was open to criticism on these lines. She was not, it is clear, indifferent to the Church principle of episcopacy; she had a genuine attachment to apostolic order; she had expounded a view of the visible Church in her *Hints*; but the Catholic aspects were not stressed in her teaching. 'Christianity', she said, 'is not a religion of forms and modes and decencies: it is being transformed into the image of God.' She referred her readers to Chapter XX of the *Strictures* as the expression of her faith, and drew from Miss Charlotte Yonge a sharp and pertinent Anglo-Catholic criticism of her book.

Considering that the authoress believed herself a thorough church-woman her views in the latter chapters of her book are curiously lacking in any references to church ordinances, or the means of grace. She had said nothing which was not borne out by the Articles and the Liturgy. The point was what she had *not* said.[6]

Equally open to the animadversions of the new age was the philosophical weakness of her homiletical writings. Always apparent, it became conspicuous in an age alive with new intellectual life and possessing in the historic method a new apparatus for finding and assessing truth. It would be unfair to condemn Hannah More for her ignorance of evolutionary theories which were to revolutionize nineteenth-century thought, or for her unwillingness to apply the remarkable work in Bible criticism, which marked the new age, to the explanation and interpretation of the traditional biblical narrative. These things were in the future. But, except in the *Hints*, there is no evidence that the new trends of thought, new widening of horizons in the last twenty-five years of her life, of which she cannot have been unaware, received a welcome. Yet Coleridge, whom she knew personally, pleading for a more profound religious philosophy, was not a dumb oracle in these years, and Dr Marsh had translated Part I of Michaelis's *Introduction to the*

New Testament, with Notes of his own in 1793. It might have been expected that any contribution which could explain and interpret the Scriptures to an earnest biblical student would have met with a measure of interest and acceptance. There is no sign of this in her writings. On the contrary she expressed in no measured terms her abhorrence of the 'new philosophical and theological speculations'.

Novelties in the sciences and in the arts may be...beneficial. Every invention may be an improvement; but in religion they are delusions. Genuine Christianity is not, as one class of men seem to suppose, a modern invention; serious piety is no fresh innovation. 'That which was from the beginning declare we unto you' are the words of inspiration. . . Though Holy Scripture was given to be searched [it] was not given to be criticized. . . Christianity is no appropriate field for the perplexities of metaphysics. . . It is not to be endured . . . to hear questions on which hang all our hopes and fears speculated upon as if they were a question of physics or history.[7]

Such an attitude of mind helps to explain her failure to make any permanent contribution to theological thought, and goes some way to justify Mark Pattison's harsh criticism of Evangelicalism in the 'thirties:

In 1833 Evangelicalism was already effete. The helpless imbecility of Evangelical writing and preaching, their obvious want of power to solve or even to apprehend the questions on which they were nevertheless perpetually talking; their incapacity to explain the Scripture while assuming the exclusive right to it; their conceit of being able to arrive at conclusions without premises, in a word their intellectual weakness contributed very greatly to the fall of the Evangelical school before a better informed generation of men.[8]

To Hannah More could be applied the criticism to which Evangelicals were exposed. She too had divorced piety from intellect.

The divorce, which it is impossible to deny, has been attributed by some of the critics of the Evangelicals to their lack of intellectual capacity. Hannah More's life as a leading Evangelical of her day throws some doubt on this estimate. She did not lack intellectual capacity. Her long and sustained friendships with men and women of outstanding qualities of mind, 'worldly' as well as 'sober', their eager desire for her opinion and support on matters secular as well as religious, the breadth of her reading, the spirited comments on men and books in her letters, and the recognition by her most adverse critic of the 'very profound remarks scattered throughout her writings' absolve her from this condemnation. Nor can a lack of power in discussing 'theological speculations' be charged against a woman who talked and corresponded with Alexander Knox and Bishop Jebb. There is in her writings none of the contempt for things of the intellect attributed to the Evangelicals of her day. 'I put religion on my right hand and learning on my left. Learning should not be despised even as an auxiliary.'[9] Yet the works of her pen, by which posterity has judged her, involved no 'intellectual exercise' and reveal no sustained intellectual power which would be of permanent value to religion. She allowed no criticism of the Bible narrative, no truck with history or the historic method. She did not 'unite the pair so long disjoined, knowledge and vital piety'.

Nor did her writings admit critical appraisement of the Church she revered. She appeared insensitive to the Church's forgetfulness of its traditional social mission and was untroubled by its 'acquiescence in the conventional ethics, class-consciousness and economic inequalities of the age'.[10] Her occasional strictures, tempered by deference, were reserved for the individual servants of the Church who neglected their duties to their flocks. Her writings offered no help wherewith the Church could meet the new liberalism and all-powerful agnosticism of the coming age.

Hannah More's distrust of intellect *applied to religion* is the explanation of the poverty of her homiletics. The strength of her teaching, as that of her fellow Evangelicals, lay in its appeal to the hearts and consciences of men to live the Christian life. In her devoted efforts to save men's souls she had concentrated all the powers of her mind on piety, mistrusting intellect as its indispensable companion in Christian apologetics. During the troubled years of the 'nineties when she could not make her peace with God, she had found it so difficult to live the Christian life that she had renounced all secular interests, and although in later years the discipline of life and religion taught her to modify her extravagance and she began again to read secular literature, the same unwillingness to allow intellect to impinge on piety is apparent in her later works. 'That I have added to the mass of general knowledge by one original idea, or to the stock of virtue by one original sentiment I do not presume to hope. But that I have laboured assiduously to make that kind of knowledge which is most indispensable to common life familiar to the unlearned and acceptable to the young . . . I will not deny to have attempted.'[11] To this end theological and historical speculations were unnecessary. 'I know no way of teaching morals but by infusing principles of Christianity, nor of teaching Christianity without a thorough knowledge of Scripture.' This was to her the work of supreme importance. All else was relatively valueless. 'Search the Scriptures, seek the help of the Holy Spirit, follow Christ's example in well-doing and stretch every faculty in the service of the Lord.'

This simple and sincere teaching came also under criticism of a new kind. John Foster's memorable essay *On the Aversion of Men of Taste to the Evangelical Religion* had already revealed and deplored the rapid development of a conventional phraseology among Evangelicals, closely connected, Foster insisted, with their lack of 'intellectual exercise'. Hannah More's essay on *High Profession and Negligent Practice* treated the same subject in a similar manner. She protested against the 'Phraseologists' who, desiring a reputation for holiness, 'picked up the idiom of a Party' and 'indulged in spiritual gossiping with a lack of taste and breeding'. To them she ascribed the unjust association which persons of refinement made between religion and bad taste. But Miss More herself was not free from the same failing. Honest and sincere, she did not always manage to avoid party slang and sanctimonious phrase. Her didactic writings and her letters are remarkably free from cant, but they are not free from religious pedantry, nor from the mannerisms which the 'unco guid' of her day introduced into common parlance. Lady Chatterton, the warm admirer of a woman who, in her opinion, was entitled to the reverence of succeeding generations, referred regretfully to the kind of 'fat complacency' which Hannah More used in speaking of the Evangelical faith.[12] This it was, perhaps even more than her narrow doctrine and neglect of Catholic aspects, which offended subsequent generations. To her contemporaries the idiom was common form. Posterity denounced it as cant.

(iii)

The social implications of Hannah More's teaching cannot be disregarded as a primary factor in the decline of her reputation. As a child of her age she shared the assumptions, unchallenged until French Revolutionary ideas threatened them, that government was the preserve of the governing classes and could not be bettered. When revolution threatened these assumptions she, like the majority of her countrymen, hastened to support the old order of things. The attempts of radical reformers to modify the political structure were to her the work of evil men out to overthrow for the sake of overthrowing. Furthermore, living in an age dominated by the all-powerful philosophy of individualism, which reduced the function of the State to its lowest terms—the maintenance of order and defence—she could not conceive of a Great Society as an association for mutual aid. And Evangelicalism reinforced her negative views, for it was the 'ally of individualism'.[13] Dicey in a brilliant passage has suggested that a theology, which insisted on personal responsibility and treated each man as himself bound to work out his own salvation, had an obvious affinity to a political philosophy which regarded men almost exclusively as separate individuals and made it the aim of law to secure for every person freedom to work out his own happiness.[14] To men of a different school of thought, passionately devoted, in the later years of the nineteenth and in the twentieth century, to concepts of Collectivism and the Welfare State, no expression of social irresponsibility could well have been more antipathetic; none more destructive of the reputation of those who taught it. That Hannah More had worked assiduously to alleviate poverty and to break down the isolation of the poor is forgotten. She was not, her life attests, in the least indifferent to the poverty and misery of the lower orders. She endeavoured to make their distress known through her parliamentary friends and by her personal efforts to alleviate it. But she lived in a static world on which the idea of social responsibility had not yet dawned, and whose social stratification and economic inequalities were accepted by the bulk of her contemporaries as the right and just order of things. She did not hold Burke's view of the 'Swinish Multitude'; she did not accept Paley's dubious thesis that the poor were to be congratulated on their freedom from the anxieties which accrued to classes burdened with wealth and harassed by the duties of office. 'The homely joys and destinies obscure' of the poor aroused her compassion. She knew, from first-hand experience, that the poor were decent, hard-working folk, who could not pay rent and feed a family on the wages paid to the West Country labourers; but she could not free herself from the assumption that the existing order of things was the ordained order of things. A woman of genuine humanitarianism, her religion never 'slipped into humanism'. Considerable effort is required today to recognize, still more to understand, that Hannah More was not primarily concerned with the incidence of wealth and poverty, but with the overriding importance of sin and redemption.

NOTES

The letters to or from Hannah More referred to in these notes, unless otherwise stated, are taken from the four volumes of Roberts's *Memoirs of the Life and Correspondence of Mrs Hannah More*. The punctuation has been modified.

CHAPTER I

1. Born respectively in 1738, 1740, 1743, 1745, 1747.

2. No letters to or from Hannah More and her parents appear in the *Life and Correspondence*. The *Quarterly Review*, no. 52 (1834), criticized their absence as a mark of filial indifference. In the Preface to the 3rd ed. of the *Memoirs* (1835), Roberts explained that he had deliberately refrained from printing intimate family letters.

3. See *Report of the Commissioners for Inquiry Concerning Charities*, 1825, x. The endowment of the Stapleton School was worth £15 p.a., but the normal custom for masters to receive pay pupils increased the emoluments.

4. Sally More from London to her sisters in Bristol, 1776 (I, 66). Sally is citing: 'When land is gone and money spent, then learning is most excellent.'

5. H.M. to her sisters, 1776 (I, 66). 'I find Mr Boswell called on you at Bristol with Dr Johnson. He told me so this morning, when he breakfasted here [the Adelphi] with Sir William Forbes and Dr Johnson.' Boswell and Johnson spent the night of 29 April 1776 in Bristol: see James Boswell, *Life of Samuel Johnson, LL.D.*, ed. A. Napier (1889), III, 94–5.

6. *The Wesleyan Methodist Pocket Book*, 1834.

7. H.M. to Mary More, 29 Mar. 1783 (I, 277).

8. J. Priestley, *Essay on a Course of Liberal Education* (1760).

9. R. Steele, *The Ladies Library* (1714), ch. I.

10. J. Swift, *Select Works* (1825), XI, 64.

11. Boswell, op. cit., III, 333.

12. Lady Mary Wortley Montagu, *Letters and Works*, II, 226, 293; see also Mrs D. Gardiner, *English Girlhood at School* (Oxford, 1929).

13. Boswell, op. cit., III, 333.

Notes

14. *Sentimental Magazine*, July 1773.

15. *A Journey through England*, 1724.

16. 'It was a singular coincidence reflecting great credit on Bristol', wrote Joseph Cottle in the 'nineties, 'that the King's poet, the King's painter, the King's physician, the King's musician, and the Champion of England should all at the same time have been Bristol men, namely Robert Southey, Sir Thomas Lawrence, Dr Henry Southey, Charles Wesley, and the Game Chicken.' *Early Recollections chiefly relating to the late Samuel Taylor Coleridge* (1837), I, 82.

17. Nichols and Taylor, *Bristol Past and Present* (1881), 200.

18. 'All the relief she [Mrs Chatterton] has procured has been from the indefatigable and unsolicited benevolence of the admirable family of the Mores, for which she was extremely grateful, though it was neither adequate to her wants, or their wishes.' Mrs Elizabeth Carter to Mrs Elizabeth Montagu, 17 Dec. 1781, in *Letters of Mrs Elizabeth Carter* (1817), III, 160. See also E. H. W. Meyerstein's *Life of Thomas Chatterton* (1930).

19. 'Perdita', *la maîtresse déclosée* of the Prince of Wales, stated in her *Memoirs* of 1785 that she had been educated at the Mores' school, and had been taken by the sisters to her first dramatic performance. Her reputation was, later, used as a stick wherewith to beat Miss More. 'I suppose', wrote W. W. Pepys satirically to H.M., 15 Aug. 1785, 'that you have received a thousand congratulations from your friends upon the discovery that Mrs Robinson has lately made known.' 'Perdita' left the Mores' school at the age of four.

20. *Public Characters*, I, 436.

21. See articles in *The Western Daily Press*, 6 Sept. 1949, on the position of the Mores' school in Park Street.

22. *Mrs Elizabeth Montagu, Queen of the Blues, Her Letters and Friendships*, ed. R. Blunt, III, 3.

23. The Dean of Canterbury to H.M., 1789 (II, 203).

24. H.M. to her sisters, 1776 (I, 78): 'Mrs Boscawen came to see me the other day with the duchess in her gilt chariot, with four footmen.'

25. See R. L. Schuyler, *Josiah Tucker* (New York, 1931), 107–8; see also *Life of Bishop Thomas Newton*, by himself (1782).

26. (See also ch. IV, note 11). The Reverend Doctor Sir James Stonhouse, Bart., Rector of Great and Little Cheverell, Wilts., and Lecturer at All Saints Church, Clifton. See *Life and Times of Selina, Countess of Huntingdon*, by a Member of the Houses of Hastings and Shirley, I and II passim.

27. Forster Papers, *Recollections of Miss Marianne Thornton*; see Dr Thomas Winterbottom, quoted by Lady Knutsford, in *Life and Letters of Zachary Macaulay*, 23.

Chapter I

28. J. C. Colquhoun, *Wilberforce and his Friends and Times* (1867), 112.

29. See H.M. to Mrs Kennicott, 1817; W. Roberts, *Memoirs of the Life of Mrs Hannah More* in one vol. (1838); Forster Papers; Lord Templewood, *The Unbroken Thread* (1949), 61.

30. 'Miss Cadogan informed us', wrote Mary Hamilton in May 1784, 'that she was acquainted with Miss H. More's sisters, who keep the school at Bristol; that the five sisters were all different, but equally amiable and clever; gave many striking instances of their genius, benevolence and excellent principles.' *Mary Dickenson, Letters and Diaries, 1756–1816* (1925), ed. E. and M. Anson.

31. Forster Papers.

32. The portraits of Hannah More by Miss Reynolds and Opie are not very satisfactory, and no remarks upon Miss More's appearance in her youth seem to be extant, except constant references to her dark and brilliant eyes. Thomas de Quincey's post-dated comment, 'She must have been very pretty when she was a girl,' appeared in 'Literary Recollections' in *Tait's Edinburgh Magazine* (March 1841). Nathaniel Wraxall's description of the Countess of Albany, wife of the Young Pretender, whom Miss More, according to her friends, strongly resembled, may be regarded as a pen-portrait of her in her early London days: 'Her person was formed on a small size, with a fair complexion, delicate features and lively as well as attractive manners, her deportment, unassuming but dignified, set off her attractions.' N. W. Wraxall, *Historical Memoirs of My Own Time* (1904), Parts I and II, 1772–84, 184.

33. Boswell, I, 235.

34. Horace Walpole to Mary Berry, 19 July 1789. The Yale Edition of *Horace Walpole's Correspondence*, ed. W. S. Lewis (1939—), I, 38.

35. H.M. to Mrs Boscawen, 13 May 1780 (I, 181). Epitaph on Mrs Patience Little, in St Mary Redcliffe Church, Bristol:

> Oh could this verse her fair example spread,
> And teach the living while it praised the dead,
> Then, Reader, should it speak her hope divine
> Not to record her faith, but strengthen thine:
> Then should her every virtue stand confest
> Till every virtue kindled in thy breast.
> But if thou slight the monitory strain
> And she has lived to thee at least in vain,
> Yet let her death an awful lesson give,
> The dying Christian speaks to all that live;
> Enough for her that here her ashes rest
> 'Tis God's own plaudit shall her worth attest.

H.M., *Collected Works* (1853), V, 181.

36. H.M. to her sisters, 1781 (I, 214): 'Mr Burke came and sat next me for an hour . . . and he repeated my epitaph in Redcliffe Church.'

37. Forster Papers.

38. *Sacred Dramas, chiefly intended for Young Persons on Subjects taken from the Bible, including Moses in the Bull-rushes, David and Goliath, Belshazzar, Daniel* (1782). Dedicated to the Duchess of Beaufort. H.M., *Collected Works*, VI.

39. Peter Pindar, Esq. [Dr John Wolcot], *Works* (1805), I, 7.

40. *The Search after Happiness* (1773). Dedicated to Mrs Gwatkin. H.M., *Collected Works*, VI.

41. See Mary Mitford, 'Our Village', in *Early Recollections* (1856), 286–96.

42. C. M. Yonge, *Hannah More* (1888), 4.

43. de Quincey, 'Literary Recollections', loc. cit.

44. Roberts, *Memoirs*, I, 34.

45. *Strictures on the Modern System of Female Education* (1799), ch. 14. H.M., *Collected Works*, III.

46. See Richard Jenkins, *Memoirs of the British Stage* (Bristol, 1826).

47. Mrs Boscawen to H.M., 1782 (I, 230).

48. Mrs Boscawen to H.M., 1780 (I, 190).

49. John Langhorne to Hannah More, 1773–6 (I, 19–28); 24 January 1775 (I, 22). *Stanzas written in the Author's Garden, on the Promise of a visit from a Lady.* For Langhorne, see his *Life* by Alexander Chalmers (1810), XVI; and H. Macdonald, 'John Langhorne', in *Essays on the Eighteenth Century, presented to David Nichol Smith* (Oxford, 1945).

50. Roberts, *Memoirs*, I, 58.

51. W. E. Weare, *Edmund Burke's Connections with Bristol, 1774–80* (Bristol, 1894); *Observations on a Pamphlet entitled 'Thoughts on the Causes of the Present Discontents'*, by Catherine Macaulay (1770).

52. Basil Willey, *The Eighteenth Century Background: Studies on the idea of Nature in the Thought of the Period* (London, 1940), 250.

53. Lord Macaulay, Review of the *Diary and Letters of Madame d'Arblay*, *Collected Essays* (1842).

54. 'I have a terror of newspapers, from which I have found by sad experience no mediocrity can secure one.' H.M., I, 301.

CHAPTER II

1. David Garrick, 1717–79; Mrs Garrick, 1724–1822: see Margaret Barton's recent study of *Garrick* (1948).

Chapter II

2. Horace Walpole to Horace Mann, 12 Aug. 1746: Mrs Paget Toynbee, *The Letters of Horace Walpole*, 1903–5, II, 230.

3. Quoted by Mrs Clement Parsons, *Garrick and his Circle* (1906).

4. H.M. to Mrs Lovell Gwatkin, Dr Stonhouse, and her sisters, May 1776 (I, 90, 88).

5. Percy Fitzgerald, *Life of Mrs Catherine Clive* (1888), 93–103.

6. H.M. to her sisters, Mar. 1776 (I, 64).

7. H.M. to David Garrick, 10 June 1776 (I, 94).

8. H.M. to her sisters, 1776 (I, 87).

9. The Rev. William Shaw, Rector of Chelvey, Somerset, *Life of Hannah More, with a Critical Review of her Writings* (Bristol, 1802).

10. Percy Fitzgerald, *Life of David Garrick* (1899).

11. H.M. to her sisters, 1776 (I, 78).

12. H.M. to Mrs Gwatkin, 9 Aug. 1778 (I, 144).

13. Percy Fitzgerald, *Life of David Garrick*, 435 et seq.

14. See Dr M. D. George, *Introduction to the Catalogue of Political and Personal Satires, 1801–1810* (1947), VIII.

15. Lines from Goldsmith's *Retaliation:*

> Here lies David Garrick, describe me who can,
> An abridgement of all that was pleasant in man;
> As an actor, confess'd without rival to shine;
> As a wit, if not first, in the very first line;
> Yet, with talents like these, and an excellent heart,
> The man had his failings, a dupe to his art.
> Like an ill-judging beauty his colours he spread,
> And beplastered with rouge his own natural red.
> On the stage he was natural, simple, affecting;
> 'Twas only that when he was off he was acting.
> With no reason on earth to go out of his way,
> He turn'd and he varied full ten times a day:
> Though secure of our hearts, yet confoundedly sick,
> If they were not his own by finessing and trick.
> He cast off his friends as a huntsman his pack,
> For he knew when he pleas'd he could whistle them back.
> Of praise a mere glutton, he swallow'd what came.
> And the puff of a dunce he mistook it for fame,
> Till, his relish grown callous, almost to disease,
> Who pepper'd the highest was surest to please.

16. H.M. to her sisters, Apr. 1786 (II, 16).

Notes

17. *Monthly Review*, Aug. 1777.

18. H.M. to her sisters, Jan. 1779 (I, 149).

19. H.M. to her sisters, 1778 (I, 132-3).

20. Patty More from Hampton, to the sisters in Bristol, 1779 (I, 68).

21. H.M. to her sisters, 1779 (I, 149).

22. *Essays on Various Subjects, principally designed for Young Ladies* (1777). Dedicated to Mrs Montagu. H.M., *Collected Works*, II. The book received a very favourable review, presumably by Langhorne, in *The Monthly Review* for Sept. 1777.

23. H.M. to her sisters from Farnborough Place, 1777 (I, 113).

24. H.M. to her sisters, 1777 (I, 51).

25. H.M. to her sisters, 1780 (I, 170).

26. H.M. to her sisters, 1776 (I, 84).

27. H.M. to Mr and Mrs Huber, 1820 (I, 101-2).

28. H.M. to her sisters, 1777 (I, 112). William Windham (1750-1810), 'Burke's political pupil', M.P. for Norfolk, 1784-1802; sometime friend and supporter of William Cobbett; strong opponent of H.M. in the Blagdon Controversy.

29. H.M. to her sisters, Apr. 1776 (I, 69-70).

30. H.M. to her sisters, 1776 (I, 70).

31. See H.M., *Collected Works*, V.

32. Sally More to Mrs Gwatkin from Bath, 8 Apr. 1775, in 'A Famous Bath Première, 1776,' by A. M. Broadley, in the *Bath Herald*, 4 Mar. 1909.

33. H.M., *Collected Works*, V.

34. Garrick to H.M., 1777 (I, 110).

35. H.M. to Garrick, 1777 (I, 110).

36. Garrick to H.M. 1777 (I, 116).

37. H.M. to her sisters, 1777 (I, 122).

38. H.M., *Collected Works*, V. See J. Genest, *History of the Stage*, VI.

39. H. V. Routh, 'The Georgian Drama', in the *Cambridge History of English Literature*, XI, ch. 12.

40. H.M. to her sisters, quoting Kitty Clive, 1778 (I, 133).

41. Thomas Davies, *Life of David Garrick* (1781), II, 33.

42. Routh, op. cit.

43. H.M. to her sisters, 1778 (I, 102, 125, 127, 128, 141). 'Miss More', wrote Mrs Barbauld to Dr Aikin, 'is, I assure you, very much the *ton*, and moreover she has got six or seven hundred pounds for her play,' 19 Jan. 1778: *Works of Mrs Barbauld . . . by Lucy Aikin*, II, 18.

Chapter III

44. H.M. to her sisters, 1787 (II, 54).

45. H.M. to her sisters, 1779 (I, 164); 1788 (II, 99); Mrs Boscawen to H.M., 1784 (I, 332).

46. *Monthly Review*, Mar. 1778; Peter Pindar, *Epistle to those Literary Colossuses, The Reviewers;* Walpole, *Letters*, ed. W. S. Lewis, I, 302; *Diary and Letters of Madame D'Arblay*, 1778–1840, ed. by her niece Charlotte Barrett, with Preface and Notes by Austin Dobson (1904–5), II, 145; H.M. to Mrs Gwatkin, 5 Mar. 1778.

47. The sisters in London to the sisters in Bristol, 1779 (I, 163); see H.M., *Collected Works*, V.

48. *The St James' Chronicle*, 7, 10, 11, 13 Aug. 1778; *The Gazetteer*, 6 Aug. 1778; *The Gentleman's Magazine*, Sept. 1779.

49. *The St James' Chronicle*, 7 and 13 Aug. 1778; see Genest, op. cit., VI, 100.

50. See Preface to the Tragedies, H.M., *Collected Works*, V.

51. H.M. to her sisters, 1780 (I, 166).

52. H.M. to her sisters, 1785 (I, 396).

53. *The Private Papers of James Boswell from Malahide Castle*, in the Collection of R. H. Isham, 20 Apr. 1781, II, 203.

CHAPTER III

1. Mrs Montagu, 1720–1800; Mrs Vesey, 1723–91; Mrs Carter, 1726–1806; Mrs Chapone, 1727–1801.

2. But see C. S. Lewis, 'Addison', in *Essays on the Eighteenth Century presented to David Nichol Smith* (Oxford, 1945): 'Everything the moderns detest, all they call *smugness, complacency* and *bourgeois ideology* is brought together in his work and given its most perfect expression.'

3. H.M. to her sisters, 1775 (I, 39, 51, 99); 1782 (I, 248); 1783 (I, 274).

4. Roberts, *Memoirs*, I, 48.

5. Sally More to her sisters in Bristol, 1774 (I, 49).

6. Roberts, *Memoirs*, I, 50.

7. Sally More to her sisters in Bristol, 1776 (I, 55, 66).

8. *Anecdotes of the late Samuel Johnson, LL.D. during the last twenty years of his life*, by Hester Lynch Piozzi (1786), ed. R. Napier (1889).

9. Boswell, IV, 251–2.

10. Boswell, III, 300.

11. Roberts, Preface to 3rd ed. of *Memoirs*.

Notes

12. *Recollections of Dr Johnson*, by Miss Reynolds, ed. R. Napier (1889).

13. Anson MSS., H.M. to Mary Hamilton, Sept. 1783.

14. H.M. to her sisters, 1776 (I, 62–4).

15.   I put my hat upon my head,
        And went into the Strand,
        And there I met another man,
        With his hat in his hand.

16. H.M. to her sisters, 1776 (I, 64); 1780 (I, 174, 175, 162); 1781 (I, 211–2); 1780 (I, 168–9).

17. Mrs Kennicott, Hannah told her sisters, was 'a very agreeable woman though she copies Hebrew'. June 1782 (I, 161–2); see Henry Thompson, *Life of Hannah More with Notices of her Sisters*, (1838), 47.

18. H.M. to her sisters, 1782 (I, 261).

19. *Bas Bleu, or Conversation* published 1786: H.M., *Collected Works*, V; H.M. to her sisters, 1784 (I, 319).

20. *Letters of Samuel Johnson, LL.D.*, ed. G. B. Hill (1892), II, 2942; Forbes, *Life of James Beattie*, 2 vols. (1806); Roberts, *Memoirs*, II, 341. The *Quarterly Review* for Aug. 1834, reviewing Roberts's *Memoirs*, cited several of her 'terse couplets, often in the mouths of people, who fancy they belong to Swift or Gay':

        He thought the World to him was known,
        Whereas he only knew the Town.

        In men this blunder still you find,
        All think their little set, mankind.

        Small habits well perused betimes
        May reach the dignity of crimes.

21. Boswell, 1 Jan. 1763 (I, 367).

22. H.M. to her sisters, 1782 (I, 236–7); H.M. to W. W. Pepys, 1788 (II, 131).

23. See Professor G. B. Tinker, *The Salon and English Letters* (New York, 1915); see also H.M., 'English Opinion of French Society', *Collected Works*, XI.

24. A. A. C. Gaussen, *Memoirs of Elizabeth Carter* (1906), 146.

25. Preface to *Bas Bleu*, addressed to Mrs Vesey: H.M., *Collected Works*, V.

26. *Selections from the MSS. of Lady Louisa Stuart*, ed. J. A. Hone (Edinburgh, 1899), 156.

27. Anson MSS.

28. N. W. Wraxall, *Historical Memoirs of my Own Time*, 1772–84.

29. H.M. to her sisters, Apr. 1784 (I, 319).

Chapter III

30. H.M. to her sisters, 1775 (I, 57).

31. Boswell, 1778 (III, 331); see General Aspinall-Oglander, *The Admiral's Wife* (1940), and *The Admiral's Widow* (1942).

32. H.M. to her sisters, 1775 (I, 56–7).

33. *Lady Louisa Stuart MSS.*, 162.

34. *Autobiography and Correspondence of Mary Granville, Mrs Delany*, ed. by Lady Llanover (1861–2), second series, I, 205.

35. H.M. to her sisters, 1775 (I, 63–4). In Dr Johnson's opinion *Braganza* was 'a one-sided play', 'paralytic on one side'; see Dr Thomas Campbell, *Diary of a Visit to England in 1775*, ed. R. Napier (1889), 157.

36. H.M. to her sisters, 1776 (I, 63).

37. *Lady Louisa Stuart MSS.*, 162. 'Hermes' Harris was Private Secretary to H.M. the Queen.

38. H.M. to W. W. Pepys, 1786 (II, 40); see Dorothy Stroud, *Capability Brown* (1950), ch. XIV, on Sandleford Priory.

39. Mrs Montagu to H.M., 1786 (II, 25).

40. A. C. C. Gaussen, op. cit.; H.M. to Mrs Carter, 1784 (I, 354, III, 254, 305); H.M. to Alexander Knox, 1809 (IV, 306).

41. H.M. to her sisters, reporting Mrs Boscawen, 11 Jan. 1788 (II, 98).

42. H.M. to her sisters, 1775 (I, 53); 1780 (I, 173); 1786 (II, 35).

43. H.M. to her sisters 1780 (I, 172, 183); Mrs Boscawen to H.M., 1786 (II, 31); 1776 (I, 97); 1780 (I, 189); 1782 (I, 225); 1784 (I, 322); 1786 (II, 35).

44. See *Diary and Letters of Madame d'Arblay, 1778–1840* (1904–5) II, 145.

45. H.M. to her sisters, 1784 (I, 357).

46. Horace Walpole to the Countess of Upper Ossory, 14 Jan. 1791: Paget Toynbee, XI, 369.

47. Mrs Vesey to H.M., May 1784 (I, 338).

48. *Bas Bleu, or Conversation* (1786). Addressed to Mrs Vesey. H.M., *Collected Works*, V.

49. H.M. to her sisters, 1780 (I, 171).

50. *Thraliana: The Diary of Mrs Hester Lynch Thrale (later Mrs Piozzi), 1776–1809*, ed. Katherine C. Balderston (Oxford, 1942), II, 1020.

51. See *Diary and Letters of Madame d'Arblay*, I, 188.

52. H.M. to her sisters, 1778 (I, 161).

53. Boswell, op. cit., 15 May 1784 (IV, 200). For Mrs Lennox, see Boswell, I, 196 note; and M. R. Small, *Charlotte Ramsay Lennox, an Eighteenth Century Lady of Letters* (New Haven, 1935).

R   245

Notes

54. H.M. to her sisters, I, 76, 230, 252, 322; II, 108; I, 184, 74, 211, 239; II, 276; I, 120, 382, 238, 274, 358; II, 348; I, 21, 105; II, 274. When Monboddo reported Hannah's refusal to Mrs Garrick he added regretfully, 'I should like to have taught that nice girl Greek.' J. S. Harford, *Recollections of Wilberforce*.

55. H.M. to W. W. Pepys, May 1811 (III, 343–9; I, 305). See A. C. C. Gaussen, *A Later Pepys*.

56. H.M. to her sisters, 1779 (I, 159); 1782 (I, 242); 1784 (I, 359).

57. H.M. to her sisters, 1784 (I, 316); 1786 (II, 12); 1788 (II, 109).

58. H.M. to her sisters, 1782 (I, 242): 'On Monday I was at a very great Assembly at the Bishop of St Asaph's. Conceive to yourself one hundred and fifty to two hundred people met together dressed in the extremity of the fashion; painted as red as Bacchanals; poisoning the air with perfumes; treading on each others gowns; making the crowd they blame; not one in ten able to get a chair; protesting that they are engaged to ten other places; and lamenting the fatigue they are not obliged to endure; ten or a dozen card tables crowded with dowagers of quality; grave ecclesiastics and yellow admirals; and you have an idea of an Assembly. I never go to these things when I can possibly avoid it, and stay when there as few minutes as I can.'

59. H.M. to her sisters, 1782 (I, 243), *Quarterly Review*, no. 52 (1834). 'She must', admitted the *Quarterly*, 'have been a delightful addition to London Society.'

60. T. B. Macaulay, *Edinburgh Review*, Oct. 1833.

61. W. Roberts, Preface to the second ed. of the *Memoirs* (1835).

62. See R. W. Ketton-Cremer, *Horace Walpole* (1940).

63. H.M. to her sisters, 1782 (I, 248).

64. H.M. to Mrs Boscawen, 1780 (I, 187); H.M. to her sisters, 1781 (I, 212); 29 Mar. 1783 (I, 277); 17 Feb. 1786 (II, 11).

65. Walpole to H.M., 6 Mar. 1784 (I, 335).

66. Walpole to Mary Berry, 10 July 1789, *Mary Berry, Journals and Correspondence*, I, 172.

67. Walpole's *Correspondence with George Montagu*, ed. Lewis, 25 Sept. 1748 (I, 77); H.M. to her sisters, 1781 (I, 213); 1783 (I, 287); Walpole to H.M., 15 June 1787 (II, 76).

68. Ketton-Cremer, op. cit., 117, 118, 119.

69. Walpole to H.M., 21 Aug. 1792 (II, 355); 1793 (II, 382); Walpole, *Letters*, ed. Lewis, II, 413; II, 276.

70. H.M. to her sisters, 17 Feb. 1786 (II, 11); 1788 (II, 109, 111); 1795 (II, 435).

71. Walpole to H.M., 21 Aug. 1792 (II, 353–5).

72. H.M. to Martha More, 1799 (III, 13).

Chapter IV

73. Robert Southey, *Lives and Works of Uneducated Poets* (1831); see also Joseph Cottle's racy account in *Early Recollections* (1837), I, 69; and for an admirable recent study see Dr J. M. S. Tompkins, 'The Bristol Milkwoman', in *The Polite Marriage* (Cambridge, 1938). A series of MS. letters in the possession of the Huntington Library, U.S.A., supplements the published letters and contemporary accounts.

74. H.M., Prefatory Letter to Mrs Montagu introducing *Poems on Several Occasions, by Ann Yearsley, a Milkwoman of Bristol* (1784).

75. Mrs Montagu to H.M., 1784 (I, 368–9); see also R. Blunt, op. cit. II.

76. *Poems on Several Occasions* (1785). Four editions were published, 1785–6.

77. See Dr J. M. S. Tompkins, 'The Bristol Milkwoman'. [*The Polite Marriage*, 1938.]

78. See Yearsley: *To the Noble and Generous Subscribers, who so liberally patronized a book of Poems published under the auspices of Miss Hannah More of Park Street Bristol, the following Narrative is most humbly addressed.* The Narrative was prefixed by Mrs Yearsley to the fourth edition of her poems.

79. Anson MSS., Mrs Garrick to Mary Hamilton, 30 Sept. 1785.

80. See H.M. to W. W. Pepys, 1785 (I, 388).

CHAPTER IV

1. The name given originally to the party which promoted the agitation in England against slavery: later popularly applied to the Evangelicals who taught world-renunciation and self-denial.

2. H.M. to her sisters, 1785 (I, 396): 'The profligacy, folly and madness of this Town is beyond the conception of those who do *not* see it.'

3. *The Life and Times of Selina Countess of Huntingdon*, I, 293.

4. *Letters of John Wesley*, ed. John Telford, 31 July 1790 (VIII, 230).

5. *The Life of William Wilberforce*, by his sons, Robert Isaac Wilberforce and Samuel Wilberforce (1838), see *errata* in Vol. I.

6. H.M. to the Bishop of Bath and Wells, 1802 (III, 125).

7. H.M., IV, 148.

8. H.M. to the Bishop of Bath and Wells, 1802 (III, 125).

9. J. C. Colquhoun, *Wilberforce: his Friends and Times* (1867).

10. See *Seventeen Sermons on some of the most important points of Natural and Revealed Religion*, by Josiah Tucker, D.D. (Gloucester, 1776).

11. Dr Stonhouse (1716–95) had been a physician of note in Northampton; he was 'converted from infidelity' by his friend Philip Doddridge. Leaving medicine he took Holy Orders, was Rector of Great and Little Cheverell,

Notes

Wilts, and follower at one time of George Whitefield; but 'worldly hopes and worldly fears', says Lady Huntingdon, 'were a perpetual stumbling block in his way'; *The Life and Times of Lady Huntingdon*, I, 138; see *Thraliana: the Diary of Hester Lynch Thrale (later Mrs Piozzi) 1776–1809*, ed. Katherine C. Balderston (Oxford, 1942), I, 94; and William Jay, *Autobiography*, ed. Redford and James (1855), 344.

12. H.M. to her sisters, 1776 (I, 57).

13. H.M., *Collected Works*, II: 'The Religion of the Fashionable World' (1791).

14. H.M. to her sisters, 1776 (I, 77); 1786 (II, 24). Captain Charles Middleton (1726–1813), created Lord Barham and First Lord of the Admiralty, 1805.

15. Wilberforce, *Life*, I, 257. See the Letters of Ignatius Latrobe to his Daughter, printed in the *Life of Wilberforce*, I, 142–6; Lady Chatterton, *Memorials of Admiral Gambier* (1861), I, 142; Sir Reginald Coupland, *Wilberforce* (Oxford, 1923).

16. Thomas Clarkson, *History of the Rise, Progress and the Abolition of the African Slave Trade by the British Parliament* (1839), 182.

17. See Sir John Clapham, *Cambridge History of the British Empire*, II, ch. VI.

18. See Clapham; Eric Williams, *Capitalism and Slavery* (University of North Carolina Press, 1944); C. M. McInnes, *Bristol, A Gateway of Empire* (1939).

19. H.M. to Mrs Bouverie, 1788, in Lady Chatterton, op. cit., I, 169; see Wilberforce, *Life*, 1788 (I, 183).

20. H.M. to Mrs Bouverie, in Lady Chatterton, op. cit.; H.M. to her sisters, Apr. 1789 (II, 152); the President of Magdalen College, Oxford, to H.M., 13 Feb. 1788 (II, 103).

21. *Oroonoko, or the Royal Slave*, by Thomas Southerne (1696), a dramatization of Mrs Aphra Behn's tale.

22. H.M. to Lady Middleton, 10 Sept. 1788, in Lady Chatterton, op. cit., I, 169–170.

23. H.M. to Elizabeth Carter, June 1789 (II, 70–1).

24. H.M. to her sisters, 1788 (II, 97–9). William Cowper, who had contemplated writing a poem on the same subject, abandoned the idea when he heard that Hannah More, 'who has more nerve and energy both in her thought and language, than half the he-rhymers in the Kingdom', was writing one: Cowper to Lady Hesketh, 16 Feb. 1788, in *The Correspondence of William Cowper*, arranged by Thomas Wright, III, 226–7.

25. See Hansard XXVII (1788–9), 495–506, 576–99, 635–52; XXVIII (1789–91), 41–67, 68–101, 311–15, 711–14; XXIX (1791–2), 258–359.

26. H.M. to her sisters, Apr. 1788 (II, 152–3); 1789 (II, 155–7).

27. H.M. to Mrs Kennicott, Apr. 1791 (II, 336). Hannah More's letters show that she retained her interest in slavery and the Slave Trade to the end of her

Chapter IV

days: MS. letter of H.M. to the Duchess of Beaufort dated 11 Feb. 1826, in the possession of Brigadier General Biddulph.

28. The *Life of Bishop Horne*, in *The Theological and Miscellaneous Works of the Rev. William Jones, M.A., F.R.S.* (1801), VI, 146. See Canon Charles Smyth's *Simeon and Church Order* (Cambridge, 1940).

29. Sir George Trevelyan, *The Life and Letters of Lord Macaulay* (1876), I, 9.

30. H.M. to Mrs Boscawen, 1780 (I, 188). For John Newton (1727-1807) see Life by the Rev. Josiah Bull (1868) and Bernard Martin's *John Newton* (1950).

31. Walter Bagehot, *Literary Studies* (1879), 43-4.

32. W. T. Cairns, 'John Newton: A Vindication', in *The Religion of Dr Johnson* (Oxford, 1946).

33. Newton to H.M. (II, 85). See Newton's *Thoughts upon the African Slave Trade* (1788).

34. H.M., Diary, 8 July 1803 (III, 196).

35. Sydney Smith in *The Edinburgh Review*, Jan. 1808: *Collected Works* (1851).

36. Dean R. W. Church, *The Oxford Movement* (1891), 3.

37. H.M. to her sisters, 1787 (II, 54).

38. H.M. to Newton, July 1789 (II, 115); 1791 (II, 237).

39. H.M., Diary, 1803 (III, 182).

40. H.M. to Mrs Bouverie, 1788, in Lady Chatterton, op. cit., I, 154.

41. Robert Southey, Preface to *Cowper's Poems*, in 15 vols. (1833-7).

42. *Letters of William Cowper*, ed. J. G. Frazer, II, 164; see also L. G. Hartley, *William Cowper, Humanitarian* (University of North Carolina Press, 1938). Neither Blake, nor Crabbe, nor Burns—humanitarians all and, in Schweitzer's phrase, possessed of 'the ethic of reverence for life'—are mentioned in Hannah More's *Works* or *Correspondence*.

43. H.M. to Mrs Bouverie, 1788, in Lady Chatterton, op. cit., I, 154; Cowper to Lady Hesketh, 16 Feb. and 12 Mar. 1788; see also *The Letters of William Cobbett to Edward Thornton*, ed. G. D. H. Cole (1937).

44. H.M. to her sisters, 1789 (II, 140). 'Mr Wilberforce', said Madame de Staël in 1814 to Sir Samuel Romilly, 'is the best converser I have met with in this country. I have always heard that he was most religious, but now I find that he is the wittiest man in England': Wilberforce, *Life*, IV, 167.

45. Wilberforce, *Life*, I, 112.

46. Wilberforce, *Life*, I, 138.

47. The *Cheap Repository Tracts on Slavery* included:
   (a) 'Babay, the true story of a good Negro woman' (1795).
   (b) 'The Sorrows of Yamba, or the Negro woman's lamentations' (1795).

Notes

(c) 'True Stories of Two Good Negroes'.

(d) 'The Black Prince: a true story, being the account of the Life and Death of Naimbanna, an African King's Son' (1798).

48. See *A Practical View of the Prevailing religious system of Professed Christians in the Higher and Middle classes in this Country, contrasted with real Christianity*, by William Wilberforce, member of Parliament for the County of York (1797).

49. Wilberforce, *Life*, I, 238. Only on one question did Wilberforce and Hannah More have any serious difference of opinion. When Roman Catholic Emancipation became a live political issue they were united in their opposition to it. Later, when Wilberforce changed his policy and supported Emancipation, Miss More remained inflexibly opposed. So vehement was she that their long friendship was in danger. But before 1829 Hannah More abandoned her hostility to the measure, saying that as so many of her friends 'whose sincerity and disinterestedness she admired'—Wilberforce, Acland, and others—were in favour of the bill, she would no longer oppose it. Dr Valpy, 'Reminiscences of Hannah More' in *The Christian Observer*, Mar. 1835.

50. H.M., *Collected Works*, IX.

51. H.M. to Alexander Knox, Nov. 1809 (III, 304).

52. (Sir) James Stephen, Essay on 'The Clapham Sect' in *Essays in Ecclesiastical Biography* (1849).

53. See W. M. Thackeray, *The Newcomes*.

54. See John Venn's *Sermons* in 3 vols. (1814–18). For an attractive monochrome portrait of this good and wise man see the *Memoirs* of his contemporary, the Rev. Charles Jerram (1855), 271.

55. *Life of Dean Milner*, by his niece Mary Milner (1842), 366.

56. Sydney Smith, in *The Letters of Peter Plymley* (1807), No. 5.

57. H.M. to Mrs Bouverie, in Lady Chatterton, op. cit., I, 277.

58. See Miss Dorothy Pym's *Battersea Rise* (1940).

59. Henry Thornton to Charles Grant, Sept. 1793; printed in Henry Morris, *Life of Charles Grant* (1904), 200.

60. H.M. to her sisters, 6 Aug. 1794: 'Wilberforce's carriage came for me after breakfast, and carried me to Battersea Rise for dinner, where were both the masters and Lord and Lady Balgonie. Wilberforce's carriage took me after dinner the next stage, where, to my great surprise, Henry was found awaiting me to carry me to my journey's end. There's politeness for you! Don't you think the masters are improving?' Forster Papers.

61. G. H. Spinney, *Cheap Repository Tracts*: 'Hazard and Marshall edition', in the *Transactions of the Bibliographical Society* (1940); see also Lady Knutsford, *Life of Zachary Macaulay* (1900).

Chapter IV

62. Maldwyn Lloyd Edwards, *This Methodism* (1939).

63. Wilberforce, *Life*, v, 71.

64. See the Note appended by Professor F. A. v. Hayek to his *Introduction to Henry Thornton's Enquiry into the Nature and Effects of the Paper Credit of Great Britain 1802* on the intermarriage of members of the Sect, and on their descendants of the second, third and fourth generations: 'T. Gisborne married Babington's sister and Babington Macaulay's, who in turn married, if not a real member of the group at least a favourite pupil of Hannah More's. James Stephen married, as his second wife, a sister of Wilberforce, who, it will be remembered, was a second cousin of Henry Thornton. James Stephen's son of the same name, the author of the Essay on the Clapham Sect, married a granddaughter of John Venn, whose son Henry was married to Martha Sykes, a niece of Mrs Henry Thornton.' Professor Hayek refers to the distinguished members of the second generation and ends with a comment on the third generation: 'There is Florence Nightingale, the granddaughter of William Smith and, in addition, James Fitz-James and Leslie Stephen. G. O. Trevelyan, A. V. Dicey and John Venn the logician may be mentioned as figures of great intellectual eminence. Of living authors the names of Mrs Virginia Woolf, as a descendant of the Stephens, and of Mr E. M. Forster as a direct descendant of Henry Thornton may be added.' So, too, may the distinguished names of Dr G. M. Trevelyan, the late Mr Robert Trevelyan and Mrs Vanessa Bell.

65. H.M. to Mrs Bouverie, 1795, in Lady Chatterton, op. cit., i, 27.

66. Archdeacon William Cunningham, *Birkbeck Lectures*, 1909; see Canon Charles Smyth, *Simeon and Church Order* (Cambridge, 1940), 13.

67. G. W. E. Russell, *The Household of Faith* (1902), 239. Mr Russell briefly summarizes the 'Gospel Plan' as follows: 'That all mankind was utterly sinful and therefore in danger of hell; that God has provided deliverance in the Atoning Death of Christ, and that if we would only accept the offer of Salvation so made, we were forgiven, reconciled and safe. That acceptance was Conversion.'

68. Trevelyan, *Lord Macaulay*.

69. Forster Papers, *Recollections of Miss Marianne Thornton*.

70. *The English Church from the Accession of George I to the end of the Eighteenth Century, 1714–1800*, by the late Canon John H. Overton, D.D., and the Rev. Frederick Relton, A.K.C. (1906), 241.

71. Bishop Handley Moule, *Charles Simeon* (1948 ed.), 78.

72. *The Christian Observer*, 1802, 15.

73. The passage reads: 'Take special care before you aim your shafts at Calvinism that you know what Calvinism is and what it is not, that in the mass of doctrine which it has of late become the fashion to abuse you can distinguish

Notes

with certainty between that part of it which is nothing better than Calvinism, and that which belongs to our common Christianity, lest when you fall foul of Calvinism you unwarily attack something more sacred and of higher origin.'

74. Newton to H.M., 1794 (II, 411).

75. G. R. Balleine, *History of the Evangelical Party in the Church of England* (1933), 135.

76. For the Five Points of Calvinism see Daniel Whitby, D.D., *A Discourse concerning the true import of the words Election and Reprobation*, etc. (1817), and A. W. Harrison, *Arminianism* (1937). The O.E.D. briefly defines the 'so-called Five Points': (1) Particular Election, (2) Particular Redemption, (3) Moral Inability in a fallen state, (4) Irresistible Grace, (5) Final Perseverance, as the particular doctrines of theological Calvinism.

77. Archdeacon Charles Daubeny, *Vindiciae Ecclesiae Anglicanae* (1803), 43.

78. Newton to H.M., 1794 (II, 411).

79. Mr Gwatkin's *Memoranda*, quoted by Henry Thompson in his *Life of Hannah More*, 339.

80. Wilberforce, *Life*, v, 162.

81. H.M. to Hart-Davis, 1821 (IV, 125).

82. Moule, op. cit., 76.

83. H.M., Diary, July 1803 (III, 196).

84. Wilberforce, *Correspondence*, 1818, II, 422.

85. *The Christian Observer*, Nov. 1803, 695.

86. Wilberforce, *Correspondence*, 1800, I, 211; 1824, II, 480.

87. Thompson, ch. X, passim.

88. *An Estimate of the Fashionable World*. H.M., *Collected Works*, II.

89. Thompson, 335.

90. ibid, 335.

91. ibid. 335.

92. Thompson, 343, quoting Osler's *Church and Dissent*, ch. III.

93. H.M. to the Bishop of Bath and Wells, 1802, in Thompson, 201.

CHAPTER V

1. Rousselot: quoted by Mrs Gardiner, *English Girlhood at School* (1929), 363.

2. See Preface to H.M.'s *Collected Works*, I.

3. Wilberforce, *Life*, 1787, I, 130.

Chapter V

4. See Prospectus of the Society in *Life of Wilberforce*, 1 June 1787.

5. D. Defoe, *The Poor Man's Plea* (1725).

6. Sydney Smith, *Collected Works* (1840), 84.

7. The Dean of Canterbury to H.M., 1786 (II, 37).

8. Bishop Porteus to H.M., 1787 (II, 83).

9. H.M. to her sisters, Apr. 1788 (II, 110).

10. See R. Blunt, op. cit., 'Mrs Montagu's set had nothing to do with Lady Townshend's set, or the Chudleigh set. She did not countenance ostentatious vice': I, 9.

11. H.M. to her sisters, Feb. 1788 (II, 103).

12. H.M. to her sisters, May 1788 (II, 112).

13. Bishop Porteus to H.M., 1789 (II, 82).

14. John Newton to H.M., July 1791 (II, 226).

15. H.M. to her sisters, Apr. 1788 (II, 20).

16. H.M. to her sisters, Apr. 1788 (II, 111).

17. H.M. to her sisters, 1786 (II, 12, 21, 24).

18. H.M., *Collected Works* (1790), II.

19. *Works of the Rev. Richard Cecil* (1816), III, 430.

20. Mrs Boscawen to H.M., 1791 (II, 230); Bishop Porteus to H.M., 1790 (II, 232).

21. John Newton to H.M., Feb. 1791 (II, 249–50).

22. Dr Watson, Bishop of Llandaff, to H.M., 1791 (II, 247).

23. Mary Berry, *Journals and Correspondence*, 5 Mar. 1791, I, 285.

24. H.M. to Wilberforce, 1792 (II, 322).

25. Rev. John Black, Rector of Bulley, Suffolk, *A Poetical Review of Miss Hannah More's Works* (1800).

26. *Thraliana*, II, 1,000, note.

27. H.M. to her sisters, Apr. 1795 (II, 434).

28. See Letters of Prince William (Duke of Gloucester) and Princess Sophia to H.M. (IV, 49, 97, 219, 265); and de Quincey for an account of a visit paid by the brother and sister to Barley Wood.

29. Waldegrave MSS., quoted by Miss Biddulph in *The Three Ladies Waldegrave* (1938), 289: 'I am afraid', wrote the Duchess of Gloucester in a footnote, 'that I wrote this in a rather peevish humour. It was written in the year 1798, at a time when many pious people were so anxious to send the lower people to Heaven . . . that they determined not to leave them any excuse to wish to remain on earth, no, not even on the Lord's Day.'

Notes

30. Charles Peguy, *Basic Verities*. Prose and Poetry, rendered into English by Ann and Julian Green (1943).

31. H.M. to a friend, 1795 (II, 451-2).

32. H.M., *Collected Works*, III.

33. Mary Berry, op. cit., II, 91.

34. H.M. to Horace Walpole, 1793 (II, 371).

35. *The British Critic*, June 1799; *The Anti-Jacobin*, June 1802.

36. Martha More to her sisters, quoting Richard Cecil, 1800 (II, 107).

37. *Life of Bishop Jebb*, by Rev. Charles Forster (1836), I, 33.

38. Alexander Knox (1757-1831), *Remains*, in 4 vols., IV, 326.

39. Charge to the Clergy of the Diocese of London, 1801.

40. *A Letter to Mrs Hannah More on some part of her late publication entitled Strictures on Female Education*, by the Rev. Charles Daubeny, LL.B., Minister of Christ Church, Bath (1799).

41. Peter Pindar Esq. (Dr John Wolcot), *Works* (1799), '*Nil Admirari*'. The Canto addressed to Miss Hannah More, a 'Rhyme and Prose Gentlewoman of Bristol', illustrates the quality of Pindar's satire:

> *Miss Hannah* has no eagle wings to flee
> Whom thus your adulation can befool;
> Alas! a poor ephemeron is *She*,
> A humming native of a Bristol pool.
> Indeed *Miss Hannah* has a so-so lyre,
> So out of tune it murders all the *Nine*.
> She really playeth not with taste or fire,
> *No, Doctor Porteus*, No, thou *Great Divine*.

42. Bishop Porteus to H.M., Oct. 1799 (III, 96).

43. The Rev. John Black, op. cit.

44. Mary Berry, op. cit., 28 Mar. 1799, II, 90-2.

45. *Letters of Anna Seward, written between the years 1784 and 1807*, III, 102; V, 412-13.

CHAPTER VI

1. H.M. to her sisters, June 1785 (I, 407).

2. H.M. to Mrs Boscawen, 1786 (II, 27).

3. H.M. to John Newton, July 1788 (II, 116).

4. H.M., Diary, 23 Nov. 1794 (III, 422); 30 Sept. 1798 (III, 62).

5. 'There is something in the genius of Bath which is opposed to my spirits

Chapter VI

and my feelings. . . I was born for the country': H.M. to Mrs Kennicott, 1789 (II, 212); H.M. to Mrs Boscawen, 27 Dec. 1797 (II, 27).

6. During the 'nineties the More sisters, having attained the age of parmanent spinsterhood, acquired the brevet rank of the married woman. Henceforward they are referred to indifferently as 'Mrs' or 'Miss'.

7. H.M., Diary, 22 Sept. 1798 (III, 61).

8. 'Had a little serious talk with the Duchess of Gloucester, Lady Amherst and the Duchess of Beaufort. Lord, let me be no mean respecter of persons': H.M., Diary, 5 Apr. 1798 (III, 58).

9. J. Cottle, *Early Recollections* (1837), I, 19.

10. Miss Mary Butt (Mrs Sherwood of *The Fairchild Family* fame), when a girl, was one of those for whom an interview was with difficulty procured. Taken to call in the 'nineties at the Pulteney Street house by her brother and Mrs King, a family friend, she relates: 'We were ushered into a large diningroom, and the four sisters came down—Miss More, Miss Kitty, Miss Patty, and Miss Sally. Miss More was the very cut of a housekeeper in a great family; the others were plain women, and by no means refined in any way. Miss Hannah was inquired after by Mrs King, who said she was anxious to introduce us, pleading that my brother was a young clergyman and that it was very desirable that Hannah should see him. 'Humph! yes, very proper,' all the sisters agreed, but she was not well they said; she was confined to her room, 'such demands upon her', 'such a tax to be the object of public attention', 'the fatigue so great, the fear of giving offence so vast'. Lady This had been refused and my Lord That put off, and even Mr Wilberforce and the Bishop of London set aside. . . The four ladies never once uttered their sister's name. It was always 'she', and the voice fell to the lowest key when 'she' was uttered. At length, when one's hopes had fallen as low as hopes could fall, a hint was given whether she could not be asked if she would see us. We were then ushered upstairs to the drawingroom, which was next the presence chamber, and after some further delay we were led into a dressing-room where sat the lady, looking very like the bestknown picture of her, though considerably older and wearing a cap. She sat in an arm-chair in due *invalide* order, though a strong-featured woman. She had a magnificent pair of dark eyes. She was very gracious to Mrs King and my brother, though she did not take the least notice of me; and she spoke oracularly. . . The issue of this visit was that I was not fascinated with Mrs Hannah More. . .' *The Life and Times of Mrs Sherwood 1775-1851, from the Diaries of Captain and Mrs Sherwood*, ed. F. J. Harvey Darton (1920).

11. H.M. to the Bishop of Bath and Wells, 1802 (III, 201).

12. H.M., Diary, 28 Sept. 1794 (II, 420).

Notes

13. Trevelyan, *Life and Letters of Lord Macaulay* (1876), 16–17; Lady Knutsford, *Life and Letters of Zachary Macaulay* (1900), 104–112.

14. See *Rex* v. *Perry*, (1794) 1. Hawk, c.41, s.13. For a report of 'The trial of Richard Vining Perry for the forcible abduction of an heiress from the Boarding School of Miss Mills of the City of Bristol, before Vicary Gibbs, the Recorder', see Bonner and Middleton's *Bristol Journal*, 19 and 26 Apr. 1794; see also *The Catalogue of Political and Personnal Satires preserved in the Department of Prints and Drawings in the British Museum* (1938), VI (1784–92), nos. 7990 (25 Mar. 1791), 7991 (17 Apr. 1791), 7992 (1 Aug. 1791).

15. H.M. to Mrs Kennicott, 23 Apr. 1791 (I, 335-6).

16. Trevelyan, op. cit., I, 20.

17. *Memoirs of the Life of Sir Samuel Romilly* (1844), Apr. 1791.

18. See M.D. Conway, *Life of Thomas Paine* (1909), I, passim; W. Roberts, *Memoirs*, II, 423.

19. H.M. to Mrs Boscawen, 1793 (II, 378).

20. H.M. to Horace Walpole, Sept. 1789 (II, 170).

21. H.M. to her sisters, 20 Mar. 1790 (II, 225).

22. H.M., *Collected Works*, II, 387; IV, 347, 355.

23. H.M., *Collected Works*, II, 221–36: *Village Politics, addressed to the Mechanics, Journeymen and Labourers in Great Britain by Will Chip, a Country Carpenter* (1792).

24. Roberts, *Memoirs*, II, 347.

25. Bishop Porteus to H.M., 1792 (II, 348).

26. Mrs Boscawen to H.M. (II, 351).

27. Bishop Porteus to H.M., quoting Cambridge, 1792 (II, 348).

28. Roberts, *Memoirs*, II, 347.

29. H.M. to Horace Walpole, Apr. 1793 (II, 360).

30. H.M., *Collected Works*, II: *Address on Behalf of the Emigrant French Clergy*, published with the speech of M. Dupont (14 Dec. 1792).

31. *Gideon's Cake of Barley Meal: A Letter to the Rev. Wm. Romaine on his preaching for the Emigrant Popish Clergy, with some Strictures on Mrs Hannah More's Remarks*, published for their Benefit (1792).

32. Bishop Porteus to H.M., 1794 (II, 361).

33. H.M., Diary (II, 417).

34. I am greatly indebted in section iii of this chapter to Mr G. H. Spinney's erudite article in the *Transactions of the Bibliographical Society*, 1940, on 'The Cheap Repository Tracts: Hazard and Marshall edition'.

Chapter VI

35. H.M. to Mrs Bouverie and Sir Charles Middleton, in Lady Chatterton, op. cit., I, 267.

36. Bishop Porteus to H.M., Dec. 1794 (II, 428).

37. H.M. to Newton, 1794 (II, 429); Forster Papers, Henry Thornton to H.M., 1794.

38. *Letters of Hannah More to Zachary Macaulay*; 14 Jan. 1796, letter of Hannah More to Henry Thornton, Forster Papers.

39. H.M. to her sisters, 1795 (II, 432); Bishop Porteus to H.M., quoting William Mason, June 1798 (III, 35).

40. H.M. to Zachary Macaulay, Jan. 1795 (II, 456).

41. See *Notes and Queries*, Series III, VI, 1864, 241–5; 290–4, 353–5.

42. H.M. to her sisters, 1795 (II, 431).

43. *The Bath Chronicle*, 4 Mar. 1795.

44. Spinney, op. cit.

45. H.M. to Patty More, 1795 (II, 431).

46. *Letters of Hannah More to Zachary Macaulay*, 8 Sept. 1797.

47. Forster Papers, Diary of Henry Thornton, 25 Apr. and 5 May 1795.

48. Spinney, op. cit.

49. Mrs Trimmer to H.M., 10 May 1787 (II, 6).

50. *Letters of Hannah More to Zachary Macaulay*, 30 Jan. 1796; 8 Sept. 1797.

51. Forster Papers, Henry Thornton to Zachary Macaulay, 6 Mar. 1798.

52. Spinney, op. cit.

53. Forster Papers, Henry Thornton to Hannah More.

54. H.M., Diary, 22 Sept. 1798 (II, 161).

55. Forster Papers, Henry Thornton to Zachary Macaulay, 6 Mar. 1798.

56. Spinney, op. cit.

57. *Letters of Hannah More to Zachary Macaulay*, 8 Sept. 1797.

58. Spinney, op. cit.

59. *Letters of Hannah More to Zachary Macaulay*, 6 Jan 1796.

60. Bishop Porteus to Hannah More, Jan. 1797 (III, 5).

61. On the back of Cobbett's letter, dated 20 Oct. 1800, Miss More had scribbled 'This flatterer, on coming to England, joined Mr Bere's party and became my mortal enemy.' See ch. VIII.

62. In 1815 the Religious Tract Society, Paris, asked permission to reprint H.M.'s Tracts: IV, 36, 121; see Jay, *Autobiography*, 343.

63. H.M., *Collected Works*, I.

Notes

64. E. Burke, *Reflections on the Revolution in France*, ed. George Sampson, 122.

65. See *Some Thoughts for the New Year*, 1796.

66. H.M. to Mrs Boscawen, Nov. 1796 (II, 386).

67. Canon J. H. Overton, *The English Church in the Nineteenth Century* (1894), 173.

68. Bishop Porteus to H.M., 1795 (II, 433).

69. John Overton, *The True Churchman Ascertained, or an Apology for those of the Regular Clergy of the Establishment who are sometimes called Evangelical Ministers* (1801), 250.

70. J. C. Colquhoun, op. cit., 122.

71. William Cobbett's *Monthly Religious Tracts*, collected in 1822 as *Cobbett's Monthly Sermons*, 1821–2; *Cottage Economy*, 1822.

72. H.M. to Lady Olivia Sparrow, 1813 (III, 390).

73. H.M. to the Bishop of Bath and Wells, 1802 (III, 132).

74. Forster Papers, Henry Thornton to Zachary Macaulay, 20 Feb. 1796.

75. William Shaw, op. cit. 25, 45, 72, 92.

76. See S. G. Green, *The Story of the Religious Tract Society* (1899). 'The Society, though conducted in a distinct circle, may be considered as pursuing a design similar to that promoted by the Cheap Repository. It does not venture so far into the field of imagination; it retires from political discussion and, taking no cognisance of what may be termed the peculiarities of a party, it aims solely at the diffusion of those principles which Christians in general acknowledge and inculcate': quoted from the early Minutes of the Committee of the R.T.S. See also Gordon Hewitt, *Let the People Read* (1949). For a list of the Cheap Repository Tracts ascribed to Hannah More see Appendix I.

CHAPTER VII

1. *The Mendip Annals, or a Narrative of the Charitable Labours of Hannah and Martha More in their neighbourhood, being the Journal of Martha More from the year 1789 to 1801*, ed. with additional matter by the Rev. Arthur Roberts, Rector of Woodrising, Norfolk (1859). The passages cited in this chapter, unless otherwise stated, are drawn from Martha More's *Journal* printed in the *Annals*.

2. See W. G. Maton, *Observations relative to . . . the Western Counties of England: Somerset* (1797), II; and J. W. Gough, *The Mines of Mendip* (1830).

3. H.M. to a friend, and to John Bowdler the younger, *Annals*, 6–9.

4. See A. E. Dobbs, *Education and School Movements* (1919); J. U. Nef, *The Rise of the British Coal Industry*, I, 166–7; T. S. Ashton, 'Coal-mines of the

Chapter VII

Eighteenth Century', in Economic History Supplement to *The Economic Journal*, 1928; J. Marshall, *Rural Economy of the West of England*; J. Billingsley, *General View of the Agriculture of the County of Somerset at the end of the Eighteenth Century* (1798), 30–81.

5. H.M. to Mrs Bouverie, in Lady Chatterton, op. cit., 1795 (I, 295–6).

6. H.M. to Mrs Bouverie and Sir Charles Middleton in Lady Chatterton, op. cit., 13 Oct. 1795 (I, 291); 20 Oct. 1794 (I, 262). See David Davies, *The Case of the Labourers in Husbandry* (1795).

7. Typhus fever.

8. In other villages also. 'We have established Female Friendly Societies in several parishes': *Journal*, 244. The Cheddar Female Friendly Society founded by the sisters was still in existence in 1951, awaiting its dissolution under the new Health Service.

9. *Journal*, 116. 'One great benefit I have found to result from our project is the removal of that great gulf which has divided the rich and poor in these country parishes by making them act together, whereas before they hardly thought they were children of one common father': H.M. to Newton, 15 Sept. 1796 (III, 465).

10. H.M. to Mrs Bouverie in Lady Chatterton, op. cit., 1795 (I, 291).

11. J. S. Harford, *Recollections of Wilberforce* (1864).

12. *Annals*, 1801, 243–4.

13. H.M. to a friend (*Annals*, 8).

14. In 1798 Wilberforce begged to be allowed to provide Miss More with a carriage for her journeys—'You are the mainspring of the machine, and it is your business to keep it in order, ours to supply subordinate movements. I did not mean a pun but a post-chaise': *Life of Wilberforce*, II, 301–2.

15. H.M. to Wilberforce, enclosing a copy of her scheme, 1801 (II, 150–2).

16. Forster Papers, *Recollections of Marianne Thornton*.

17. E. M. Forster, *Abinger Harvest* (1936), 234.

18. Martha More to H.M., 18 Aug. 1795 (439–43).

19. Maton, II; Gough, 221–4; Billingsley, passim.

20. During the outbreak of typhus fever in 1798 the sisters sent a wagon of coal to the village, which Jones distributed. 'The schoolmistress entered so tenderly into their wants and they would send to fetch her at midnight and she supplied all the sick with broth, medicines etc.' H.M. to a friend, 1798 (II, 315). See also ch. x.

21. H. O. Papers, 42, 21, quoted by J. L. and B. Hammond, *The Town Labourer*, 227–8.

Notes

22. See R. N. Boyd, *Coal-pits and Pitmen* (1892); J. U. Nef, op. cit.
23. H.M. to a friend, 1796 (*Annals*, 181).
24. H.M. to a friend 1798 (*Annals*, 211).
25. H.M. to William Wilberforce, 1795 (*Annals*, 168).

CHAPTER VIII

1. Pamphlets on:
    (a) 'The Controversy between Mrs H. More and the Curate of Blagdon, relative to the conduct of her teacher of the Sunday School in that Parish, with the Original Letters and Explanatory Notes by Thos. Bere, Rector of Butcombe, 1801.'
    (b) 'A Letter to the Rev. Thos. Bere, Rector of Butcombe, occasioned by his late unwarranted attack on Mrs H. More, with an Appendix. By the Rev. Sir Abraham Elton, Bart, 1801.'
    (c) 'An Appeal to the Public on the Controversy between Hannah More, the Curate of Blagdon, and the Rev. Sir Abraham Elton. By T.B., A.M., Rector of Butcombe. Bath, 1801.'
    (d) 'Expostulatory Letter to the Rev. Sir A. E., Bart., in consequence of his late publication addressed to the Rev. Thos. Bere. Bath, 1801.'
    (e) 'The Blagdon Controversy, or Short Criticisms of the late Dispute be-between the Curate of Blagdon and Mrs H. More relative to Sunday Schools and Monday Private Schools, by a Layman. 1801.'
    (f) 'A Statement of Facts relative to Mrs H. More's Schools, occasioned by some late Misrepresentations. Bath, 1801.'
    (g) 'A Letter to the Rev. T. Bere, Rector of Butcombe, by the Rev. J. Boak, Rector of Brockley. Bristol, 1801.'
    (h) 'The Something Wrong developed: or Free Remarks on Mrs H. More's Conventicles etc. Seasonably addressed to the Blagdon Controvertists; and inscribed to the Bishop of Bath and Wells. Bristol 1801.'
    (i) 'An Address to Mrs H. More on the Conclusion of the Blagdon Controversy. With Observations on an Anonymous Tract, entitled "Statement of Facts". by Thomas Bere, M.A., Curate of Blagdon. Bath, 1801.'
    (j) 'The Force of Contrast, or Quotations accompanied with Remarks, submitted to all who have interested themselves in what has been called "The Blagdon Controversy". Bath, 1801.'
    (k) 'Truth respecting Mrs H. More's Meeting Houses, and the Conduct of her Followers; addressed to the Curate of Blagdon. By Edward Spencer. Bath, 1802.'

Chapter VIII

(l) 'Elucidations of Character, occasioned by a Letter from the Rev. R. Lewis, published in the Rev. T. Bere's Address to Mrs H. More, with some Remarks on a Pamphlet lately published by Edward Spencer of Wells. By the Rev. John Boak, Rector of Brockley. Bath, 1802.'

(m) 'An Alterative Epistle, addressed to Edward Spencer, Apothecary. By Lieut. Charles H. Pettinger, Bristol, 1802.'

(n) 'Illustrations of Falsehood, in a Reply to some Assertions contained in Mr Spencer's late Publication. By the Rev. Thomas Drewitt, A.M., Curate of Cheddar. Bath, 1802.'

(o) 'Calumny Refuted, in a Reply to several Charges advanced by Mr Spencer of Wells, in his Pamphlet called "Truths", his Advertisements and Handbills. By the Rev. John Boak, Rector of Brockley. Bath, 1802.'

(p) 'Candid observations on Mrs H. More's Schools, in which is considered their supposed Connection with Methodism. Recommended to the attention of the Public in General and particularly to the Clergy. By the Rev.——Rector of——. Bath, 1802.'

(q) 'The Force of Contrast Continued, or Extracts and Animadversions. With occasional Strictures on the Contraster and others of Mr Bere's opponents. And observations on the Effects of Mrs H. More's Schools. To which is added a Postscript on the Editors of the "British Critic". Respectfully submitted to the Consideration of those who have interested themselves in the Blagdon Controversy. By a Friend of the Establishment. Bristol, 1802.'

(r) 'Animadversions on the Curate of Blagdon's Three Publications, entitled "The Controversy between Mrs H. More and the Curate of Blagdon" etc: "An Appeal to the Public" and "An Address to Mrs H. More" with some allusions to his Cambrian Descent from "Gwyr Ap Glendour Ap Cadwallader, Ap Styfnig", as affirmed and set forth by himself on the twenty-eighth page of his "Appeal to the Public". London, 1802.'

(s) John Duncan. 'Seasonable Hints etc.' 1802.

2. 'The Anti-Jacobin', wrote H. M. to Wilberforce, 'is spreading more mischief over the land than almost any other book, because it is doing it under the mask of loyalty. It is representing all serious men as hostile to the Government': 1799 (III, 102). See in particular Anti-Jacobin, v, 80, 314, 340, 359; IX, 277–96; XI, 13, 87–99, 195, 199–201, 326, 530; and The British Critic, XVII, 444; XVIII, 216; XIX, 90.

3. Charge of the Bishop of Rochester to the Clergy of the Diocese, 1800.

4. Letter of the Rev. T. Bere, Curate of Blagdon, to his Rector, the Rev. Dr Crossman, 21 Aug. 1800. Printed in 'The Controversy between Mrs H. More and the Curate of Blagdon'.

Notes

5. Thompson, *Hannah More*, 192–3.

6. Sir Abraham Elton: Letter to the Rev. Thomas Bere (1801).

7. 'An Appeal to the Public' (1801).

8. 'A Statement of Facts relative to Miss H. More's Schools (1801).'

9. Edward Spencer: 'Truth respecting Miss H. More's Meeting Houses, and the Conduct of her Followers (1802).'

10. H.M., III, 122.

11. Bishop Porteus to H.M., III, 143.

12. H.M. to Wilberforce, II, 147.

13. *Life of Mrs Hannah More, with a critical review of her writings*, by the Rev. W. Shaw, Rector of Chelvey, Wilts (Bristol, 1801).

14. Patty More to her sisters, 1802.

15. H.M. to the Bishop of Bath and Wells, 1802. The letter is given in full in the Rev. Henry Thompson's *Life of Hannah More*, 200–22. Comparison of Miss More's letter as printed by Roberts in the *Memoirs*, III, 123–39, reveals that he omitted to record H.M.'s statement to Bishop Beadon that she had attended Jay's Meeting House at Bath, and had on one occasion received the Sacrament at his hands. It runs as follows: '. . . I was not prepared for the shock, when a charge of sedition, disaffection, and a general aim to corrupt the principles of the community, suddenly burst upon me. In vain have I been looking round me for any pretence on which to found such astonishing charges. One circumstance which is now made a ground for past accusation is but recently brought forward. The circumstance I allude to is, my being charged with having constantly attended and received the sacrament at Mr——'s Chapel at Bath for fifteen years. The simple fact is this: The novelty and talents of Mr——, a celebrated dissenting Minister at Bath, were considered as such an attraction, that I, in common with a number of strict Church people, frequently went to hear him preach. It was chiefly at six o'clock in the evening, an hour which did not interfere with the Church Service. It was not unusual to see, perhaps, near half a score of clergymen, who, I presume, no more thought they were guilty of disaffection than I myself did. I went, of course, to Church as usual, except that the extreme nearness of this Chapel drew me a few mornings, in severe weather, when my health was bad. At one of these times I unexpectedly found they were going to give the sacrament. Taken by surprise, in a moment of irresolution, never having been used to turn my back on the Communion at Church I imprudently stayed. How far this single irregularity which I regretted, and never repeated, deserves the term of constant, your Lordship will judge. My eldest sister has been accused of denying it. She well might deny it, for she never knew it till now. I believe it to have been nine or ten years ago. Again, I

Chapter VIII

did not begin to reside part of the winter at Bath till about the beginning of 1791. I never go thither till near Christmas, and at the time alluded to I always left it, and went to London in February. During a part of this short season I was generally confined by illness. When the interests of the Church became a question (I cannot be quite accurate as to the time, but I think it was either seven or eight years ago) I ceased entirely to go to Mr——'s. How far this justifies the charge of fifteen years constant attendance, your Lordship will judge. And is it unfair to request your Lordship to draw your own conclusions concerning the accuracy as well as the candour of my accusers?'

Hannah More's letter to the Bishop of Bath and Wells decides the long and embittered controversy concerning Miss More's association with William Jay and the Dissenting chapel at Bath. The several differing accounts given during her lifetime may be attributed to her critics' ignorance of the contents of her letter to Bishop Beadon. Roberts's truncated transcript of her letter in the *Memoirs* was not corrected until the publication of Henry Thompson's little known *Life of Hannah More* in 1838. The chief references to this much debated incident are as follows:

Martha More's letter to the Rev. T. S. Whalley in the *Journals and Correspondence of Thomas Sedgwick Whalley*, ed. Wickham Hill, II, 224–6.

Jay, *Autobiography*.

Richard Polewhele, quoting (or misquoting) Jay, in the Introduction to his edition of Bishop Lavington's *The Enthusiasm of Methodists and Papists considered* (1820), 231.

Dr Richard Valpy, 'Reminiscences of Hannah More' in *The Christian Observer*, for Mar. 1835, 165.

William Jay's rejoinder to Dr Valpy in his *Autobiography*.

16. Bishop Beadon to H.M., III, 140–1.

17. See Dr M. D. George, Introduction to the *Catalogue of Political and Personal Satires 1801–1810*, VIII (1947).

18. H.M.'s letters record her unflattering opinion of the 'Worldly Clergy': lazy, sullen, drunken, card-playing, artful, are among the terms used.

19. 'She [Mrs Hannah More] has been indelibly stamped as a Methodist, and all the waters of the Atlantic will not wash her clean from the "foul blot". How often has she struggled to throw off the vile imputation? This is the weakness of her character.' *The Life and Times of Selina, Countess of Huntingdon*, I, 293.

20. H.M. to John Bowdler, *Mendip Annals*, 21.

21. *The Christian Observer*, 1805, 94.

22. Miss More's biographer explains this term as follows: 'Mr Wilberforce, considering the Methodists as Churchmen, had recommended Miss More to procure a Wesleyan Master for her school at Cheddar': Thompson, 355.

23. *Mendip Annals*, 18.

24. *Mendip Annals*, 24.

25. H.M. to Martha More, 4 Mar. 1790 (*Annals*, 25). 'It was at first thought very Methodistical,' wrote Miss More to Wilberforce, 'and we got a few broken windows': 1791 (IV, 303).

26. E. Spencer, op. cit.

27. The term 'intrusion' is used in its ordinary and not in its legal meaning.

28. Rev. John Boak, Rector of Brockley, and Fry, 'the youthful father of a nursery of thoughtful young men in Oxford': H.M. to Sir Charles Middleton, 28 July 1797, in Lady Chatterton, op. cit., I, 32.

CHAPTER IX

1. 'Animadversions on the Curate of Blagdon's Three Publications entitled "The Controversy between Mrs H. More and the Curate of Blagdon etc"; "An Appeal to the Public", and "An Address to Mrs H. More with some allusions to his Cambrian Descent from Gwyr Ap Glendour, Ap Cadawaller, Ap Styfing", as affirmed and set forth by himself on the twenty-eighth page of his "Appeal to the Public" ' (1802).

2. H.M., Diary, 1 Jan. 1803 (III, 182); 6 Oct. 1803 (III, 198); 2 Jan. 1803 (III, 185); Roberts, *Memoirs*, IV, 92.

3. H.M., Diary, 5 May 1803 (III, 195); 5 Jan. 1803 (III, 184).

4. H.M., Diary, 14 Jan. 1804 (III, 213).

5. Dr Valpy, 'Reminiscences of Mrs Hannah More' in *The Christian Observer*, Mar. 1835.

6. Jay, *Autobiography*, 332, 339.

7. Bishop of Bristol, 1827–34.

8. H.M., *Collected Works*, IV. The *Hints* were published in two volumes at 12s.

9. Bishop Jebb to Alexander Knox, 4 June 1805; *Life of Bishop Jebb*, by the Rev. Charles Forster (1836) II, 55.

10. H. Thompson, *Hannah More*, 236.

11. Knox to Jebb, May 1805; *Remains*, II, 301 (in 3 vols, 1834–7).

12. Acton, *Inaugural Lecture on the Study of History* (1895).

13. *Monthly Review*, June 1805.

14. [In the *Hints*] 'Mr Knox took peculiar interest having been on a visit to the author when engaged in the composition of this work, which was materi-

Chapter IX

ally benefited by his strictures, and enriched by his suggestions'. Editorial note to *The Correspondence of Bishop Jebb and Alexander Knox*.

15. *Edinburgh Review*, 5 Oct. 1805.

16. *Letters of Princess Charlotte 1811–17*, ed. A. Aspinall (1949), 16 Nov. 1812, 39.

17. James Stephen to H.M., 26 Jan. 1809 (III, 291). '*Coelebs in Search of a Wife*, Comprehending Observations on Domestic Habits and Manners and Religion': H.M., *Collected Works*, VII.

18. *Strictures*, passim.

19. See Allardyce Nicoll, *Eighteenth Century Drama 1750–1800*, 67, on Hannah More's contribution.

20. *Strictures*, passim.

21. H.M. to Sir W. W. Pepys, 13 Dec. 1809 (III, 313).

22. 1810 (III, 318).

23. The reference is to James Bean's widely read book *Zeal without Innovation or the Present State of Religion and Morals considered; with a view to the dispositions and measures required for its improvement. To which is subjoined, an Address to Young Clergymen, intended to guard them against some prevalent errors* (1808). The book was a favourite of Hannah More, see Letter to Lady Olivia Sparrow, 27 Dec. 1813 (III, 407).

24. In 1820 Miss More declined membership of the Royal Society of Literature on the ground that membership was an impropriety for women.

25. 'It has always been the practice of the better kind of country ladies to distribute benefactions,' wrote Lucy Aikin to W. E. Channing, 'but Hannah More by representing her pattern young lady as regularly devoting two evenings to making her round among the village poor has unfortunately made it a fashion and a rage': *The Correspondence of W. E. Channing and Lucy Aiken*, ed. Laetitia le Breton (1876), 396.

26. Roberts, *Memoirs*, IV, 205, quoting Hannah More.

27. John Venn to H.M., 30 Apr. 1810 (III, 323).

28. Pepys to H.M., 14 Mar. 1809 (III, 295).

29. The *Constitutionnel*, no. 18, 18 Jan. 1817.

30. R. W. Chapman, *Letters of Jane Austen*, I, no. 65.

31. Knox to Jebb, 1807, I, 527.

32. Wilberforce, *Life*, III, 399.

33. Forster Papers, 30 Dec. 1808. Remarks upon Roman Catholicism in *Coelebs* brought Miss More a rebuke from the Pope's Vicar-General in England, Monsignor Joseph Berrington. She had, he held, assumed the high office of a

Notes

censor morum, and a censor also of religious practices and religious beliefs, without accurate knowledge. In the correspondence which followed, Hannah More apologized if she had offended against Christian charity and undertook to modify her unguarded expressions in future editions of *Coelebs*: Correspondence of H.M. and the Rev. Joseph Berrington, 1809 (III, 276–88).

34. *Edinburgh Review*, Apr. 1809.

35. *London Review*, 1809. 'My early foe Richard Cumberland has kept alive all that rancour which he exerted against me thirty years ago, because *Percy*, with perhaps less merit, had more success than the *Battle of Hastings*': H.M. to Sir W. W. Pepys, 13 Dec. 1809 (III, 314).

36. *Christian Observer*, Feb. 1809.

37. *Letters of Hannah More to Zachary Macaulay*, Mar. 1809, 29.

38. *Coelebs* and its author evoked extraordinary interest. 'Mrs Clifford tells me', wrote Maria Edgeworth, 'that Hannah More who was lately at Dawlish excited more curiosity there and engrossed more attention than any of the distinguished personages who were there not excepting the Prince of Orange' (Jan. 1810): *Life and Letters of Maria Edgeworth*, ed. A. J. C. Hare.

39. James Stephen to H.M., 30 Apr. 1811 (III, 327).

40. Preface to *Christian Morals*: H.M., *Collected Works*, IX.

41. *Baroness de Bunsen*, ed. A. J. C. Hare (1822), I, 82–4.

42. *Practical Piety*: H.M., *Collected Works*, VIII.

43. 'The best of all your performances', W. W. Pepys to H.M., 27 Mar. 1811 (III, 335); 'The most valuable of all your works', Lord Barham to H.M., 1811 (III, 335); 'There is scarcely a page which does not contain just and valuable observations,' Robert Hall, *Eclectic Review*, May 1811.

44. H.M. to Mrs Kennicott, 1811 (III, 347).

45. H.M., *Collected Works*, IX.

46. H.M., *Collected Works*, X.

47. Miss More's *Moral Sketches* (1819), *Collected Works*, XI, include essays on: French opinion of English Society; English Opinion of French Society; England's Best Hope; On Domestic Errors in Opinion and Practical Habits; On Soundness in Judgement and Consistency in Conduct; On Novel Opinions in Religion; Ill Effects of the Late Secession; On the Exertions of Pious Ladies; High Profession and Negligent Practice; Auricular Confession; Unprofitable Reading; The Borderers.
The Spirit of Prayer (1824), *Collected Works*, X. (This was H.M.'s last work.)

48. *Practical Piety*.

49. Lady Chatterton, *Memorials*, Preface.

Chapter X

50. H.M. to Pepys, 24 Jan. 1817 (IV, 471).

51. 57 Geo. III, c.3 (Habeas Corpus Suspension Act); 57 Geo. III, c.6; 57 Geo. III, c.7; 57 Geo. III, c.19 (Seditious Meetings Act).

52. E. Halévy, *History of the English People, 1815-30*, 30-2.

53. H.M. to Pepys, 24 Jan. 1817 (III, 473).

54. H.M. to J. S. Harford, 21 Apr. 1817 (III, 480).

55. H.M. to Pepys, 8 Mar. 1817 (III, 477).

56. Wm. Cobbett, *Weekly Political Register*, 20 Apr. 1822.

57. Wilberforce, *Life*, 1817, IV, 308.

58. *The Loyal Subject's Political Creed* (1817): H.M., *Collected Works*, X, 277.

CHAPTER X

1. H.M., Diary, 25 Nov. 1803 (III, 202).

2. H.M. to Lady Olivia Sparrow, 23 Nov. 1813 (IV, 403).

3. H.M., Diary, 14 Jan. 1804 (III, 212).

4. H.M. to Sir W. W. Pepys, 19 Aug. 1822 (III, 480); see C. Creighton, *History of Epidemics in Britain*, II, and M. C. Buer, *Health, Wealth and Population in the early days of the Industrial Revolution* (1920).

5. H.M. to J. S. Harford, 21 Apr. 1817 (III, 480).

6. See W. Canton, *History of the British and Foreign Bible Society*, 5 vols. (1899), I, 1805-10; Eugene Stock, *History of the Church Missionary Society*, 3 vols. (1899), I.

7. H.M., Diary, 8 July 1803 (III, 46); see D. A. Winstanley, *Early Victorian Cambridge* (1940), for an account of the struggle to set up an auxiliary Bible Society in Cambridge; see also H.M.'s letter to Daniel Wilson, 2 Sept. 1825, deploring the 'unhappy schism' in the Bible Society on the question of the inclusion or exclusion of the Apocrypha in the Bibles published by the Society. 'If the Papists will not take a Bible without it, is there any comparison between having a Bible with it and having no Bible at all?' said Miss More.

8. Quoted by Thompson, *Hannah More*, 31.

9. Knox to Jebb, I, 211, quoted Canon Overton, *English Church in the Nineteenth Century*, 291.

10. Archdeacon Thomas, *Collected Tracts* (1817); see also Archdeacon Daubeny, *Reasons for Declining Connection with the Bible Society* (1814).

11. H.M. to Sir W. W. Pepys, 1819 (IV, 48).

12. Knox to Jebb, Sept. 1817 (II, 336).

267

Notes

13. 'I have spent a day with Hannah More and her four sisters at her charming cottage under the Mendip Hills which she has named Barley Wood, and what is equally the seat of taste and hospitality,' wrote Mrs Barbauld in 1813. 'We have had a meeting here for an auxiliary Bible Society. Many ladies went not indeed to speak but to hear speaking. I honour the zeal of these Societies, but it is become a sort of rage'; *Works of Anna Laetitia Barbauld* (1825), III, 107.

14. H.M. to Wilberforce, 1816 (III, 442).

15. Eugene Stock, op. cit., I, 110. The C.M.S. was organized in 1799, established in 1801, and became known as the Church Missionary Society in 1812.

16. See G. W. E. Russell, *The Household of Faith*, 235.

17. H.M. to Daniel Wilson, 1818 (IV, 36–7).

18. H.M. to Daniel Wilson, Apr. 1826 (IV, 259).

19. For the 'Home Heathen Problem', so called by Thomas Chalmers, 'the moral engineer of Scotland', see his *Christian and Civic Economy of Large Towns, 1823–8*, I and II. 'The militant advocate of the old Parochial System', [of the Church of Scotland] as Sir John Clapham called him, detested the humiliating, degrading and impersonal English method of poor relief as a cure for pauperism, and demanded in its place the New Testament method of the prevention of poverty by love and organized service to the poor. Nothing, in his opinion, could make up for love and service.

20. *A Memoir of the Rev. Henry Budd* (1855).

21. J. Bateman, *Life of Daniel Wilson, 1778–1856, 5th Bishop of Calcutta*; see also M. L. Loane, *Oxford and the Evangelical Succession* (1951).

22. Canon Charles Smyth, *Cambridge Historical Journal*, VII, no. 3, 161.

23. Bateman, I, 232.

24. H.M. to Miss Roberts, 1821 (IV, 129).

25. H.M. to Wilberforce, 1823 (IV, 173).

26. H.M. to Wilberforce, 1823 (IV, 174).

27. H.M. to Sir W. W. Pepys, 15 Oct. 1821 (III, 139).

28. H.M. to Sir W. W. Pepys, Dec. 1820 (IV, 120).

29. Jebb to Knox, *Correspondence*, Oct. 1804, I, 150.

30. Knox to H.M., *Remains*, III (1806); IV (1809–10).

31. Knox to Geo. Schoales, *Remains*, I, 48–62.

32. Knox to H.M., *Remains* (1809–10), III, 130.

33. Knox to Mrs La Touche from Barley Wood, 10 Sept. 1804, *Remains*, IV.

34. Knox to Geo. Schoales, Sept. 1804, *Remains*, IV, 172.

35. Jebb to Knox, *Remains*, June 1806, I, 255.

Chapter X

36. Knox to Jebb, Sept. 1817, *Remains*, II, 336.

37. Knox to Rev. W. Stedman, Mar. 1806, *Remains*, IV, 207.

38. Knox to Jebb, Sept. 1817, *Remains*, II, 336.

39. John Stoughton, D.D., *Religion in England from 1800 to 1852*, 2 vols. (1854), I, 47.

40. Dean Church, *The Oxford Movement* (1891), 29.

41. J. Braithwaite, *Memoirs of J. J. Gurney*, Norwich (1854), I, 230.

42. *Life and Correspondence of John Foster*, by J. E. Rylands, 2 vols. (1848), I, 16; *Eclectic Review*, May 1811.

43. J. W. Morris, *Biographical Recollections of Robert Hall, A.M.* (1832), 491; *Eclectic Review*, May 1811; H.M., 1800 (III, 107).

44. William Jay, *Autobiography*, 329–47; Roberts, *Memoirs*, IV, 207–9.

45. H.M. to Sir W. W. Pepys, 5 Apr. 1808 (III, 255).

46. J. S. Harford, *Recollections of Wilberforce* (1864), ch. XII.

47. H.M. to Mr and Mrs Huber, 3 Aug. 1825 (IV, 241). 'I was amused,' wrote H.M. to Zachary Macaulay, 'by an American gentleman who called yesterday. He said "We publish all your Works except your *Hints*. Thank God we have nothing to do with royalty"': 8 Sept. 1827 (IV, 207).

48. Charles Simeon, *Sermon preached before the University of Cambridge* (1837).

49. H.M. to Mr and Mrs Huber, 3 Aug. 1825 (IV, 240).

50. Forster Papers, *Recollections*.

51. Lady Trevelyan.

52. Sir George Trevelyan, *Life and Letters of Lord Macaulay*, I, 34–5.

53. *Letters of Hannah More and Zachary Macaulay*, 1812, 45, 54, 85.

54. See William Vincent, D.D., Headmaster of Westminster School, *Defence of Public Education, addressed to the Most Reverend the Lord Bishop of Meath*. In a letter to the Rev. William Jones, Dr Vincent denied the charges made against the School and explained his methods of instruction. Mr Jones accepted his explanation. See also H.M.'s contribution to the controversy, 'England's Best Hope', *Collected Works*, XI.

55. *Letters of Hannah More and Zachary Macaulay*, 1819, 132.

56. Sir George Trevelyan, *Lord Macaulay*, 24 Mar. 1831, I, 188.

57. Madam de Bunsen, *Life and Letters*, I, 32.

58. de Quincey, *Tait's Edinburgh Magazine*.

59. H.M. to Mrs Henry Thornton, 1802 (III, 170–2); to Lady Olivia Sparrow, (III, 357); to Wilberforce, 16 Oct. 1805 (III, 234); to Knox, 30 Nov. 1809

Notes

(III, 304); H.M., Diary, 12 Mar., 5 May 1803 (III, 191, 195); H.M. to Knox, 30 Nov. 1809 (III, 305).

60. H.M. to Pepys, 1 July 1823 (IV, 183); to Miss Roberts, 9 Feb. 1820 (IV, 84); to Pepys, 5 Apr. 1820 (III, 250); to Wilberforce, 1814 (III, 409); to Pepys, 19 Dec. 1808 (III, 259).

61. S. T. Coleridge, *Miscellaneous Criticism*, ed. T. M. Raysor (1906), 313.

62. de Quincey, *Tait's Edinburgh Magazine*.

63. H.M. to Lady Olivia Sparrow, 1813 (III, 389); H.M. to Daniel Wilson, 1822 (IV, 145, 168–9).

64. H.M. to Daniel Wilson, 1822 (IV, 144, 165–70).

65. Sir Herbert Grierson, 'The English Bible' in *Impressions of English Literature*, ed. W. J. Turner (1934), 52–3.

66. James Hogg, *De Quincey and his Friends* (1875), 153–4.

67. *Letters of Dorothy and William Wordsworth*, 1811–20, ed. E. de Sélincourt, 651.

68. Forster Papers, *Recollections*.

69. H.M. to Wilberforce, 1825 (IV, 237); H.M. to Miss Roberts, 25 Aug. 1822 (IV, 165).

70. H.M. to Lady Olivia Sparrow, Dec. 1825 (IV, 252).

71. Lady Knutsford, *Life of Zachary Macaulay*, 447.

72. H.M. to Wilberforce, 27 Oct. 1828 (IV, 293).

CHAPTER XI

1. Quoted in *Notes and Queries*, II, Series XI, 13 Mar. 1915, 215.

2. Forster Papers, *Recollections*.

3. Warre Cornish, *The English Church in the Nineteenth Century* (1910), pt. I, 19.

4. Forster Papers, *Recollections*.

5. W. E. Gladstone, *Gleanings of Past Years*, VII, 207: 'The Evangelical Movement; its Parentage, Progress, and Issue", reprinted from *The British Quarterly*, July 1879.

6. C. M. Yonge, *Hannah More* (1888), 129.

7. H.M., *Essays, Collected Works*, XI.

8. Mark Pattison, *Essays*, collected by H. Nettleship, in 2 vols (1889), I, 269. See also John Foster on 'the discourse of sincere Christians whose religion

involved no intellectual exercise. . . There are Christians who have never even
suspected that knowledge could have any connection with religion': 'On the
Aversion of Men of Taste to the Evangelical Religion', *Collected Essays* (1805).

9. H.M., *Essays: Collected Works*, IX.

10. R. H. Tawney, *Religion and the Rise of Capitalism* (1926), sect. iii, ch. III.

11. H.M., *Essays: Collected Works*, I, Preface.

12. Lady Chatterton, *Memorials*, II, 357. See also Viscount Templewood, *The
Unbroken Thread* (1949), quoting Miss Sarah Hoare on Hannah More's 'party
slang offensive to good taste'.

13. R. W. Dale, *The Old Evangelicalism and the New* (1899), 11.

14. A. V. Dicey, *Law and Public Opinion in England during the Nineteenth
Century* (1905), 400–1.

APPENDIX I

Cheap Repository Tracts ascribed to Hannah More

The Apprentice's Monitor; or Indentures in Verse.
The Carpenter; or the Danger of Evil Company.
The Gin Shop; or a Peep into a Prison.
The History of Tom White, the Postillion.
The Market Woman, a true tale, or Honesty is the Best Policy.
The Roguish Miller; or Nothing Got by Cheating.
The Shepherd of Salisbury Plain. Part I.
The Two Shoe-makers.
The Lancashire Collier Girl.
The Shepherd of Salisbury Plain. Part II.
Patient Joe; or the Newcastle Collier.
The Riot; or Half a Loaf is better than no Bread.
The Way to Plenty.
The Honest Miller of Gloucestershire.
The Two Wealthy Farmers; or the History of Mr Bragwell. Part I.
The Two Wealthy Farmers; or the History of Mr Bragwell. Part II.
Robert and Richard.
The Apprentice turned Master.
The History of Idle Jack Brown.
The Shopkeeper Turned Sailor. Part I.
Jack Brown in Prison.
The Hackney Coachman, or the Way to get a Good Fare.
Sunday Reading: On Carrying Religion into the Common Business of Life.
Turn the Carpet; or the Two Weavers.
Betty Brown, the St Giles's Orange Girl.
Sunday Reading: The Grand Assizes; or General Gaol Delivery.
The History of Mr Bragwell; or the Two Wealthy Farmers. Part III.
A Hymn of Praise for the Abundant Harvest of 1796.
The History of the Two Wealthy Farmers. Part IV.
The Two Wealthy Farmers, with the sad Adventure of Miss Bragwell. Part V.
Black Giles the Poacher. Part I.
Sunday Reading: Bear Ye One Another's Burdens; or the Valley of Tears.
Black Giles the Poacher. Part II.
The Cottage Cook, or Mrs Jones's Cheap Dishes etc.
The Good Militiaman.

Appendix I

Tawny Rachel, or the Fortune Teller.

The Sunday School.

The Two Gardeners.

The Day of Judgement.

The History of Hester Wilmot.

Sunday Reading: The Servantman turned Soldier.

The History of Hester Wilmot. Part II.

The Lady and the Pye; or Know Thyself.

Sunday Reading: The Strait Gate and the Broad Way.

The History of Mr Fantom, the new fashioned philosopher and his man William.

Sunday Reading: The Pilgrims. An Allegory.

Dan and Jane: or Faith and Works.

The Two Wealthy Farmers. Part VI.

The Two Wealthy Farmers. Part VII.

The Plum-cakes.

APPENDIX II

Hannah More's major writings as published in her lifetime

1773 The Search After Happiness.
1774 The Inflexible Captive. A Tragedy.
1776 Sir Eldred of the Bower and the Bleeding Rock. Two Legendary Tales.
1777 Ode to Dragon, Mr Garrick's house-dog at Hampton.
1777 Essays on Various Subjects, principally designed for Young Ladies.
1778 Percy. A Tragedy.
1779 The Fatal Falsehood. A Tragedy.
1782 Sacred Dramas, chiefly intended for Young Persons, to which is added Sensibility, A Poem.
1786 Florio. A Poem.
      Bas Bleu or Conversation. A Poem.
1787 The Slave Trade. A Poem.
1788 Thoughts on the Importance of the Manners of the Great.
1789 Bishop Bonner's Ghost. A Poem.
1790 An Estimate of the Religion of the Fashionable World.
1792 Village Politics.
1793 Remarks on the Speech of M. Dupont, made in the French Convention.
1795-8 Cheap Repository Tracts. For a list of the Tracts see E. Green, *Bibliotheca Somersetensis* and G. H. Spinney, *The Bibliographical Society*, London, 1940.
1799 Strictures on the Modern System of Female Education.
1805 Hints towards Forming the Character of a Young Princess.
1808 Coelebs in Search of a Wife.
1811 Practical Piety.
1812 Christian Morals.
1815 The Character and Practical Writings of St Paul.
1817-8 Tracts and reprints of the Cheap Repository Tracts.
1819 Moral Sketches.
1821 The Feast of Freedom.
1821 Bible Rhymes.
1825 The Spirit of Prayer.

INDEX

Index

Index

Index

Index

Index

Index

Index

Index

For EU product safety concerns, contact us at Calle de José Abascal, 56–1°,
28003 Madrid, Spain or eugpsr@cambridge.org.

www.ingramcontent.com/pod-product-compliance
Ingram Content Group UK Ltd.
Pitfield, Milton Keynes, MK11 3LW, UK
UKHW040617240426
470322UK00010B/170